Recollections of
a Civic Errand Boy

the autobiography of John Henry Hauberg, Junior

ACKNOWLEDGMENTS

Many thanks to the following people, without whom this book would still be a collection of notes and journals handwritten over an eighty-six year lifetime.

To Corrine Reinbold-Ford, for her hard work in organizing mountains of handwritten notes, scanning hundreds of photographs, and bringing it all together as the foundation for the book you hold in your hands.

To Margaret Marshall for editorial expertise and helpful advice.

To Darlene Lyman for the initial editing.

To Tracy Salter, for her final editing that so well preserved John Hauberg's voice.

To Susan Miller for her incredible job of indexing.

To Steven Ford Photography and Jill Sabella for the photographs of the contemporary art collection, Paul Macapia for the photographs of Northwest Native Art from the Seattle Art Museum, Alan Staringer for the cover photograph, Mary Randlett for the back cover photograph, and the numerous family members whose photographs appear in this book.

To Cath Carine for designing the book to resemble the family photograph albums that John Henry Hauberg so enjoyed during his life.

And to John Henry Hauberg, Senior, and the librarians of Augustana College, for the use of his albums and journals dating from 1911–1915 and now stored in the archives of Augustana College.

Recollections of
a Civic Errand Boy

the autobiography of John Henry Hauberg, Junior

Introduction by Ralph Munro

Designed by CC Design, Seattle
Printed and bound by
C&C Offset Printing Co., Ltd., China

ISBN: 0-295-98364-7

Distributed by the University of Washington Press,
P.O. Box 50096, Seattle, WA 98145-5096
www.washington.edu/uwpress

Contents

*Ralph Munro and John Hauberg examine a
bucket of clams at John's 85th birthday party*

INTRODUCTION

John Hauberg, A Remarkable Man

fIRST A TRUE AND HUMOROUS STORY, THEN A FEW MORE WORDS ABOUT MY FRIEND JOHN. The Director of the Washington Department of Vocational Rehabilitation was having a "tizzy-fit." Yelling loudly, he paced the halls around his office in Olympia. His secretary, Miriam, ran behind him, closing doors and windows, for fear that someone across the street in the Governor's office might hear the ruckus.

You see, John Hauberg, parent of a handicapped child, was proposing to build a "facility in a normal setting" for disabled youngsters in Snohomish County, and, according to the Director, *"Hauberg is not following the rules."*

"What the hell does he think I've been doing here all these years," the Director shouted. *"Doesn't he realize that if he expects taxpayers' money for that damn thing he calls a 'village' then it is going to have to have a name that meets my approval. The rules are the rules."*

True indeed. John had been studying something the experts called 'normalization.' Instead of placing disabled citizens in institutions with names like 'Center for the Retarded,' the idea is to treat them as normally as possible. Provide settings where they can live normal lives and give those settings names that are 'normal' as well. John was proposing a facility where seven or eight disabled men would live and receive work training. Eventually they would commute to jobs. He wanted to call it Victoria Village.

"He's not going to get away with this! That village is going to have a name that meets the guidelines of this department! I don't give a damn if he's a big shot. I don't care if he's one of the Governor's friends. He's not going to bully me. I run this department...."

A few days later, John Hauberg arrived in Olympia. Hat in hand, he climbed the stairs of the state office building to acquiesce to the director's demands. "The name has been changed," John told the director. "We have dropped Victoria Village and will follow your guidelines. We have decided to name the facility 'Snohomish Handicapped Institute of Training,' and, because you are being so helpful, we are planning to put your name on the sign as well. A thank you for all the assistance you have provided."

The director beamed as he thought, "What a wonderful name, and my name will be on the sign as well. I hope the Governor himself can come to the dedication and see my name on the sign." As John was saying his good-byes, he mentioned that the lumber for the facility's sign had been ordered for months. There would be room for the director's name, but only room for the initials of the new facility. "Oh, that will be fine," the director replied. John headed for Highway 99 and the long road back to Seattle. The director mused to himself, "Imagine, my name on the sign. With the initials of this brand-new facility. Snohomish Handicapped Institute of Training. That name has a real ring to it. Let's see, the initials will be S. H. I.....

"This can't be true. That damn Hauberg has screwed me again. Does he know what this will do to my reputation, my career. That son of a bitch.... He's beaten me at my own game."

Miriam ran from room to room again, closing the doors and windows. She could see another "tizzy-fit" coming on. A few days later, State of Washington policy changed on the naming of facilities and Victoria Village was born.

I first met John when I was a youngster at Bainbridge High School. My family had lived at Crystal Springs for generations, and John had just completed a new home at Beans Bight, near the Country Club. We always called his neighborhood "Poverty Flats" in jest for all the wealthy people that lived there.

John was having one of his many parties. Margaret Sandberg, the Island's best caterer, hired me to cook fish, prepare clams, serve corn on the cob, and wash dishes. John would wander through the kitchen, talk to us, want to know about our families, where we lived, etc. I had dug three buckets of clams, and John loved them. After the party, he wrote down my phone number and shoved it in his pocket. "There's no clams on my beach," he said. "I'll give you a call."

A week later, the phone rang at our house. John's booming voice came across the line. "Say, Ralph, this is John Hauberg. How about us digging some clams in about 30 minutes. The tide is low at 9:17." My parents simply couldn't believe it. John Hauberg from the Country Club was coming to our house. This was unheard of.

We had a great time and a lifetime friendship was born. My parents stood in disbelief as John's Rolls Royce (formerly owned by King Farouk) pulled out of our driveway. The clams were sloshing around in the trunk, spilling water and seaweed on the carpet.

This was the John Hauberg I knew all my life. Making friends wherever he went. When you read this book, what comes through loud and clear is how John viewed life. Most wealthy and influential people spend their lives building relationships with others of their position and level. Not John. It didn't matter what station in life you held, when you came in contact with John Hauberg, you were his friend for life.

Years later, I looked around the room at John's 85th birthday party, a lovely dinner party at the Sunset Club in Seattle. I saw roommates from college days, folks who had worked in his kitchens and homes, foresters and loggers from the tree farm, leaders in the struggle to provide a better life for the disabled, struggling artists and those of world acclaim. Regular folks who had touched his life. And I thought to myself that evening, "We have had the pleasure of living with a great man, John Henry Hauberg, in our midst." I only hope I can accomplish one tenth of what he did for his fellow man.

—*Ralph Munro*

Recollections of a Civic Errand Boy

the autobiography of John Henry Hauberg, Junior

Here's to you and all your family,
    Cheers from us and all our animaly.
          ☆
From John who this year cap and gowned it,
    From Anne with whom he New York town'd it.
          ☆
From Fay, the mistress of her dollies;
    From Suby, pink-cheeked Junior Follies.
          ☆
From Jazz, our bouncing poodle mop;
    From Judy, whitest of a crop.
          ☆
From Dickie, unframed carols warbling;
    From fishes, ditto joyous bubbling.
          ☆
From our Gallery we join to cheer
    For MERRY CHRISTMAS and
        a HAPPY NEW YEAR
          1949

CHAPTER 1

Thirty-three & Looking Back Already

1950

t HE THIRTY-THIRD YEAR OF A MAN'S LIFE IN 1950 IS PROBABLY NO TIME TO WRITE AN autobiography. It's too confusing. With medical research extending our life span and with atomic research threatening to shorten it, one hardly knows whether the thirty-third year represents life near its close or life near its beginning. Thus each day of life going by has a different weight of importance depending on whether one is optimistic or pessimistic. One must have some faith, however, and so, in short, let me be brief.

After all, I'm lucky to be here at all. Almost two generations of normally measured time separated me from Mother and Dad, who sponsored my arrival in their early forties to the fascination, no doubt, of several aunts and uncles in their sixties, and first cousins in their forties who might resent such a latecomer into their generation. However, there I was. And so I should be optimistic, I suppose, since I'm here.

DENKMANN SISTERS AND THEIR SONS, 1930. *Front: Apollonia (Lonie Tom) Davis, Marietta Reimers, Carl Denkmann, Sue D. Hauberg, Elise Marshall. Back: Tom Davis, Jr., Charles Reimers, Fred W. Reimers, John Hauberg, Jr., Robert Marshall. Missing is Aunt Catherine Wentworth, living in Paris, France and without children. Carl Denkmann is the son of Uncle Ed Denkmann, alive but not in Rock Island on this occasion.*

During my childhood in Rock Island, Illinois, the world began to shrink in size at an accelerated pace. This was due not to my arrival but to the arrival of the radio and the airplane upon the domestic scene. These had been tested during the first war, and now we were to be afflicted with the results. Each member of our family had a pair of earphones that could be plugged into the new radio, and if one listened hard one could hear KDKA Schenectady above the static. Our horse, Pet, still took Henry Frank and me down to the Sash & Door Works to get artesian drinking water in big earthenware jugs, but Pet's days were numbered and the new streetcars on the 25th Street hill used to scare him so that Frank would leap out of our buggy and hold his head until the trolley was well past us down the street.

Roads began to be paved and cars were more numerous. We kids knew the names of them all—Velie, Reo, Packard, and the survivors — Fords, Chevies, and Buicks. The last horse pulled the junkman's wagon as he called out, "Rags, old iron; rags, old iron!" The iceman's wagon gave up with the coming of the new fangled electric Frigidaire, replacing the icebox.

Growing up is a very painful process. Falls, tears, frustration, spankings, shyness, pimples, adjustments, popularity or lack of it, stage fright, relatives, girls, and parents – what problems! If six years old is a terrible age, think of sixteen! And the sifting and sorting problems that culminate happily (everybody hopes) in finding the "One and Only Girl." If life before marriage is a headache to be remembered with pain then I have only eight or nine years of life to talk about with pleasure, and three of those were spent in the army, a nightmare existence.

The Lyford Farm

However, there was a lot of fun. The fun of the Hauberg Farms—Grandpa's Sugar Grove the day after Christmas, Aunt Anna's cheerful, hearty greeting, Uncle Louis and Dad taking me hunting or sleigh riding, Aunt Nora Lyford with good-natured Uncle Ed squirting milk straight from the cow into the cat's mouth or putting me on a horse, and cousins Helen and Ada, such pleasant company. The House-in-the-Woods, so dark and damp (before Annie and I let in the light) but so lovely in its

Above: Pushing the truck out of the mud. My father's "Band Boys" on a hike. Below: Day after Christmas hunt with Uncle Louis & Dad. Photo by Uncle Louis Hauberg

beautiful woods, the home of flying squirrels, "coon," and "possum." We went "up to the country" many times behind Andrew Rietz, our gardener-chauffeur, who one winter day struck an enormous hog sleeping on the Hillsdale road and sent Mother up through the canvas top of our Packard twin-six touring car, whose isinglass side curtains didn't do much to keep out the winter cold. We went up country many times over the old river road and had to detour in the spring around the flooded miles. And the mud! The big laundry basket of picnic groceries always rested on some shovels which were carried just in case...and were used more often than not, it seems (and still are today), for the Haubergs have always seemed an adventurous group, pioneers, liking the outdoors, and keen to find out what lies on the other side of a mud hole. The dirt roads were full of horseshoe nails so flat tires were expected. The tire was removed from the wheel's rim, the inner tube inspected to find the hole, then patched, pumped up by hand, re-inserted in the casings, and on to the next "flat."

Then there was a pony from Uncle Will Schmoll and Aunt Amelia, who lived in Ward, Colorado. Her name was Lady, but we didn't treat her like one. We rode her like fury for a while and then overgrazed her to death. She made us cowboy daredevils and circus riders for a short time. May she rest in peace.

Then a boat, the *Catherine*, came along. She was a square, oily, noisy, ugly bathtub, and like other bathtubs I hated to get into her and then hated to get out. Dad took the whole family on many adventures which were fun, but the best of them went to Joe Meenan and me. On one venture, when we went up to LaCrosse, Joe and I were straining our eyes for the next bridge across the Mississippi, for Dad had a standing offer of a root-beer ice-cream soda to the one of us who saw a bridge first. Then in 1927 we went all the way to Mammoth Cave, Kentucky, down the Mississippi and up the Ohio, with a hundred incidents. Eighty mosquito bites on an arm carelessly left outside my bedroll! My first speakeasy when Dad, who either was at the time or had been president of the Illinois AntiSaloon League, was innocently taken there by a boat repairman in Quincy.

(Yes, we had taken a "short cut" on the Mississippi River—a liberty not taken without reprisal—and the old river had brought up a wing dam to ruin our propeller.) This repairman had said, "You can have any drink you want." And Dad said, "I'll have lemon soda." As I recall, even in my age of innocence, I was disappointed in Dad. The thrill of quick action. I had firmly tied the *Catherine* to a cleat inside a lock on the Green River and as the water went down, the front of the boat went up! I grabbed an axe and severed the line with a blow. Self-confidence grew a notch. We learned how embarrassing it can be to run out of gas in midstream of a swelling river. We got soaking wet and bitter cold on windy days. We learned how to work together to make a good landing at a current-swept dock, and to spell each other at the steering wheel, and to get along with the people we met along the rivers who were so different from the folks at home. Yes, that old boat was a wonderful thing.

The Denkmanns were different from the Haubergs, except that they, too, were interested in civic matters and church. Aunts and uncles and cousins were all pleasant to a small boy who loved their big houses, fine linens, beautiful silver, glass, and chinaware; their big yards, lawns, and trees; their wonderful presents at Christmas and birthdays; their pleasant talk and laughter. The Denkmann sisters and their cousin, "Cousin Lonie Sam" Davis, divided the holiday dinners among them. Mother always had the family on Christmas Day, Aunt Elise Marshall on Christmas Eve, Aunt Marietta on New Year's Day, Cousin Lonie Sam at Easter, and Aunt Lonie Tom on Thanksgiving. The dinners were all alike to me, none leaving a single individual impression, but a cumulative one of quiet dignity, good taste, and pleasant society. They were all catered by a cook, Mrs. Nelson, and a waitress, Annie Wells, working with the regular cook and maids in each house.

Aunt Catherine Wentworth was a Denkmann who was different. She was a nebulous character who lived in Paris and painted. Of our visit to her in Paris in 1926 I remember only her Pekinese dog which sat on a silk cushion beside her at the table, and a pheasant, skinned, with feathers intact, roasted, carved, and pieced back together feathers and all with toothpicks, and placed before Uncle Ned (who is even more shadowy in memory) as if it were a bird straight from the field. He "carved" by removing the toothpicks and taking the bird apart.

Sister Catherine and I went to Audubon School when it was still a frame building, and got to ring the big handbell that the janitor rang or was supposed to ring, except that he usually passed on the privilege. Mother's good friend, "Aunt Jane" Wilcox, was principal, and the teachers were very good. School was almost always fun. One time when it was not, was when I called Miss Brennan, teaching 4-A, a dirty name I had heard a teamster use and didn't know the meaning of. I got a D in conduct for the period and several other punishments besides. The old Audubon School was moved across 18th Avenue about 1926 to become an apartment, and a fine brick structure arose in its place with a big gymnasium. We began to play basketball year-round from then on. One winter Audubon played Longfellow School on a day that was so cold that Billy Robinson and Dick Kennedy and I had to ring doorbells about every other block on the walk down to Longfellow and ask to come in and thaw out for a few minutes. We lost to Longfellow 1-0 when Chubby Hubbard made a free throw for them. I don't remember what position I played, but it didn't matter that day. In 6-A Miss Spry read *Treasure Island* to us, about three or four pages at the end of each day. She made it last all semester, and we were thrilled by it, hanging on to every word.

Then on to Washington Junior High where most of my memories revolve around the lightweight basketball team. We won the city championship three times in a row, I believe, and our whole team also played as the YMCA "Midgets," and won several tournaments for the Y. Our greatest thrill at school came when we caught our coach, Mr. Helms, kissing Miss Mitchell, the math teacher, on the stair landing between floors when they thought we were still in the locker room after practice. We didn't know they were engaged, and would have been thrilled anyway.

Mother wanted me to go east to Hotchkiss School in Connecticut where Carl Denkmann had gone. Because I knew very little Latin I was sent to Fessenden School near Boston in 1930 to prep for prep school. I roomed with John Good of Moline and was scared to death of most of the Eastern boys there for several months. However, I joined the soccer squad for some reason and learned to kick others in the shins as hard as they kicked me.

At Hotchkiss, the Fessenden Latin preparation sent me into an advanced class from which I never escaped. In senior year we read the poetry of Horace and Catullus with Mr. "Aggie" Maitland, the master of our little class of seven. We met in the luxurious comfort of his private suite in one of the dormitories, where we played with his silver Persian cat, Xerxes, while doing our Latin translating. Occasionally Aggie would get a long letter from his brother in India who was a high administrator of some sort in one of the back provinces. The whole hour would go to the reading and discussion of that letter, the tiger hunts, and British policy, while Horace was completely forgotten. (This sometimes took quite a bit of engineering on our part.) John Shedd Reed, Ted Beal, and Bill Scranton were three others in the class and our paths crossed many times later in life.

Two things stand out in my mind about Hotchkiss. One was that scholarship was made to seem desirable as well as interesting, and exciting instead of something invented by grown-ups to torture boys. The other was that the teachers, or masters as we called them, lived with us in our dormitories and took a personal interest in us. I got interested in listening to good music on records because we could go into the room of the master on our floor and make ourselves tea and cinnamon toast while playing his large collection of records. If food had to be the inducement, who cares? The choir had several privileges, too, so I tried out for it and eventually became tenor soloist, although I'm glad no recordings of my high-pitched quaver exist. From the choir was drawn an Opera Club of about ten boys who went one Saturday a year with Mr. Fish, our choirmaster, to New York where we sat in a box in the fabulous Diamond Horseshoe at the Metropolitan. One year we saw *Die Meistersinger* and got so excited about it that Gus Swift of Chicago fell full length (all six foot five) down one flight of the grand staircase.

I learned to ice skate and to ski because there wasn't a basketball team, and for the same reason I finally played football on the class team and found it the best game of all. But track was my best sport and I became captain just before the last season when the regular captain left school. There was only a handful of us out for track and we all did at least three events, mine being the high jump, discus, and high hurdles. The four years at Hotchkiss were very fine, very few of us realizing that the Great Depression was occurring beyond the borders of the clipped lawns.

Those years were the biggest in influence, from zero to nineteen. There were other great events, but not so influential—summers on Cape Cod, trips to Europe and Hawaii, jobs in the Sash & Door Works and in the great woods of the West Coast and the sawmills, the years at Princeton where social functions relegated scholarship to a dim corner.

A happy day was hiding around that corner. I found that One and Only Girl, Anne Westbrook Gould, at Vassar and later in Seattle, and now we have "Two and Only Girls," so far—Fay Westbrook, born February 4, 1944, and Sue Bradford born October 3, 1948. Our eight-plus years of marriage have been very wonderful. Enough said.

The war was an intermission. I served in the field artillery and the infantry in the States for two years and in occupied Germany for fourteen months with the Third Army. Then back to Seattle and graduation from the University of Washington College of Forestry with membership in Phi Beta Kappa, scholastic honorary; Phi Sigma, biological studies honorary; and Xi Sigma Pi, forestry honorary. I found motivation to study, at last, in the devastated logged-off lands of the Denkmanns in the South, the Weyerhaeusers in the West. The beautiful forests and professional forestry of Austria, Germany, and France convinced me that something had to be done to re-create our family forests.

Since forestry college I have been engaged in acquiring timberlands for research in regeneration and management and the production of saw logs, Christmas trees, telephone poles, fence posts, and pulpwood. Civic activities include membership on the boards of the Seattle Art Museum, the Arboretum Foundation, the Seattle Symphony Orchestra Association, and the Helen Bush School. For further details consult my obituary in the year 2016.

Mr. John H. Hauberg
and
Miss Susanne C. Denkmann

announce their marriage

on Thursday, June the twenty-ninth

nineteen hundred and eleven

Rock Island, Illinois

*Mom, Susanne
Denkmann Hauberg*

*Dad, John Henry
Hauberg, Senior*

CHAPTER 2

How I Came to Be

OW I AM EIGHTY-THREE, AND "LOOKING BACK," PERHAPS IN THE NICK OF TIME, brings to mind far more details of my life that seem to fall into a pattern and fulfill a purpose, neither of which I perceived at age thirty-three.

There have been Hauberg family and Denkmann family reunions in those fifty years. Members of both families have been fascinated by our ancestors who braved ocean crossings in sailing ships in the 1830s and 1840s. Even today, in 1999, there are a few of us whose fathers and mothers knew the details of their parents' adventures. My own range of family knowledge spans over one hundred fifty years. Current family members are greatly interested in how the Frels and Haubergs and Denkmanns and Weyerhaeusers came over from Germany and prospered in a relatively new and exciting country.

I will write only of my own years, letting the other living and the dead speak for themselves. All of us have memories, and not a few libraries around the U.S.A. hold archives of many of our members. It's fun to be a Hauberg and a Denkmann. I hope these pages will reflect that joy.

With that introduction out of the way, let me tell you how I came to be, and that story has to start with the intertwining of my mother and father's lives. How and why did they meet each other?

How Mother and Dad Met

Mother was born Susanne Christine Denkmann in 1872 in the Denkmann home in Rock Island, Illinois, across the railroad tracks from the Weyerhaeuser and Denkmann sawmill which, in turn, was on the bank of the Mississippi River. She attended Rock Island schools and went east to Miss Brittingham's in Philadelphia and on to Dana Hall in Wellesley, Massachusetts. She made numerous trips to Boston to its symphony concerts. Her scrapbook of those years is filled with concert programs and dance cards from Dana Hall proms. She then went to Wellesley College briefly but was called home to be with her mother. Later, she attended Radcliffe College.

Kindergarten work appealed to Mother. She enrolled in a Chicago Kindergarten College. After a year there, she went to New York and was on the payroll of an organization doing "settlement" work in a very poor district. Her year there convinced her to create a similar organization in Rock Island, starting the "West End Settlement" in 1909 in an area not far from the Weyerhaeuser and Denkmann sawmill. The West End Settlement helped battered women and children, as mill workers spent their weekly paychecks in saloons and came home to irate wives whom the fathers beat up. From her I inherited a strong streak of caring for others.

Along with this, she and two older sisters became very active in the Broadway Presbyterian Church and the new YWCA of which she was the first president. And from these activities she then joined the board of the Bethany Home orphanage.

Top: Grandpa Marx D. Hauberg; Bottom: The farmyard at Sugar Grove

My father was born in 1869 at Sugar Grove Farm in the "upper end" of Rock Island County. He was the fourth child of Marx D. Hauberg and Anna Margaret Frels, and the first to be born in the new "stone house," thereby missing out (for himself and all of us) on the virtues of being born in his grandfather's and father's log cabin. His older sisters, Amelia, Emma, and Anna were so honored.

Dad spent his first twenty-five years on that farm. Grandpa and Uncle Louis Hauberg and he were the only men. All were sorely needed to "lift the mortgage" so Dad was tied to that until 1894, finishing only five years of formal schooling. I spent one

Top: Grandpa Marx Hauberg's stone house on Sugar Grove Farm; Bottom: JHH, Sr.'s photograph of Niagara Falls, circa 1895

month on that farm and from that experience I learned why "sorely needed" is an appropriate phrase.

John H. Hauberg, Sr., however, was a voracious reader of history and books about geology and botany, not to mention the poetry of his time. While his seven sisters and brother were chattering, he was always "in a corner reading a book" according to Aunt Emma years later. He had bought a bicycle and a box camera, and using both tirelessly he had biked over dirt roads to Niagara Falls, Boston, New York, Philadelphia, Washington D.C., and many other places. He kept a minute-by-minute diary and cash journal, which, along with his photos, have created an enormous archive at Augustana College in Rock Island. From him I inherited a great curiosity.

After his twenty-five years on the farm, he exploded to a "hurry-up degree" at Valparaiso College in Indiana, and a law degree from Michigan in 1900. I will not dwell on his life's details here other than to say that in due course he was elected to the board of Bethany Home, a church-supported orphanage.

Sue Denkmann's and John Hauberg's board membership at Bethany Home turned into friendship. Both of them were in their late thirties, both deeply involved in church and Sunday school work, each living in two small cities whose boundaries touched in the vicinity of Bethany Home.

Dad wrote to his mother, "I have made the acquaintance of a Miss Sue Denkmann." Years later Dad told me, "I realized that she was lonely." He asked her at the end of a board meeting if he could escort her to her family home at the far west end of Rock Island—by streetcar, of course. He then had to return by the same trolley past Bethany Home to his rented room in Moline.

Sue Denkmann was building the biggest house Rock Island was ever to see—still true in 1999. The house was begun in 1908. My guess is that she and Dad became engaged in 1910 with a year to go before the house was finished. (See *his* archives for details), and their marriage date (June 29, 1911) and honeymoon schedule were set by the contractor's prediction of the end of his work.

The Denkmanns didn't think much of her choice. Wedding photos show them looking at Dad's farm sisters and brother with more than a little snootiness. But both Grandmother and Grandfather Denkmann were gone and Mother's sisters had not married well themselves—small town men who pretty much retired from "business" after marrying these high-powered, well-off Denkmann girls. Dad had a law degree, a terrific sense of organization, and tons of energy. The Weyerhaeusers soon found him interesting and competent and soon he was on the board, and in time, president of all the Weyerhaeuser and Denkmann enterprises still operating in Rock Island.

Sister Catherine Denkmann Hauberg was born April 11, 1914, and I came along June

Top: The Great House begins, circa 1908
Bottom: John Henry Hauberg, Senior, and family

Grandpa Marx Hauberg holding Ada Mary Lyford, Grandmother Anna Frels Hauberg, Helen Lyford, and in front, Hazel Schmoll holding John H. Hauberg, Jr. beside Catherine D. Hauberg. These are all the grandchildren there ever would be of Marx and Anna Margaret Frels Hauberg.

24, 1916. Mother had just passed her forty-fourth birthday, Dad was almost forty-seven. My birth, I believe, but without knowledge, was very difficult for her and she never recovered vigorous good health. Both she and Dad were involved in the active leadership of all sorts of organizations. I'm going to pass up listing these because this writing is about me, but my story will refer to how that affected me over the years.

The name Marx, or Mark, alternated with John on the Hauberg family tree. I was supposed to be Mark. It was his turn. But I was born on St. John's Day and my guess is that Mother insisted on John, Jr. So that was that.

Where Does the Name Hauberg Come From?

Our name, Hauberg, derives from the name of this type of Holstein farm building. Set in the lowlands of North Germany with its many dikes and waterways, the land was exclusively agricultural. These farmhouses, with their appearance of large pyramids, were scattered about and were called "Haubargs."

Haubargs in Holstein

"To this very day they have again and again been called the most beautiful, the greatest, the most imposing farm houses in the world", so says *Architektur Zeitschrift* magazine of January 1983. Many of them have become inns and "bed and breakfasts."

I suppose one of our Hauberg ancestors lived in one of these. These pictures show the front of one and the back of another. There was ample room for the family, farm equipment, animals, and hay storage. In this rather bleak North Country, it made good sense to have animals and humans keeping each other warm.

Another more romantic account has it that the highest window in the gable of these huge buildings was known as the Haubarg, through which, if left open, the Devil would swoop in and seize the farmer's fairest daughter. Or a swain, unwanted by the farmer, would have a rendezvous with the daughter in the haymow, and upon being caught the two lovers would leap to their deaths through the window.

Either way, Hauberg is an interesting name. And there are no high mountains in northern, low Germany.

Sis and I

CHAPTER 3

Early Days & Early Memories:
Hyannisport, 1924–1925;
Audubon & Washington Schools, 1926–1930

I DON'T REMEMBER EVER BEING HELD BY EITHER MOTHER OR DAD. NOR PLAYED WITH. Nor read to. My parents were absorbed in their missions. They had married late in life, probably attracted to each other because of mutual interests more than because of love. Each had already made a name not only in local affairs, but statewide. But many photographs show that we were with them constantly.

Sex was a taboo matter in our house. To Mother, all horses were horses, not mares, stallions, or geldings. Dogs were dogs, there were no bitches, chickens were not divided into hens and roosters—very Victorian. Dad, a farm boy, must have laughed inwardly about all this.

1921: Wading in the Mississippi

Dad abhorred doctors. His older sisters, Amelia and Emma, had become Christian Scientists. They lived year-round in Ward, Colorado, which had been a silver mining town in the 1890s, at about seven thousand feet elevation, and were endlessly cheerful in their efforts to convert Dad to their beliefs. He was always half there already.

Mother and Dad slept in separate beds with a sturdy three-fold screen between them, and locked their bedroom door when they retired. Perhaps Miss Ross was with us because of Mother's seizures, although Kay and I never heard of any. I saw Mother in a nightgown and Dad in pajamas only once. I saw my father naked only once when he was seventy or eighty, and he was horribly embarrassed. I had been in many locker rooms in school and college and the army, as well as those where my school friends' fathers changed clothes for squash, tennis, (or golf) at their clubs, so Dad's embarrassment brought back a flood of questions I had about why he found such a normal experience to be so painful to both of us.

Having children must have been an equally painful duty for Mother and Dad. Two such pious and outstanding leaders knew they had to produce children to show the world that they "did it." And the Victorian taboos about expressing love and devotion were an abetting influence.

Well, you are impatiently asking, when did we discover our parents?

The answer is 1922. Sis was eight and I was six. My earliest memories are of the six winter months we spent in Pasadena at the lovely Huntington Hotel. There I became aware that Miss Ross was not only our governess, but that Mother needed her care. I know now, but not then, that Mother never regained her health after (maybe even before) I was born and suffered "petit mals" the rest of her life. She took medications for this and we children never saw any of these seizures. Miss Ross was extremely discreet and self-effacing, but Dad never liked her. The eucalyptus trees in southern California had a compelling fragrance, so my first memory is an olfactory memory. We walked from our cottage to the hotel for meals and drove around the area in a rented car with a driver. And that's all I remember of that.

Aunt May was another spinster scheduled to live out her life with Mother in the Great House.

Miss Ross more or less took the place of my parents for several years, enabling them

Miss Ross

John H., Jr., Miss Ross, "Aunt May" Blanding, & Kay

to do their civic work together without having to pay much attention to Kay and me. She never married although she had some dates and Kay and I would tease her about that. She had a very slight Canadian accent. I think she did a lot for Mother in the health field.

Mother wanted Miss Ross to sit at the dining room table with her, which put her in a difficult position. I think the fact that she sat at the table irritated my father. She basically was a servant, but here she was dining with the family. She never said anything during dinner, but then my father did so much talking that none of us could get a word in. After the meals were over she didn't stay with Mother and Dad at all. She was always with Kay and me. She had a good relationship with the cook, Mrs. Pearl Bennett, who was with us for years.

Because my mother was so busy with church and YWCA and her settlement work, Miss Ross was the one who put us to bed and tidied up after us. She read to Kay and me, usually in my room before the two of them retired across the hall to Kay's bedroom. She read such works as *Black Beauty*, the Albert Payson Terhune books about collies, *Treasure Island*, *Gulliver's Travels*, *Swiss Family Robinson* and so on. There were wonderful illustrations by N.C. Wyeth. Those books would be collector's items now. We both loved to hear them read to us by Miss Ross.

My sister and I later went our separate ways for reading. Kay read the Bobbsey Twins, and I read countless books about Tom Swift and his wonderful inventions, and the bad guys who were trying to steal his ideas from him or put his life in jeopardy. I also read western books by Zane Grey. I took at least two magazines. One was called the *Youth Companion*, to which I think every boy of my kind in the United States subscribed. We also read *Popular Mechanics*. When I was eight or ten years of age, the advertisement on the back cover of *Popular Mechanics* was always about how to build up your body so you could look attractive to girls. The slogan of this ad was, "I was a

98 lb. weakling until I took Charles Atlas's course." Some poor underdeveloped young fellow was always getting sand kicked in his face by a strapping bully on the beach. Once he had taken the Atlas course, however, all that intimidation ceased. I did not subscribe.

Miss Ross took care of Kay and me through all the assorted illnesses of those days. Whenever we got sick, my father's first cousin, Dr. George Hauberg, who incidentally had brought me into the world in my mother's bedroom, treated us. He had a wonderful voice. The minute the front door was opened to let him in and I heard Dr. Hauberg arriving, I felt completely well. This was probably frustrating to him when he had been called to treat me.

We were in public school in the early years, and brought home all of the common diseases, such as measles, mumps, whooping cough, and chicken pox. Our doctor was required to report our contagious conditions to the health department, and up went the famous red card on our front door, proclaiming to one and all that something contagious was in the air and they should proceed at their own risk.

Being sick in those days was really kind of fun. You got to stay in bed and be waited on by Miss Ross and Mother's staff of people. And you got to stay home from school…although both Kay and I liked school. After a week or two of sick leave we were always glad to rejoin our classmates.

But then Sis and I began to go on the fortnightly Saturday afternoon hikes of the newly created, by Dad of course, Black Hawk Hiking Club, which began in September and went on through May— rain, sleet, snow, below-zero weather never canceled a hike. Dad's motto was "all weather is good weather." The worse it got, the more enthusiastic he became. Sis and

I loved these hikes. Dad probably kept a close eye on us, but we never felt it. The bachelor and spinster hikers were mostly professional people, some of them Europeans who had hiked a lot over there. We hiked, we sang: "There's a long, long trail a winding into the land of my dreams, where the nightingales are singing and the bright

moon beams," converting that into "There's a long long nail a grinding into the sole of my shoe..." Others were "Bicycle Built for Two, Daisy, Daisy..." and the Sergeant Major song. And songs from World War I like "Long Way to Tipperary," "Pack up Your Troubles in Your Old Kit Bag" and "Give My Regards to Broadway." Every hiker knew all the words and every hiker sang. If anyone was off key, it was never noticed. The hikers took care of Sis and me as we tried to be grown-up and need no looking after. No flowers were ever picked, no gate was ever left open, we all, grown-ups and kids, rolled under the lowest barbed wire of every fence. Every farmer was asked for permission to hike on his premises. The club had a terrific reputation and permission was usually granted. Of course Dad knew almost every farmer in the county from his Sunday school work, and that helped. The warmth and enthusiasm of the hikers to Sis and me got both of us off to a great start in dealing with "grown-ups."

Hyannisport—1924, 1925

In the summer of 1924, the excitement about the discovery of King Tut's tomb persuaded Mother and Dad to go to Egypt to see the tomb and the beautiful artifacts, and ride camels. Dad photographed everything there. The next stop, the Holy Land of Bethlehem, Golgotha, and Jerusalem, was the real reason for the trip. Again Dad's camera recorded everything. He turned these photos into glass "lantern slides" for a lecture he gave about the trip to well over fifty audiences, Rotary Clubs, church groups, etc. When schoolwork permitted, I was his slide-machine operator, making fifty cents per show. He shook his bundle of keys in his pocket for me to change slides. I learned to identify his jingling keys from others who thought it would be fun to hurry the show along. These illustrated talks were expanded to include Dad's Indians. They kept me busy for three or four years in the '20s.

While Mother and Dad were in the Middle East, Miss Ross took Sis and me to Hyannisport on the southern side of Cape Cod. Mother's niece, Anna Davis, and her companion, Gertrude Eustace, a hearty Englishwoman, and also an RN (cousin Anna also was subject to seizures as was Mother), had been at Hyannisport already for several summers. So we took a house nearby and close to the beach. We were to take the same house in 1925. I learned to swim in these sparkling waters, and to sail a tiny "catboat," and to avoid horseshoe crabs with stiff spines that one did not want to step on. There were also "puffing pig" fish, easily caught by hand, that would bloat up tremendously when tickled on their tummies.

I met new boys from Chicago, Indianapolis, and Cleveland at Hyannisport, several of them later going to Hotchkiss and Princeton with me. We were either swimming, sailing, and looking for rocks on the beach or at the nine-hole golf course club house, a one-room shack where the players stored clubs, bought balls, drank "pop," and smoked cigars. We boys collected pop bottle tops—cream soda, sarsaparilla, root beer, strawberry soda, etc., and cigar bands whose names I can't remember. It was an early form of baseball cards.

Sis and I were signed up for riding lessons. Since we had ridden horses on Grandpa's and Uncle Ed Lyford's farms and in the Colorado national parks, we thought we knew all we needed to know. The first lesson was a disaster. While the rest of the children were learning to post, hold the reins just so, etc., Sis and I galloped off down the road. Naturally the other school horses followed us. At the following "round up" we were told not to come back. Miss Ross was chagrined, but Dad was secretly pleased to hear the story when he and Mother returned from Dam-

On the beach at Hyannisport

Left: Sis in riding clothes; Above: her riding teacher

ascus to spend a week or so with us on Cape Cod before returning to Rock Island. "Eastern" riding to him, who had been a cowboy on the Swann Land and Cattle Co. in Chugwater, Wyoming, in the late 1880s, was for sissies.

So these are the principal memories of my life's early days. I don't seem (at age eighty-one) to remember much of anything before 1922. What comes next will begin about 1926 and continue to 1930 when the Crash of 1929 affected almost everyone else in the U.S.A. Mother sent Sis and me to private schools in the East where my horizons expanded geometrically as I entered into an entirely different kind of life, almost diametrically opposed to Dad's experiences.

School in Rock Island

The fall of 1922 saw me going off to Audubon School. I think Mother drove me there in her electric car to introduce me to "Aunt Jane" Wilcox, the principal, and one of Mother's dearest friends. Aunt Jane was one of the spinsters who was going to live with Mother in the Great House. If she was at all disappointed that I had taken her place, it never showed. After Aunt Jane retired from being principal at Audubon, Mother bought fifteen or twenty John J. Audubon bird prints and gave them to the school in honor of Jane Wilcox.

The first grade was large, probably thirty to thirty-five of us, and I do not remember the teacher's name, nor anything of the teaching. But by the end of the year the class was smaller and it continued to get smaller as the six years went by. The dropouts were needed at home. I remember no trouble among the teachers and fellow students. But boys eight to twelve years old learned to repair cars. There were few auto repair shops. Mostly, cars were "fixed" by a man in the back yard of his house. Our family mills also hired boys of this age at a dollar a day. Girls helped frail or ailing mothers. An education was not considered to be terribly necessary or important. Later in Seattle, I learned that some of the most successful men had not gone beyond the sixth grade; for example Joshua Green, Sr., the mighty banker, and D.K. MacDonald, the insurance man, whose daughter Janet was one of Annie Gould's bridesmaids.

I learned to play marbles. At recesses outdoors, we all ran our legs off in "Cowboys and Indians" and "Cops and Robbers." I got roughed up once by a larger bully and went home to tell Mother why I got so dirty. She praised me and told me always to "turn the other cheek." Fortunately, I did not follow her heartfelt Christian belief, and at an early opportunity, had at the bully to the cheers of my little friends.

Most of the boys at Audubon lived close to our big (eleven acres) yard so winter snows brought a throng to our hill for sledding. In the spring and summer, my pals and I built little roads near the house and ran our toy cars and trucks over them.

The old wooden "Audubon" was replaced about 1927 with a handsome brick building with a gymnasium/meeting room. We boys became instant basketball players and played year-round.

The school would let us play after school hours, but we wanted to play on weekends as well. The Presbyterian Church on top of the hill had a gym. We had to figure out ways to get into that building so we could play basketball in the gym. We found we could send one boy sliding down the coal chute and he would go through the building to open the side door so we could get in. Strangely enough we were never caught. We also snuck into Audubon School through the coal chute. There must have been at least one mother who wondered how her son managed to get his clothes so dirty.

Aunt Jane retired and was replaced by Miss Ellen Fried. I began to remember the names of some of the teachers. We did group singing in the fourth grade under Mrs. Whitney and began competitive drills in math and spelling in the fifth grade under Miss Spry. Miss Young of the sixth grade began to expand our sense of the universe with geography. I ate it all up and was an enthusiastic student with a little band of buddies, cousin Carl Rochow, Bob Hubbard, Billy Robinson, Joe Meenan, Dick Kennedy, and others. After school I used to stop at Joe or Dick's house for a cookie and a chance to talk to a grownup. Sis and I had graduated from the kitchen to the dining room in our house but we were not invited to talk.

One day, after we had our showers, we caught Mr. Helms, our junior high coach, kissing Miss Mitchell. We were shocked! It was just the most amazing thing. We all rushed home and told our parents. Of course they got married—had to! And when

Miss Mitchell became Mrs. Helms she could no longer be a teacher, as married women could not teach. She became a cashier in the Denkmann family bank, so I used to see her later in life.

I was also on the track team for Washington Junior High School. We had an annual meet with Lincoln Junior High and Franklin Junior High. I high-jumped against a Lincoln student named Arnold Dennecke. He and I became friends and would have sodas together at the Greek's. Later on he became the chief justice of the Supreme Court of the state of Oregon. He was on the Reed College board, and he got me to join him on the board. So here was a friendship that survived a long time.

We loved to go to the movies. The Fort Armstrong Theater was too expensive so we went to the Riviera farther downtown. For ten cents on Saturday morning at the Riviera we saw Wild Bill Hart and Tom Mix, who became great heroes to us. Tom Mix

1930 Championship Lightweight Team. Left to right, top row: Coach Helms, Walt Anthony, Jack Brown, Claire Hoogerwerf, Dick Kennedy, Ed Lavell. Bottom Row: Chink Ankney, Kenny Johnson, John Hauberg, Jr., Lawrence Murphy, Chubby Hubbard.

in particular did spectacular stunts. His horse would jump right through a boxcar that was supposed to be traveling at thirty miles per hour.

At Washington Junior High I met Dolores, who was the school cheerleader. I became the team captain and occasional high point man, and Dolores led the cheers for me. One day we went downtown to the Greek's ice cream and soda fountain where there was a coin-operated photo machine. I put in quarters, Dolores and I squeezed together, and six stamp-size photos of us emerged. Wow! But if I sought out Dolores, I was not unaware of Billy Robinson's cousin Mildred, who became the recipient of Valentines surreptitiously slid under her door. I would ring the doorbell and run away. My fickleness was not discovered. Mildred also proposed "spin the bottle" at other parties. Blushes all around.

At the junior high level we could join the YMCA with its gym and its pool. The Rock Island Y had a trained athletic coach who recruited our Washington lightweight basketball team in toto to play also for the Y. He coached us into the best lightweight school team in Rock Island, and a quite successful team for the Y, playing as far away as Sterling, Illinois. He also taught us to tumble and to dive. The Y was about twelve to

Aunt Elise Marshall (back row, second from left), Susanne Denkmann Hauberg (back row, fourth from left) and a Sunday school class. John Henry Hauberg, Jr. (on his mother's lap) and sister Kay (Catherine Denkmann Hauberg) (front row, right) were not part of this class.

sixteen blocks down the hill from our house so that the Audubon/Washington gang spent a lot of time there. A natatorium had been built on the Davenport, Iowa levee. It cost a nickel to cross the Mississippi on the ferryboat *Quinlan* which landed next to the pool. So by 1930 we were all good little athletes and great friends.

However, there was another school that I didn't like at all—Sunday school. It was divided into three parts: primary, intermediate, and senior. Mother was head of the intermediate, Aunt Elise Marshall headed the primary, and Aunt Lonie Tom Davis the senior. A formidable trio of sisters. The Broadway Presbyterian Church ministers fawned on them as well they should have, but even at a tender age I was disgusted. I also refused to put a dime in that part of the contribution envelope slated for missionaries in China.

SEVENTEENTH ANNUAL **INDIAN POW-WOW**

CEREMONIAL DANCES by Members of SAUK & FOX TRIBES

L A B O R   D A Y   W E E K   E N D

S O U V E N I R   P R O G R A M

BLACKHAWK

10c Per Copy

BLACK HAWK STATUE
(see page 18)

SEPTEMBER, 1-2-3, 1956

BLACK HAWK STATE PARK

ROCK ISLAND, ILLINOIS

SPONSORED BY THE INDIAN POW-WOW COUNCIL

CHAPTER 4

My Father's Indians & My Mother's Church:
The Denkmanns & the Haubergs

My Father's Indians and His Museum

I
T WAS INEVITABLE THAT I WOULD BECOME A COLLECTOR OF INDIAN ARTIFACTS, considering my early exposure to my father's intense interest in the Indians of his community and his own collection of their work. My father was named Chief Standing Bear as a result of his interest in the Sauk and Fox Indians and efforts on their behalf.

They occupied the region of western Illinois, eastern Iowa and Wisconsin, and perhaps the eastern part of Minnesota. In 1800 there was a band of these Indians living in Rock Island County. It was splendid hunting country with a tremendous deer population. The soil was very fertile for their cornfields. Black Hawk was the war chief for this particular band of Sauk and Fox Indians. The Sauk chiefs signed a treaty agreeing to move to reservations in Iowa and Oklahoma, but Black Hawk felt the chiefs should not have sold out the tribe. He found several hundred braves willing to go to war against the U.S. Government. The so-called Black Hawk War of 1830-32 became a political hot potato, which involved all the men who became leaders of the country for the next thirty years, including Abraham Lincoln, Jefferson Davis, Ulysses S. Grant, Robert E. Lee, and William Henry Harrison.

Chief Black Hawk was Dad's hero. My father became the authority on the Black Hawk War and published a book about it. In the 1930s, he located the direct descendants of Black Hawk who were living on reservations in Iowa and Oklahoma. About 1936 he invited these direct descendants of Chief Black Hawk to come to Rock Island to put on a powwow during the Labor Day weekend. Dad did it all by himself to start with, paid their travel and living expenses while they were in Rock Island. He complained about the amount of money they were spending in the local drugstore on a new product called Geritol. He was an ardent Prohibitionist but he didn't know about the high percentage of alcohol in Geritol, assuming it was necessary medicine. So the Indians had their firewater and sold their baskets and beads, and then in the afternoon and evening of the weekend, maybe two or three days in a row, they did their dances in costume. It was very impressive.

Dad had quite an extensive collection of Indian material—wonderful feathered war bonnets, muskets, and bows and arrows. I don't know whether he bought them

In Memoriam
JOHN HENRY HAUBERG
HONORARY CHIEF STANDING BEAR
NOVEMBER 22, 1869 — SEPTEMBER 13, 1955

IN RECOGNITION of the founding of the Indian Pow-Wow by Mr. and Mrs. John H. Hauberg, their great efforts for its successful continuation, and their continued financial support, The Indian Pow-Wow Council dedicates this year's Seventeenth Annual Pow-Wow and future Pow-Wows to the memory of Mr. and Mrs. John H. Hauberg.

Dad's "Indian Room"

from the Indians or from dealers. He also had acquired oil portraits of the many leaders in the Black Hawk War.

Dad also collected Lincolniana, as they called it. The poet, Carl Sandburg, who wrote a many-volumed work on Lincoln, sometimes came to our house when I was a youngster to sit with Dad in his "Indian Room" and discuss their hero by the hour.

Another man who shared Dad's love of Lincoln lore was Governor Henry Horner, a Democrat. While Dad was a Republican, they shared a fascination with Lincoln material, and Horner thus was a frequent visitor to Dad's Indian Room.

There was a high bluff between the confluence of the Rock River and the Mississippi, right in the heart of Black Hawk's village. It served as a watchtower for the Indians in Black Hawk's time. Dad and some local Rock Island people, Walter Rosenfield and Harry Cleveland, caused this bluff to become the Black Hawk Watch Tower State Park. He took a lot of pictures of his Indian friends in costumes standing on the bluff or walking on forest trails beside Rock River.

During the Depression, the Civilian Conservation Corps showed up at the park prepared to build what would become several small, handsome limestone buildings on Dad's bluff. He immediately called his friend, Henry Horner, the governor, to ask what was going on in "his" state park. The governor explained that he needed to keep the CCC boys busy and thought the buildings would be an improvement. Dad wasn't so sure about that.

When the buildings were completed, Governor Horner called Dad and said, "I want you to meet me at the Watch Tower State Park with the State Parks Commission and some local people." At this meeting he gave Dad the keys to the buildings and said, "John, these buildings are for your Indian collection."

My father was elated about the possibilities this gift offered. I was nineteen at the time, and I remember as we sat at the dining room table discussing his plans for the project, he took out an envelope and sketched out rough plans. One of his ideas was to have the Indians themselves build a winter house as well as a summerhouse. Just as the Pacific Northwest Indians moved out of their big houses in small family groups to summer places on many beaches where they picked berries and fished for salmon, the Sauk and Fox Indians also left their winter houses and scattered about.

In 1936 Dad hired two elderly members of the Sauk and Fox tribe, living on their reservation at Tama, Iowa, to build both a winter house and a summerhouse inside the new museum spaces. They would get the material needed to

Jim Powisherk and Sam Slick

build—100-percent Indian style, no nails, screws, boards, doors, windows, screens, or white man's hardware—from our House-in-the-Woods property along the River Road beside the Mississippi. I was to drive them back and forth in our old Reo truck, give them a hand if necessary, and buy them whatever they needed, such as chewing tobacco, soft drinks, etc.

Structural pieces were of one-inch willow, tied together by shreds of elm inner bark. There were few upright pieces needed to support the roof. The winter house was larger, with side benches for sleeping and storage. The summerhouse was much more informal, a round igloo-type structure, meant to be used perhaps once and replaced the next summer. The covering of the frame was to be sheets of elm bark. The girdling of these trees killed them, of course. Dad winced, but the Indian way had to prevail.

I was pleased to be part of the process. It was my first behind-the-scenes museum experience. The Indians and I exchanged very few words. The drive to our woods was a bit over a half hour, the Indian "chiefs" sitting in the open-air seats behind the cab. But we were comfortable with each other. I learned that one could build a house with nothing more than a long-handled axe and a sharp knife.

When Governor Horner said, "It's yours," Dad took that seriously and played an active role as director, head curator, and manager of the museum. The Indians appreciated his interest in their way of life, and as an expression of their thanks he was named Chief Standing Bear. My father's collection is still on exhibit at Watch Tower State Park, and it is a wonderful memorial to him.

The Labor Day powwow he established continues to be a popular event to this day. Although the early powwows were paid for by my father, he gradually got a committee together which managed the powwow and raised the funds to make it an ongoing affair. The state built a small outdoor amphitheater that seats several thousand people. Visiting Indians pitch their tepees nearby and sell their wares. It's a great tourist attraction to which people come from a long way off. Dad was on hand for every single powwow until his death in 1955.

By that time I had just begun my own collection of Northwest Indian artifacts, but my father didn't get to see much of it. I have an idea he wouldn't have been too impressed with it, however. He was just not interested in any Indians but the Sauk and Fox. When he came to Seattle in 1949 to attend my graduation from the University of Washington, I took him to some Indian reservations and he was not interested at all. His life was bound by the borders of Rock Island County, its Indians, its flora and fauna, its history, and the great people who came there to fight the Black Hawk War.

The one thing he was interested in out here was the height of the bracken fern on my tree farm. He always carried a tailor's tape measure, and he took it out to measure the height of the bracken fern. He said, "I just want to see if it's taller than the bracken fern we have in Rock Island County." And he was happy to find that it was not.

My Mother's Church

Broadway Presbyterian Church

A good part of my growing up was connected with Broadway Presbyterian Church and its Sunday School. Mother and two of her sisters were the pillars of Broadway Presbyterian, and felt keenly the necessity of attending all of its functions. Mother's life was entirely focused on that church, its ministers and its problems. It's where I went to Sunday School and earned my Bible from my mother because I had memorized certain passages. We were thoroughly grounded in the Bible stories. I don't think we were troubled with too much high thinking about the meaning of religion, but Mother was very pious.

Mother stood at the door with the minister at the end of services and shook everyone's hand as they left. She knew everyone in the congregation by name. If someone was all of a sudden not there, Mother would have Andrew, our chauffeur, take her around to this person's house to discuss why. No threat was intended. Mother was just sure that something had happened and that she might be able to help.

Even though my mother had never had any hardships in *her* life, except for her health problems, she had a very strong streak of humanity. But it never occurred to her what impact her descent from a Cadillac at the front door of a modest home would have on the inhabitants. What shocked her the most was the response to her question that they couldn't afford to keep up with Broadway Presbyterian Church any more, the rest of the congregation wore better clothing, and they felt they were looked upon as poor people who really weren't worthy of attending.

My Sunday School Teacher

In those days Sunday School work was very big in all churches. I was in the primary department and my teacher was William McLean Stewart, who was Mother's insurance agent. Mother received Bible-study guides from the State Sunday School Association and the National Presbyterian Church. I think it's tragic that children today don't learn the Old Testament stories. We got through Joseph and his coat of many colors, Noah's ark, Daniel in the lion's den—a lot of wonderful stories. Mr. Stewart was very good at getting us kids to read these out loud and talk about them. He had great illustrations of these stories. If it was a beautiful Sunday morning he took us out to sit on the lawn to discuss Bible stories and watch the cars go by.

Attending so many church services, I knew the litany and most of the hymns by heart. I thoroughly enjoyed the singing, and I really enjoyed the relatives and friends that surrounded us. Broadway Presbyterian Church has been a touchstone for many relationships, all my life.

The Denkmanns

Almost all of Mother's brothers and sisters had been well educated. Uncle Frederick graduated Phi Beta Kappa from the University of Iowa, I think in 1879. He succeeded his father in managing many businesses along with his cousins, the Weyerhaeuser sons. Mother was the youngest of her own family and the seven Weyerhaeuser cousins. There was such a huge group of Denkmanns and Weyerhaeusers that their main socializing was with each other.

Mother went on to Dana Hall, after which she spent at least one year at Wellesley. Her older sisters, except for Aunt Marietta, the oldest member of the family, had been to Wellesley.

She enjoyed her year at Wellesley, which gave her an opportunity to attend the Boston Symphony concerts. In her scrap album she pasted up the entire symphony programs. She apparently enjoyed going to dances, which were card dances. Those attending were given a dance card on which would be listed one's partner for each dance. These were decorative little cards, with a tiny pencil attached, and everyone was busy getting paired up so the dance card was full. Some of Mother's cards were among

A DENKMANN GROUP, 1930

Standing, left to right: Carl Denkmann, Anna Reimers Richardson, Fred W. Reimers, Susanne Davis Shuler; H.J. Richardson, Catherine Hauberg Sweeney, Charles Shuler, Catherine Marshall Shuler and R.D. Randall. Seated: Tom Davis, Jr., Apollonia (Lonie Tom) Davis, Marietta Reimers, Sue D. Hauberg, Helen Davis Stibolt-Johnson, Elise D. Marshall, V.A. Stibolt; on the ground: John H. Hauberg, Sr., Charles Reimers, John Shuler, and John H. Hauberg, Jr.

the contents of her box of souvenirs, and apparently she didn't have any trouble filling out her dance card.

Her Wellesley education was cut short because her sister Catherine decided to go to Paris and be an artist. She and Mother were the only unmarried children at that time so it became Mother's role to take care of her aging mother, Anna Catherine Bloedel Denkmann, back in Rock Island, which she did as a dutiful daughter until her mother's death in about 1910.

Her other sisters married local people and lived in big houses. They all were very interested in church work. Her brothers were involved in various aspects of the lumber business.

There were steamboats which moved logs up and down the river from the timberlands in Wisconsin, Michigan, and northern Minnesota to all the mills along the Mississippi River. The two families converted one of their steamboats into a pleasure boat with many staterooms. The Denkmann  and Weyerhaeuser cousins would take annual boat trips up and down the Mississippi between St. Paul, where the Weyerhaeusers lived, and Rock Island, where the Denkmanns lived.

The Denkmanns and Weyerhaeusers were prosperous. The Denkmann children were quite elegant. They had lots of books and pictures, beautiful houses, and they all had chauffeurs. The Weyerhaeusers loved Mother because she was the youngest of the cousins.

Mother also had lots of friends in Rock Island. She joined the Rock Island Arsenal Golf Club when it was formed and became charter member No. 7. She was an enthusiastic winning golfer and won the ladies' club championship in 1905. We have the silver cup that she won. Although Mother had school friends, during her growing up years her social life was with her aunts and uncles and cousins, as well as with her brother and sisters, whom she loved.

Grandfather and Grandmother Denkmann

In the early 1850s, Grandfather Denkmann was working in Erie, Pennsylvania, when he got a call from his brother in Davenport, Iowa, that the government had built a railroad bridge across the Mississippi. With the new bridge, mills could now be built on either side of the Mississippi in the Davenport-Rock Island-Moline area. This meant that you could ship products from either side of the river, to Chicago and on to the East, as well as to the rapidly expanding West.

As a result of the bridge, my grandfather and grandmother came to Rock Island to take whatever work he could find. One of his first jobs was working for John Deere in his forge, making iron and steel for the plows John Deere had invented and was producing. The total employment at Deere and Company when Grandfather joined up was only fifty-five men so he must have known John Deere personally.

Frederick Weyerhaeuser formed a partnership in 1860 with my grandfather who was to run sawmills in the Tri-Cities area of Davenport, Iowa, and Rock Island and Moline,

Illinois. Mr. Weyerhaeuser bought the logs for the mills and also sold the lumber. Mr. Weyerhaeuser, fourteen years younger than Mr. Denkmann, moved to St. Paul about 1880 to be closer to the timberlands and sources of capital. But most of his children were born in Rock Island and the fourteen first cousins were very close to each other.

The Haubergs

Mother, Cousin Emil Bracker, Aunt Anna Hauberg, Uncle Louis Hauberg, "Uncle" Charlie Walther, Dad. In front, John H. Hauberg, Jr., Kay, Grandpa Hauberg, Don Bracker (killed in WWII), Mrs. Walther, Ada Bracker.

My father's family were good, hardy people. The Haubergs came from an area near Kiel in Germany—a little town called Raisdorf. Great-grandfather John Detlev Hauberg was a blacksmith. He took care of all the ironwork for the farmers' wagons, and their tools, shovels, picks, crowbars, and horseshoes. He did the same thing for the men who worked in the Vogelsang forest, which was adjacent to his own fields. He worked in the planting and harvesting as well as making the ironwork for forest work, too!

He left his farm to his younger brother in 1848 to escape the militarism that was rampant over all of Europe and brought his immediate family to America. [Photos of the Vogelsang Forest on the following page by John H. Hauberg, Jr. in 1988, 140 years later.]

The Haubergs were Lutherans and worshiped in the church at Preetz, about a two-and-a-half-mile hike from their house. The house and the church are still there. Dad visited it in 1900 and took photographs of it. When my second wife, Ann, and I went over there in 1988, I was able to find the house and fields and the forest beyond from the picture Dad had taken. We introduced ourselves as Haubergs to the owner of the house and his two sons. We talked a little bit about the Hauberg family, conversing in his bro-

Vogelsang Forest in 1988; forerunner of Pilchuck Tree Farm

ken English and my broken German. He knew all about the family. I asked if there were any relatives around and he said there were lots of them. My cousin, Steven Scott, went over there in 1996 and found one hundred fifty Haubergs in the local phone books.

Here again was a very strong German background. The towns of Kiel and Preetz were both located in Holstein. The Holsteiners were at war with Denmark because they wanted to join the Prussian Empire. My great-grandfather, John Detlev Hauberg, emigrated to America in 1848 because he was fed up with all of the militarism. He was married, so perhaps would have been exempt from the draft, but his younger brother, Dave, was in the Army at the front. My great-grandfather went to the front to say goodbye to his brother before he and his family boarded the ship at Hamburg. That must have been a sad farewell between the two brothers.

Great-grandfather Hauberg became an indentured worker (not a servant) on Mr. Nervi's fifty thousand acres of farmland and forest in Tennessee. Nervi probably paid either all or a major part of the travel expenses from Germany.

He crafted the ironwork for all the operations of the estate. At the end of a year, someone told him he could apply for citizenship, which required a year's stay and a permanent residence. He signed all the necessary documents, but when he told his boss about this, Nervi said, "I cannot employ you any more, because now you will be my equal as a citizen of the United States and I can't employ equals." It was a very interesting attitude. The year was 1850.

The family got back on a riverboat and went down the Tennessee River to the Ohio, then down the Ohio River to the Mississippi River at Cairo, Illinois, then up the Mississippi River to Davenport, Iowa. There they disembarked because there was a Hauberg living nearby.

They settled first in Moline in a very small twelve-by-fourteen-foot house. Great-grandfather hired out his two sons—my grandfather (who I think was ten years old) and his younger brother Dave (who was about eight). For a dollar a week they worked as farm hands, sometimes in Iowa, sometimes in Illinois, wherever great-grandfather could sign the boys up. Their father must have had a job in Moline. The boys came home on Sundays.

Moline was a very Swedish town. The Germans were looked down on by the Swedes. My grandfather Hauberg reported in his memoirs that in a Moline beer hall one of the Swedes called him a German squarehead to which he took offense. Grandpa hit the offender so hard that he knocked him through the window of the beer hall. So he had a temper. He was always a tough man. When he was seventy years old he won an old settlers' fifty-yard race. He was very hardy, and a wonderful man. In 1851 Great-grandfather Hauberg homesteaded one-hundred-sixty acres of land still owned by the government. He walked forty-eight miles from Rock Island to Dixon, the county seat, and back in twenty-four hours to register his claim.

Grandpa Hauberg farmed something like three-hundred-sixty acres of the high prairie. Grandmother Hauberg was not born in Germany, although her parents were. She had a great curiosity, and maybe that's where Dad's and my curiosity came from. She obtained a patent for an improvement to the sewing machine in the late 1890s. She had eight children so one can picture her using her improved sewing machine to help clothe her family.

Grandpa was very active in all sorts of functions of the farm people. He ran for sheriff of Rock Island County because he was so well known from his attendance at county fairs. He spoke up and wanted to talk to everyone he could find. He was very congenial and gregarious. My dad was somewhat aloof whereas Grandpa Hauberg wanted to sit right down with people and talk to them eye-to-eye and hand-to-hand.

Dad had two sisters in Colorado. After Mother and Dad were married, Mother used to buy a Pullman seat on the Rock Island Railroad to Denver so that Grandpa could visit

Haubergs, Frels, Walthers, Brackers, Stiltzes, Pearces, all descendants
of my Great-Grandfather, John D. G. Hauberg

his daughters out there. Apparently Grandpa would turn that ticket in and get a coach seat, pocketing the difference. He said nobody wanted to talk in the Pullman car, but everyone wanted to talk when you were riding coach.

Grandpa Hauberg died at the age of ninety in the winter of 1927, when I was eleven. He had been out in the fields in July of that year cultivating the corn. At ninety he still had muscle and was a hale and hearty man. He was much loved in the community. The funeral service was held on a very cold and snowy day. The neighbors shoveled the snow on the road from his house on the hill down to the county road at the bottom, then up the hill on the other side where the local cemetery was. I remember what a tremendous number of people were there under those terrible conditions.

Dad was the oldest boy of eight children. They all stayed close to each other throughout their lives. He was very attached to Aunt Emma and Aunt Amelia, because they were the oldest, and to Aunt Ada, who was the youngest. They had to work hard for a living. I felt very intimate with them and enjoyed their company. They were fun to be with. They laughed and let me ride the horses on their farms. Occasionally I went out and tried to ride a pig just for fun.

Uncle Ed Lyford, married to Aunt Nora, was an enthusiastic farmer, and was quite jolly. When we kids showed up, we would go out and watch him milk the cow, and, of course, the cats all came out there. He would shoot milk into a cat's mouth from a distance of ten or twelve feet. I was very impressed by that. Uncle Louie had a beautiful singing voice and sang the *Messiah* with the Augustana chorus at Christmas. Dad was in that chorus too for a while. Aunt Anna won the chicken-calling contest at the county fairs, and Uncle Louie would win hog-calling contests.

Mother, Dad, and Cousin Hazel Schmoll

Aunt Amelia Schmoll and Aunt Emma Fairhurst lived in Ward, Colorado, which was more than seven thousand feet above sea level. They were part of a year-round community of only seven people who lived in Ward after the silver mines were exhausted and everybody else moved away. We went out several times by train to visit them. Uncle Will would meet us at Denver. He would drive us to Boulder, then up Left Hand Canyon to Ward. I guess we stayed with Aunt Emma. She had the Columbia Hotel, made of stones, every one of which had flecks of gold in them, which was about what the hotel was worth. The business had collapsed as soon as the silver got mined out, but Aunt Emma continued to live there. Her husband had been killed in a mining accident.

Aunt Amelia lived not too far away. Uncle Will Schmoll had a stable and a gas pump and sold all the gas in town. He had a Dodge truck and would drive to Boulder to get provisions for the miners in Ward. He had a droopy mustache and was a very thoughtful chap. I don't remember his talking very much because Aunt Amelia was a great talker, like a lot of the Haubergs—but they got along fine.

So these were the two German families in my background—Mr. Denkmann getting into business, and the Haubergs becoming farmers. Coming from these disparate backgrounds, my parents were worlds apart, not just miles apart. Both families were 100-percent German, but pursuing far different lifestyles. Mother and Dad found common ground in church work and such related activities as YWCA, YMCA, supporting evangelical work, and church-affiliated colleges such as Augustana. Mother never became an enthusiastic hiker, and Dad never became a golfer.

EARLY PHOTOGRAPH OF Denkman House shows trellis no longer there with seats overlooking view. House was completed in 1911.

Prairie School Mansion in Rock Island

Famous Illinois Architecture: XXXI

By Paul E. Sprague

SUZANNE Christine Denkmann (1872-1942) began her palatial brick mansion in 1909 high on a hillside overlooking Rock Island, Davenport, and the Mississippi River valley. She was the youngest daughter of Frederick Carl A. Denkmann (1822-1905) and Catherine Bloedel Denkmann (d. 1907), a prominent and wealthy Rock Island family. In 1860 her father had formed a partnership with his brother-in-law, Frederick Weyerhaeuser, in a lumber business that prospered and still survives today under the Weyerhaeuser name.

Suzanne Denkmann studied at Dana Hall, Wellesley College and the Chicago Kindergarten College before returning to Rock Island. There she became active in civic projects.

The house she commissioned in 1909 was finished in 1911, just in time for her and her new husband, attorney John Henry Hauberg, to move into following their wedding in 1911. Designed for her by Prairie School architect Robert C. Spencer Jr., close friend of Frank Lloyd Wright and a resident of River Forest, the house is a mature work of early modern architecture.

Stimulated by the idea of a modern architectural style, Spencer gradually modified his historically-oriented picturesque buildings of the 1890's into the severe geometry of the Denkmann House. Although there are still reminiscences in it of the historic styles,

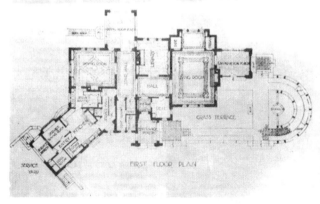

FIRST FLOOR PLAN

CHAPTER 5

The Great House: A Description

THE GREAT HOUSE I WAS BORN IN HAD FOUR STORIES. THERE WAS THE BASEMENT, which contained the huge laundry with its many irons and mangles. The steam arose, and Marie, the Swedish lady who was the empress of the lower regions, contended with sheets, tablecloths, towels, blankets, and clothes. Another room in the basement contained three huge tanks that treated the city water, which was very hard. The water was pumped by the city waterworks from the Mississippi River, then treated with many chemicals—first of all to get rid of the silt, and then to get rid of the pollution. By that time it wasn't fit to bathe in or drink, so our private water softening system was operated by Frank, the houseman, who arrived daily at 4 a.m. Also, my father had a darkroom where he enlarged his photographs and developed the glass plates that he used for taking pictures of groups.

In another basement room was the heating system. Grandmother Denkmann's collection of shells was kept in this room, in a gigantic cabinet that must have weighed a thousand pounds. Every drawer was crammed with a variety of shells from all over the world. My friends and I didn't pay much attention to that. We were more interested in the furnace room, which was also the base of all the organ pipes that extended up into the living room above. Upstairs they were concealed by slotted doors which let the sound escape. In the basement, the pipes looked like a forest of trees whose tops you could not see, and we boys were fascinated by them. We knew we shouldn't touch them, and we didn't, but it was always fun to go down there and play in that make-believe forest.

The Great House consisted of the owner's wing and a servant's wing. On the main floor, the owner's wing had a huge living room directly below Mother's bedroom suite above. There were several halls. The library was off one hall, which led to the living room. The large dining room contained a table, which would seat twenty, or maybe twenty-four if you put in enough leaves. Mother had beautiful lace tablecloths, which Ann Homer Hauberg and I have used in the 1990s, but which cannot be laundered anymore because nobody has the right equipment. A grandfather clock in another hall faced the dining room. There was an upright piano, which I believe is now at the Pilchuck Glass School. Off that hall and the dining room was a sun porch with two huge plate glass windows. At the other end of that hall was the grand stairway.

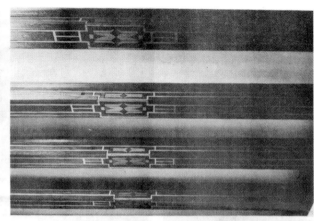

TULIP GRILLE COVERS organ pipes in living room.

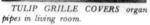

(UPPER RIGHT) PAINTED beams of library, designed by the architect, repeats highly stylized theme.

LIVING ROOM LOOKING toward porch on northeast side. Organ grilles (left), plaster work, chandeliers, rug, wall surfaces, ornamental glass designed by the architect.

LIVING ROOM LOOKING southeast, with portiers, drapes, rug and fireplace designed by architect.

*ORIGINAL LIVING ROOM fire-
place, now replaced with imported fireplace, repeated tulip motif in mosaic.*

*DINING ROOM FIREPLACE,
again with tulip motif.*

*TULIP PANELS AT front entrance.
Note bronze and glass lamp now missing from pedestal (right).*

*ORNAMENTAL geometric grille
above stairway.*

*LIVING ROOM CHANDELIER de-
signed by architect.*

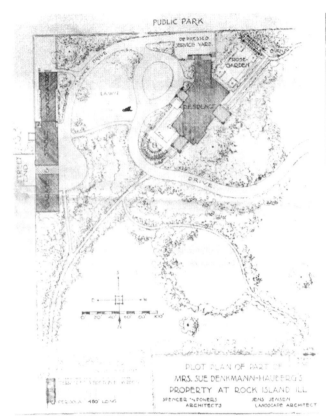

PLOT PLAN OF PART OF
MRS. SUE DENKMANN-HAUBERG'S
PROPERTY AT ROCK ISLAND ILL
SPENCER & POWERS   JENS JENSEN
    ARCHITECTS   LANDSCAPE ARCHITECT

LIBRARY FIREPLACE designed by architect Robert C. Spencer Jr. Note tulips used in design.

especially in the medieval half-timbering of some walls and gables, even these have here become disciplined exercises in a rectilinear subdivision of surface. In place of traditional architectural ornament, Spencer designed a stylized tulip, Miss Denkmann's favorite flower, as theme for nearly all the decorative details.

The siting of the house is splendid. It wraps around the top of a curving hillside following a highly disciplined yet quite irregular plan. The service wing, placed at an angle to the main part of the house, follows the sweeping curve of the hilltop while, at the same time, providing a functional visual separation between the two parts. Jens Jensen, the famed Chicago landscape architect, laid out the ten-acre site, using as his theme a Wisconsin woodland predominating in birches and evergreens.

The interior planning is varied and irregular. At one end of the living room there are on each side handsome wooden screens with tulip decorations designed by Spencer. These cover the pipes of a built-in organ. Spencer's modern fireplace was replaced in 1926 by an historic one imported from England. The fireplaces in the library and

UPPER LEFT IS plot plan by famed landscape architect Jens Jensen. Lower photograph from the period, looking southeast past drive with Jensen landscape in foreground.

*DINING ROOM AND library, with
all furnishings and surfaces including
fireplace designed by architect and executed by Niedecken & Walbridge of
Milwaukee.*

dining room are still the originals designed by Spencer. Painted decorations
on the beams of the library ceiling, the
geometric screens in the ceiling of the
main staircase, the decorative plaster
borders of the ceilings and the art glass
windows are other innovative touches
by the architect. No longer in the house
are the rugs, portieres, drapes and
chandeliers that were made by the Milwaukee firm of Niedecken & Walbridge
from Spencer's designs.

In 1956 the house and grounds were
given by the Hauberg heirs to the City
of Rock Island for use as a civic center.
This house, perhaps the largest ever
built by Spencer and one of his finest
works, is an important milestone in the
outward spread of early modern architecture in America from its midwestern
center at Chicago. As the home of one
of Rock Island's most prominent families and one of the largest and most
distinguished residences in that city, it
is also a monument of considerable local interest.

*DENKMAN HOUSE LOOKING
northeast to garage/ stable. Originally
a greenhouse was attached at right.*

51

On the second floor, there were four major bedrooms. Perhaps because Mother had planned to live there with her three friends, each bedroom had its own personality, which might be read as a status symbol. The master bedroom, occupied by Mother and Dad, had a huge dressing room on one side of the hall, and a big bathroom on the other side. The bedroom stretched from one side of the house to the other with lots of windows and a sun porch.

I slept in what was called the Green Room. It had a very small bathroom and overlooked the porte-cochere. My sister and Miss Ross slept across the hall from me in what was known as the Blue Room. The tiled fireplace showed little girls dancing and picking daisies.

There was a huge guest room, the Brown Room, with a very large bathroom. The rug from the Brown Room now fills our living room, extending from the sofas to the west wall. Why this room was so large I don't know. I never really bought the story that Mother was going to live in that large house with three other spinsters, which seemed so ridiculous. But here we had a giant suite, then my little room, then Miss Ross and Kay's room, which had a dressing area as well as a bathroom and was a little suite all of its own, in addition to my parent's suite.

A playmate and I were sitting on the grand stairway one day trying to hit some cans with our slingshots. One of the stones went wild and broke a huge plate glass window in the sunroom. Both my friend and I were "tanned" by Dad and realized we had made a big mistake, but we paid for it.

In the servant's wing, the kitchen was over the basement laundry room. There was a pantry filled with china, glassware, and large vases. Mother was fond of organizing flower arrangements of peonies with all the ants in them, and roses and so on. She was very good at it. Then there was the servants' dining room. We normally had six or seven servants eating six days a week in that dining room. There was Frank, the houseman, Mrs. Bennett, the cook, a second girl who waited on table and helped make the beds, etc. Then there was Marie, the laundress, Andrew, the chauffeur, and a couple of gardeners. They all were faithful employees, and Mother in turn was very loyal to them. When the Crash came in 1929 and her income was reduced by something like 95 percent, she still kept everybody on, and it was deeply appreciated.

Off the living room was Dad's Indian Room, with bows and arrows and Civil War rifles, eagle-feathered war bonnets, beaded leather gauntlets and trousers. He also had all kinds of books about Abraham Lincoln. Some rather famous people came to talk to Dad about his Lincoln collection. One was Carl Sandburg, the poet, who wrote extensively about Lincoln. Later on there was Henry Horner, a Democrat who became governor of the state of Illinois. He and Dad used to sit and talk about the latest items in their collections of Lincolniana—letters, documents, photographs, and so forth.

There was a courtyard off the end of the house, concealed by a brick wall, but you could drive into it. That's where Marie hung the sheets out to dry. The oak firewood was kept in the courtyard also. The oak trees had been cut down near the House-in-the-Woods, a house the family owned about fifteen or twenty miles upriver. Dad and Mother had fires almost every night. Frank laid fires with these four- to five-foot split logs.

There was a coal chute from outside to the coal pile in the basement. When Frank arrived in the morning he would shovel coal into the hot-air heating system. By the end of winter the living room walls were somewhat darkened by soot, and Mother supervised an annual spring housecleaning that took care of all those problems. The use of coal was discontinued, probably in the late thirties, when Mother switched to oil heat.

The other major building on the property, in addition to the house itself, was a garage for six cars and stables for four horses. It had the re-charging equipment for Mother's electric car, of which she was an excellent and fearless driver. Aunt Elise Marshall also had an electric car. They charged them up every night. The car had a steering bar, and another bar beneath that for speed. You pushed the bar ahead for more speed, and pulled it toward you to slow down. There was a foot brake and a parking brake, I believe.

When I was six or seven, I was with Mother one day when she drove to the drugstore across from Audubon Elementary School. As she pulled away from the curb, a car zoomed up 18th Avenue. I was just terrified, but Mother calmly pushed the bar as far ahead as possible. The electric car responded with a splendid surge and she shot across the street out of the way of this madman's rush, just in the nick of time. I never got over how cool Mother was that day. Not only was she fearless, but also she was very quick-witted. I think the other car probably had the right of way, but Mother didn't see him coming and started out. Then instead of ducking, she just threw on all the power and got out of his way. It was a close call, but she just said, "He was going too fast." All the blame was on him.

The garage also housed our Reo truck with a cab and open seats in the back and was used by Dad to go down to the YWCA in Rock Island and pick up people who wanted to go on a hike but didn't have cars to reach the hiking location. Someone drove the truck with Dad in the other front seat while the "fresh air" benches faced each other, room for a dozen of us. Kay and I always rode in the back. The truck was one of our favorite vehicles. We had some happy times on those hikes.

There was a tool bench in the garage, with all kinds of tools. We boys used them at our peril however, because Andrew, the chauffeur, didn't like little boys. We would tease him and he always had an oily rag that he would rub our faces with if he caught us. Andrew had been Grandfather Denkmann's driver. He was a "teamster" and had driven a team of horses for Grandfather's three carriages. Andrew never got over the fact that automobiles were not being pulled by horses, which knew when, and how to turn. We had several close calls because Andrew forgot that he was supposed to turn the steering wheel, the car went where it wasn't supposed to go, and we almost got smashed. After Andrew retired, Dad did the driving for Mother, and was happy to be promoted to that job, as well as enjoying Mother's company without Andrew's comments. Andrew really never got used to the title of "chauffeur"—he was our "driver."

There was a tunnel through this building, which was the only entrance to the property for many years. There were also stables, with box stalls for two horses, and standing stalls for two others. Above this area was a space for hay and grain that could be accessed by a second floor opening out to 13th Street. There was a pulley arrangement which could raise a bale of hay or sack of oats to be stored above the stalls.

Beyond the stables was a greenhouse, which was probably sixty to eighty feet long. Andrew was in charge of that, but was never a good gardener. Mother never did hire an expert gardener to care for our eleven acres. The only things Andrew knew how to grow were geraniums, so the house was always full of geraniums.

Across 24th Street there was a tool house with a place for a buggy, but the buggy had

The greenhouse along 24th Street

been removed so that Dad could pile all of his law books in this space, along with old family Bibles, etc. Unfortunately, all of those got eaten up by mice before we discovered that a mouse was even around. The other part of the tool house was occupied by the two yardmen, both of whom had worked at the Rock Island Sash & Door Works for Grandfather Denkmann. Mother took them on as retainers to keep them employed after they retired from the Sash & Door plant.

Near the tool house was a vast vegetable and flower garden, part of it given over to the Reverend Williams of the Broadway Presbyterian Church to grow flowers for the church. Just as Andrew could only raise geraniums, Reverend Williams seemed able to grow only gladiolus. I've hated that plant ever since, because I never liked him.

We grew all the vegetables and berries for our household. We had fruit trees—apples, peaches, pears, etc. I don't know how productive they were, but the berry bushes were very productive. All the carrots, potatoes, and so on came from our own garden.

Frank would dig them up and bring them to Mrs. Bennett. We also had a pasture for our horse, Pet, and Lady, my pony, and the cow that Frank milked.

As is usual when you have large staffs like that who became quite intimate in their service relationships, they always squabbled with each other. The cook complained that Frank would bring her things she didn't want, and Frank would complain that she wanted things he didn't have.

There was a chicken house in the courtyard, where Frank would sometimes kill a chicken. That was a fascinating experience for me to watch the famous headless chicken rushing around until the body finally died.

Also across 24th Street from the house, beside the garden and pasture, was a play yard for Kay and me with a marvelous little playhouse—an early Johnson prefabricated house. Kay had a group of kids known as the So-Sew Social Club, and I had my boy friends. Our parents built a tennis court in 1927, so we played tennis. On a grassy area we put up basketball standards at either end, and we had a ping-pong table under the trees. In the summer we always had ten or fifteen boys from the neighborhood taking turns playing tennis, ping-pong, basketball, etc. By that time the chicken house had been cleaned up and Kay took that over as a clubhouse for her So-Sew Social Club. She had ten or twelve girl friends from Audubon Elementary and Washington Junior High School. The playhouse then kept us dry during rain showers.

The long grape arbor at Sue Denkmann Hauberg's house
being constructed in the background, circa 1910

The garden was a huge place. The hillside was landscaped by Jens Jensen, the famous Mid-western landscape architect. He designed it to be a Wisconsin type of forest. It became overgrown, but at the time we boys were sliding on our sleds down the hill, it was still quite open space. The whole neighborhood came with their sleds and toboggans to use our hill. You could go through the gate on 22nd Street and, if it was icy, you could probably add a quarter of a mile to the ride on your sled.

We never did any ice-skating, although the Mississippi and the Rock River and all the sloughs would freeze over. We walked on the Mississippi when it was frozen.

The garages were also used for rehearsals by Dad's United Sunday School Fife, Drum and Bugle Band, made up of boys who were teen-agers. The forty or fifty members had to have a perfect attendance record at whatever Sunday School they attended, whether they were Jewish, Catholic or Protestant, white or black. Dad taught each one to play an instrument. They marched in all the major parades downtown, whether Memorial Day, Fourth of July, Columbus Day, or Armistice Day. They disbanded before I was old enough to be eligible to learn an instrument. In 1923, when I was seven, the band was in its last year. That year, much to my delight, I was allowed to carry the flag in two different parades, along with two other boys who carried flags. We marched in front of the band, just behind Dad, who sometimes walked backwards taking photographs and waving his arms to direct the band. We boys felt pretty proud and happy to be a part of this fine group.

I am the little boy struggling with the flag, but still keeping step

Mother and Dad were not social and were violently opposed to alcohol and to smoking so we had very few private functions, but there were big affairs at the house, sponsored by various organizations. The Tri-Cities Garden Club would meet out on the big front lawn if the weather was fine, with numerous folding chairs being borrowed from funeral homes and churches. But mostly they met in our living room.

The Ladies Musical Club would meet there also. There were some fine organists in town, and our organ was always kept tuned and ready for such events. It was very much appreciated by everybody. Quite a few houses in the Tri-Cities area also had organs. I'm not sure how many of the people who owned the organs could actually play them. The organ with its numerous pipes was installed when our house was built. A later addition was a dresser type of thing. You lifted the lid to insert a roll of slotted paper which would automatically play the organ music. Mother also bought a Steinway player piano, which was hooked up to this so we could actually play piano concertos by Mozart and Beethoven.

In 1928, when I was twelve years old, Augustana College learned it was to be favored with a visit from Crown Prince Gustav Adolf, who later became King of Sweden. Mother agreed to use our house for a reception and tea. A multitude of people connected with Augustana College were invited to join Prince Gustav Adolf, along with other leading citizens.

Up to that time, the entrance to the Great House had been through the tunnel in the chauffeur's quarters and stables. Mother didn't think it was fitting for the crown prince to have to take this rather gloomy route, so a new entrance was planned and built off 24th Street and was called Prince William Drive.

The day arrived when the great man came to the house, and, of course, at some point Dad was eager to display his collection of Lincoln material and his Indian artifacts. The men headed for my father's study, which the prince mistakenly thought would be a male bastion where men could relax and have a smoke. Everyone in the room but the prince knew of the taboos in our house about smoking. So when the prince took out a long, elegant cigar from the case in his coat, a gasp went up. Prince Gustav Adolf was very sensitive. He quickly put the cigar back in the case, replaced the case in his pocket, and everybody heaved a sigh of relief.

It was a house that lent itself beautifully to large groups of people. Dad was fond of having the hiking club there. This was his interest, although Mother was never really up to hiking very much. Most members of the club were single men and women who enjoyed walking the woods and hills bordering the Mississippi, on both the Iowa and the Illinois side. They also traversed the hills of the Rock River, which bounded the city of Rock Island on the west and south sides.

When ladies' groups convened at our house, I had been taught to bow to the ladies, to hold out my hand and look them in the eye. I had to wear neat little pants and be a little man at an early date. I hated it, but I was secretly proud of the fact that Mother wanted to show me off. I think that was my first lesson in being proper and social.

My sister and I spent almost all of our time in the kitchen—sort of an "Upstairs-Downstairs" type of thing. The second girl was usually young, and Mrs. Bennett, the cook, was a chatterbox. Kay and I always got jelly bread or a biscuit or maybe the cook had made fudge. The stove was along the front wall and the kitchen sinks were in front of the windows so the cook could watch cars coming up the driveway. Across the

Top: The old entrance to the Great House through the garage-stables off corner of 13th Avenue & 24th Street; Bottom: New Prince William Drive entrance to the Great House off 24th Street

kitchen was a counter, under which was the radiator. The counter was quite wide and supported a large roll of wrapping paper. Mother sent lots of presents to people and used a great deal of wrapping paper. All the gifts that went out of our house were wrapped in the kitchen and sent on their way, usually through Henry Frank, the houseman.

Kay and I had a hideaway under that counter. We would laugh and talk and listen to the chatter of the second girl and the cook and the houseman, and maybe Marie, the laundress. They knew we were there, of course, but we were out of sight and out of the way. It was better than being in the living room, where Mother and Dad were quite austere. They would usually just be sitting and not talking too much. It was an old-fashioned way of growing up, probably adopted by most families who had the means to live the way Mother and Dad did. We didn't feel left out; we just felt it was more fun in the kitchen.

At the dining table Dad did most of the talking, and it would be about the hiking club or his other activities. He was head of the YMCA, and Mother was head of the YW. She was deeply involved in church work. At meals there was family talk and there was church talk, and talk about drinking. Dad was very much involved in the Prohibition movement. He was a close friend of Congressman Volstead, who sponsored the Volstead Act which brought about Prohibition. Mother was very involved in her shelter program for battered women, the West End Settlement.

I would say that Mother ran the house. Of course, Mother had all the money. Dad gave up his law practice because his income was minuscule compared with Mother's vast fortune, which came from the various Denkmann and Weyerhaeuser enterprises. The Weyerhaeuser Company had been founded in 1900, but didn't really produce much revenue until the mid-twenties. Before that, most of Mother's money came from just the Denkmann family enterprises, consisting of sawmills and timberlands in Louisiana and Mississippi. Mr. Weyerhaeuser wasn't involved in those things at all. They were entirely Denkmann properties, and they were very lucrative.

Kay and I were expected to listen to the grown-up talk at the dinner table and were not encouraged to talk ourselves. We never were asked how our day went or what went on at school. That reinforced our pleasure at being in the kitchen where there was a lot of laughter and chatter and we were free to say what we wanted. We thought Mother and Dad were wonderful and we never had anything bad to say about them. I think secretly, however, we were rather lonely for affection from our parents that wasn't really forthcoming.

John, Mother and Kay

The Great House in 1911

CHAPTER 6

The Great House & How We Used It

IT WAS ALWAYS MOTHER'S HOUSE, OF COURSE. WHY SHE BUILT SUCH A HUGE HOUSE was never discussed. But she and Dad loved it and Sis and I did too. The Great House was spectacular even to us boys of six to ten or eleven. It was so big that we kids, playing basketball in the halls (using a tennis ball and hoops to match), never seemed to disturb Dad in his cubbyhole office on one side of a hall or Mother in her library directly across from Dad. The house was located on the brink of a knoll commanding the valley below. Our view was filled with a shady residential area of houses immediately below. Then the downtown of the city of Rock Island. The broad Mississippi with Davenport, Iowa and its shady hills above that city gave us a mighty scope by day and by night.

I don't know (and never will) how Mother came to build such a house. She said often that it was built to bring together herself and her three other spinster "best friends" where they could enjoy a lifetime together. She was thirty-six in 1908 and without prospects for marriage. She was quite social, a charter member (No. 7) of the Rock Island Arsenal Golf Club and its Ladies Champion in 1905.

I don't know when she bought the eleven-acre tract at the top of 23rd Street. How did she wind up with a leading firm of architects, Spencer and Powers, of Chicago, who built many Midwest Prairie School houses? The four-spinster theory breaks down when one examines the bedrooms and baths on the second floor. The four bedrooms bear no relationship to how she felt about herself and her three friends, each is most different in size and facilities. Each would speak to a different level of affection for each friend.

The principal of Audubon School was Miss Jane Wilcox, one of Mother's closest friends. The others were Miss Mae Blanding, who was principal of Hawthorne school, and Miss Haverstick, who was a secretary. Reportedly, the four of them planned to remain maiden ladies and live there for the rest of their lives in Mother's huge house. Then Dad came along and upset the plan.

Dad loved the house. Never in his life before Mother did he think about such a beautiful thing. Dad was not "social" so the house never saw parties of friends. No smoking was permitted and drinking was never even thought about. These taboos resulted in no invitations to social parties for Mother and Dad. But my Audubon

Also known as the House on the Knoll

School buddies and I were permitted to play almost all over the house except for the bedroom floor. We all loved the elevator, the laundry chute for secret messages, the organ pipes rooted in the cellar and rising behind the wooden screens in the living room, and the "echo" pipes in the attic with invisible outlets over the grand stairway. There were the back stairs, from service delivery door up to the third floor attic and down to the basement, where Marie and Frank toiled. I had a tool bench next to the water tanks that helped us boys nail together pieces of wood for boats, bird houses, etc.

Dad had a darkroom in the basement where he enlarged his photographs and developed the prints. His collection of his early (pre-1900) glass plates and negatives were labeled on shelves. Most of his enlarging came from pictures taken on the Saturday hikes or the annual (1920-on) "Big Hikes." The Black Hawk Hiking Club had an annual "photograph hike" in which everybody competed with his or her best pictures. Dad was an ardent contributor and competitor for a ribbon.

There was actually a skeleton in a closet in the basement! He was the murderer of Colonel George Davenport, and was hung in Rock Island. Somehow or other the remains were on display in the Rock Island County Courthouse until somebody complained. Dad rescued the skeleton, with the broken neck bones clearly visible, for some future disposal. But there it was, next to our elevator, for us boys to show our pals.

We boys were permitted to use the "front hall" to put up hoops that were sized for tennis balls so we could play indoor basketball with a tennis ball. Since there was an upright piano and the grandfather clock in this hall too, we had to be careful—and we were. Dad saw, or heard, to that.

Dad's office (he never went downtown to work after two years of marriage) was just off this hall. When our noise got too loud, or we failed to heed warnings from his office, he would appear, collaring the nearest culprit and giving him a few whacks. We had our own alarm system however. He spent most of the time typing letters, historical data, minutes of meetings on a very old and noisy machine and when that noise stopped we boys *knew* that trouble was coming. Much of his correspondence was with the various Weyerhaeusers, especially F.E. and Rudolph in St. Paul and John P. in Tacoma. The telephone was more costly and still not entirely private.

He also typed interviews with "old settlers" from a personal shorthand and illustrated by his photos of them. And he was writing about "The Black Hawk War: 1830-32" as part of his presidency of the Illinois Historical Society in the 1920s and 1930s. Not to mention his association with the Rock Island YMCA and other organizations from the Rotary Club to the Chamber of Commerce. He was a very busy, self-started man. In his office, just off the front hall, his typewriter was going many hours every day.

Mother, across the hall, read books on teaching Sunday School and required a weekly meeting with her six teachers to develop lesson plans. She took a keen interest in bright young ladies and put more than twenty-five of them through Augustana College. Along with Aunt Elise Marshall and Aunt Lonie Tom Davis she "ran" Broadway Presbyterian Church. The three sisters terrified the Broadway minister, although he was a frequent visitor to Mother's library. In addition there were visits from the best fund-raisers in the country from the National YMCA and National YWCA, the United Negro College Fund, and Billy Sunday's evangelical missions and others. Mother and Dad were thrilled to put Billy Sunday up for the night. He played the piano and we sang "Brighten the corner where you are …… someone far from harbor you may guide across the bar, brighten the corner ……." No one went away empty-handed, even during the Depression.

The living room was huge and the center of all evening activities. The lamp bases looked like Ming dynasty vases and the lampshades let little light through. The two twenty-five watt bulbs in each lamp ruined the eyesight of all of us. But we gathered around them to do our reading.

Both Sis (the Kay came later) and I loved the nights when Dad turned on the Aeolian organ and chose the grand marches by Verdi and music by Wagner. There was also a big stand-up Victrola which had to be cranked up to play the records with the logo of the dog listening to a loudspeaker mounted on a Victrola. "His Master's Voice" was the slogan, even though Enrico Caruso and Madame Schuman-Heink made pretty scratchy renditions. Then came the radio, at first a four- or five-foot long box with glowing tubes and receptacles for three or four plug-in lines to head sets through which one occasionally recognized voices and music. KDKA Schenectady was first, then an evangelist from Memphis. The Victrola and this early radio were soon turned in for a more useful radio. We laughed to *Amos and Andy*. Dad hated Bing Crosby's "croon-

ing." "That's not singing," he'd say.

I am seated with my collie dog, Prince, at lower right

Just off the living room below and Mother and Dad's big bedroom above were two glassed-in garden rooms, one above the other. Neither was ever used as a place to enjoy a sunny rest. My parents were far too busy to sit down and rest. The upstairs room stored all sorts of things from linens to books to excess furniture.

The downstairs room, off the living room, was Dad's library and his "Indian Room," with cabinets for his eagle-feathered war bonnets, Indian bows and arrows, dozens of chipped flint arrow heads

and spear points, Civil War rifles, Indian beaded vests and breeches, and many other artifacts. Homemade bookshelves along every wall concealed the glass doors and windows. The journals of various Midwest State Historical Societies reflected his tenure as president of the Illinois State Historical Society during the 1920s. Hundreds of books bought in rare book stores which had perhaps only one reference to Rock Island County's history, geology, crops, flora and fauna crammed the shelves. His hero, Abraham Lincoln, was represented by Dad's collection of his letters both before and during Lincoln's presidency.

Our table in the kitchen

Andrew Reitz, driver for Grandparents Denkmann and chauffeur for our family

So the "Indian Room" had magic that everyone felt, whoever came to the house, and along with the skeleton in the basement closet, these two rooms were unforgettable. We boys, in the 1920s, were permitted to take the bows and arrows outdoors to play "Indians at war," as long as we put them all back in their cabinets. Somehow, we never managed to "shoot" each other.

Outdoors, the hill below the knoll was pretty steep. It became the sledding area for the whole neighborhood. Prince would follow me on my sled all the way down barking furiously. If the snow became hard, we could even exit our property onto 22nd Street and get another block or two of sledding. No one had skis in those days, but there were always a few toboggans. The numerous trees made for some turning to make the descents more interesting. But every so often a tree would move into some kid's path and knock out a few teeth.

We made Eskimo igloos out of chunks of heavy snow when such fell. The soot of Rock Island's coal furnaces turned these igloos black very quickly, while the dogs peed on the entrances until they were bright yellow. The things one remembers!!

The pergola between the house and the driveway

In 1927 Mother built us a tennis court, clay and sand surface, and hired a young man to care for it during the summer. Between the tennis court and the chicken coop was an open, but small, lawn. The lawn became an outdoor basketball court. Nearby, under trees, we had a ping-pong table. Some ten to fourteen boys gathered every day all summer long to enjoy the sports. Sis cleaned up the chicken coop which became headquarters for her So-Sew Social club. We boys felt that "girls" were a waste of time and we offered a few remarks from time to time. Since the girls were our sisters or neighbors, the remarks were guarded.

In another area just below the pergola beyond the house, we boys built endless roads with toy bulldozers, dump trucks, cranes and graders. These little wonders were made in Moline by a steel manufacturer named Lundahl for his son Buddy. The line was called Buddy L, and later in my teens at dancing parties, lo and behold there was Buddy Lundahl, just my age! These activities kept Bob Hubbard, Billy Robinson, Carl Rochow—all neighbors—and me, busy for at least two years, if not three, until we were probably all ten or eleven years old.

Our lawn across the driveway down to 22nd Street

Waimea Canyon, Island of Kauai

CHAPTER 7

Family Travels

Europe 1926

d AD TOOK MOTHER, KAY, MISS ROSS, AUNT ANNA HAUBERG, AND ME TO EUROPE in 1926 for almost the entire summer. After a New York Central train trip to New York City, we sailed on the SS *Adriatica* and landed in Liverpool. It was a fascinating experience. Kay and I had never been on such a big ship before. Mother and Dad had gone to Egypt, the Holy Land, and to Europe in 1924, so this was not new to them. Kay and I explored every cabin in every class of the boat that we could. We were amazed to learn that there were people crowded together in the lower regions of the *Adriatica*. The difference between our luxurious first-class accommodations and those in steerage was astounding to me.

During the ten-day passage, everyone in first class got to sit at the captain's table at least once. When it was our turn, the Archbishop of Dublin joined us. He asked the Captain if another Irishman, who was a great tenor, could sing for the guests on board. John McCormick sang Irish songs — "Mother Machree" and "When Irish Eyes are Smiling." Soon the Archbishop was in tears and almost blubbering. When McCormick bent over and kissed the Archbishop's ring, my parents couldn't hide their displeasure with this whole Catholic business.

My first photos: Top left: Buckingham Palace; Bottom left & right: Changing of the guard at Buckingham Palace

This presaged my mother's reaction to the presidential election of 1928 when Al Smith, the Democratic candidate, an ardent Catholic who was determined to scuttle Prohibition and bring back good Irish whiskey, opposed Herbert Hoover, a staunch Republican and the very symbol of correctness. Mother said if Al Smith won the election we would all move to Bermuda. I had no idea until then what strong feelings Mother had about the Catholics, let alone Mother and Dad's strong support of "prohibition."

From Liverpool, we took the train to London and began a sightseeing tour of England, including a trip to Stratford-upon-Avon to visit Shakespeare country. We certainly saw every sight in London, including Westminster Abbey, the Tower of London, and the changing of the guard at Buckingham Palace. We took a boat across the English Channel and spent several days in Paris, of which I have only a few recollections.

Mother's sister, Aunt Catherine Wentworth, and her husband were living in an elegant house in Paris. She was a very good portrait painter, doing pictures of people of status, including some of the Catholic higher clergy and prominent Parisians. She pooh-poohed Mother's ties to the church, and pretty soon Mother was in tears because of her sister's scorn of Mother's efforts on behalf of the church and Sunday School. It wasn't a very pretty scene.

My other memory of Paris is of the Louvre, where I felt challenged to run through every room so that I could say I had seen everything in the Louvre. I believe I actually succeeded in visiting every room open to the public. I stopped at only two displays for a longer look: The Winged Victory and Venus de Milo.

While in France we visited Verdun and saw the remains of the battlefield where so many soldiers had so recently fought and died. We went on to Rheims where the cathedral was being restored and saw the statue of Joan of Arc on horseback in the plaza. Miss Ross had given my sister and me little cameras. I took pictures of the fortifications at Verdun, and of the changing of the guard at Buckingham Palace, and other scenes. She had also given us diaries with "My Trip Abroad" on the cover. It was my first and I cherish it.

Top: The fortifications at Verdun; Bottom: The statue of Joan of Arc stands defiantly before the ruined Rheims cathedral

A high point of the 1926 trip was Helsingfors (now known as Helsinki), the capital of Finland. Dad was a delegate to an international YMCA convention. The secretary of the Rock Island YMCA joined us there, Dad having funded his trip. We stayed at a hotel outside the city. Due to the language barrier, Mother, Aunt Anna, Miss Ross, Kay and I didn't get around very much while my father attended the convention sessions. There was a creek running through the hotel grounds and Kay and I spent almost the entire visit building a little dam across it. We were barefoot and having a wonderful time.

The only sight in Finland I remember seeing was a sensational watercourse called the Imatra Falls in the forest of northern Finland. The rapids were at least a mile long, with a tremendous chute of water coming out through that gap and plunging into the valley. I believe those falls have been dammed now to create much of the power needed by Helsinki.

Things got very interesting after that. Our family took its first flight in airplanes, from Helsingfors to Riga, Latvia. They were single-engine Fokker floatplanes made of corrugated aluminum, also known as wrinkle-tin. There was room for only four passengers. My parents engaged in quite a debate as to whether we should all get on the same plane,

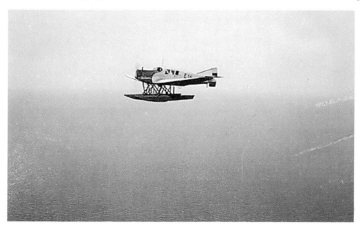

We flew in two identical airplanes. This is Dad's photo of the plane with Mother, Aunt Anna, Miss Ross, and Kay

because in case of a disaster we would all perish together, or whether we should divide up. My 1926 diary reveals that Dad and I went in one plane, the four ladies in the other.

At Riga we boarded a train for Berlin. It had compartments glassed off from the companionway which went up one side of the car. American trains had a central aisle with open seats on either side. We went through what was then the separate enclave of Danzig. After World War I, the Treaty of Versailles set up Danzig as a neutral country, because there was a big squabble over it between Poland and Germany. The Allies did not want to do anything to enrich Germany, but they weren't keen on doing much for Poland either. When the train went through Danzig all the shades were pulled down, which seemed a strange situation.

I remember the Brandenburg Tor in Berlin, the huge old gates that had been used in the days when European cities were walled. The gates had become sort of a

*Above: Dad, Kay, and I built this cairn for the photo with
the Jungfrau behind us. Right: John H. Hauberg, Jr., in
Bavarian clothes with an ice axe*

splendid monument to German victories and thus were not favored by the Allies. Dad,
of course, was an enthusiastic German who felt that Britain had started World War I,
and that Germany had been forced to defend itself. He thought Germany was wonderful, and we felt that way too.

Another memory is of the splendid Gates of Pergamum, which were from an ancient
Near-Eastern civilization, possibly Hittite. They were located in that part of Berlin which
later fell under communist domination. The museums were great. I began to take an interest in the big paintings I saw, although I have specific recollections of only one.

In Munich we visited the Museum of Industry and Science, where they had an
elevator that simulated a mineshaft. You went down one floor, but the elevator's sidewalls

were rolling screens that went whirling up and we felt as if we were descending into the depths of the coal mine. I was thrilled with that. We were each given a miner's helmet with a little light on the top.

Dad had climbed the Jungfrau Mountain in 1924 at age fifty-four(!) and felt that Kay and I should experience the high mountains of Switzerland. We arrived at Grindelwald where we boarded a train that took us up to a hotel inside a mountain. Much of the trip was inside this mountain but every now and then there would be a "window" with spectacular views of the mountain range. Dad proposed that Kay and I join him in a short climb of a peak not far from the hotel. A guide was hired and we all rented appropriate boots and roped up behind the guide with Dad bringing up the rear in order to take pictures. It was a great thrill for us to stand on the peak, although a very easy time for our guide. We saw the Jungfrau off in the distance and were properly awed that our Dad had climbed it.

During our visit to Dresden, a curious thing happened. We went to the great collection of old masters, of which the image of Raphael's *Sistine Madonna* was deeply engraved on my memory. Later in my life, after I had been to Italy a number of times and had seen many Raphael Madonnas in Florence, I realized there must have been something different about that Madonna. In 1988 my second wife Ann and I revisited Dresden and the *Sistine Madonna*. What was different about her was that she was a peasant woman looking out of the canvas at you, and indicating great trepidation about the future of the baby and her own life. The baby was more of a peasant baby, showing some worry about the future. The Florentine Madonnas were aristocratic ladies, who seemed assured that everything was going to be all right.

We visited Haubergs in Kiel. Dad had been there in 1900, and he and Mother visited Kiel again in 1924. We also met the Frels. Dad's mother was a Frels. Kiel and the surrounding countryside were loaded with people named Frels or Hauberg. My strongest memory of that is going into the house of Henry Frels, who spoke no English. He promptly trotted out schnapps for Dad and Mother, who of course were ardent Prohibitionists. To the delight of my sister and myself we were given tiny little cups of schnapps. Before Mother and Dad could stop us we downed our peppermint schnapps and thought they were wonderful.

As in the United States, the Haubergs and Frels were hearty people, big-nosed, tall and broad, and prone to lots of laughter. Kay and I were just very pleased to meet these wonderful people who were so like our relatives back home, even though we couldn't understand them, as they spoke very little English. We didn't look up the Denkmann background at all. I'm not sure where Grandfather Denkmann was born and raised.

During our ten-week sojourn we saw a lot, got used to foreign languages, and enjoyed a variety of hotels. Dad and Mother had no trouble with German, as both were brought up with that. I think it's too bad they didn't speak German around the Great House so Kay and I could have learned something of it. We returned to the United States on a different ship.

Hawaii 1928

The next big trip the family took was to Hawaii on July 14, 1928. We stayed for ten weeks there also, spending time on all the major islands—Oahu, Maui, the big island of Hawaii, Kauai to the north. It was our first visit to the tropics.

At Waikiki on Oahu, we stayed at the Royal Hawaiian, which had just opened in 1927. We had the Presidential suite, with Mother and Dad looking out over the ocean, and across the hall Miss Ross and my sister and me looking out over the hotel gardens, which were splendid. Even though our room was on the landward side, we could hear the waves crashing on the beach. Kay and I could hardly wait to get into our suits and go down to the wonderful beach at Waikiki. We loved the help in the hotel. They were all pure Hawaiians—very handsome people, and talented in making grass hats, splitting coconuts, climbing palm trees, swimming, surfing, dancing, singing, and playing ukuleles.

I turned absolutely black. At one point I had a heat stroke and had to stay in the hotel for a couple of days, but soon I was back out on the beach digging in the sand and playing with a Hawaiian chap, a hotel employee who I believe as a youth had broken his jaw. His name was Hawkshaw. He taught us to do the hula, how to climb the palm trees, and took us out on his surfboard.

The sand at Waikiki was absolutely riddled with cigarette butts. Mother and Dad were upset about that but it didn't bother Kay and me. In those days everybody smoked, and the hotel didn't have any equipment to filter the sand. When Mother came to the beach she wore an old-fashioned bathing suit, while the younger gals were all in skimpy suits for those days. Mother must have felt terribly old at that point, but she had been brought up in the days when bathing suits were designed to cover everything but the lower legs.

That was a great beach, with the hotel overlooking the inlet and Diamond Head beyond. We took a two- or three-day trip all the way around the island by limousine, staying at tiny, almost motel-like hotels tucked among the palm trees, not too far from the beach. Pure Hawaiians ran them. They are wonderful people with a great presence and were very caring. You felt almost that they were members of your family who were devoted to looking after your best interests, and I guess they felt that way too.

When we drove through the pineapple fields, the driver got out and cut a few pineapples. He had a little machete and would take the prickles off, and we ate the pineapple right in the fields. It didn't seem to matter to the owners. The idea in those days was that everybody liked everybody. You respected everybody. That was a great time to see all of this. I think living on an island creates a sense of intimacy and familiarity that one doesn't find in big cities today.

In the Royal Hawaiian dining room we were delighted with new things to eat like papaya and fresh pineapple. There was always entertainment, mostly with wonderful Hawaiian songs. All the children staying at the hotel were taught to do the hula to such songs as "Lovely Hula Hands," "Little Grass Shack," and the "Hukilau Song." We were taught to play little ukuleles and learned the words to all the songs, even the Hawaiian words. They were always mixed in with a little English. It was the first chance Kay and I had to really get into a foreign language, and, because it wasn't important to learn it, we were eager to do so.

There was no air transportation between islands then, so we traveled by small boat. We went to the big island, Hawaii, and drove up to Mauna Loa and Mauna Kea, seeing an active volcano for the first time. We visited the great hole in the ground, Hale Mau Mau, where they had a little concession at which you would tee up a golf ball and could make a hole in one by just dribbling the ball off the tee. I remember, however, that I whiffed! I took a big stab at it and missed. Everybody roared with laughter because I didn't get my hole in one when it was so easy.

Our stay in Hilo was at another of these tiny hotels, almost totally covered with palm fronds, hibiscus and flowers of every sort. The Hawaiians did the cooking and waited on the table, carried the bags, and became your instant friends.

On Maui we disembarked in the Kihei area and got on horses. Dad, Kay and I rode up to the rim of Haleakala and back the same day. The ride was rather strenuous. Going up on horseback was wonderful, but coming down wasn't so great. Seeing this enormous crater was very impressive, with lots of steam coming out.

On Kauai we spent three or four nights at Lihue, and here, too, we were driven all around the island. Kay and I had lots of fun sliding down the sand dunes. The sand particles were of such shapes and sizes that when you shoved your foot into it, it barked. They were called the barking sands. We went out on a boat with some fishermen and I had my first experience with seasickness.

That first visit to Hawaii was memorable for me, and I'm glad I had an opportunity to see that beautiful part of the world in its more natural state. I have visited it many times over the years, and although it is a far more crowded tourist destination today, there still is the charm of the islands which draws one back for yet another visit.

Going Home

Map of the Fourteen hundred mile cruise of the
"Catherine" of Rock Island,Ills. July-August,1929.
    The distance is Nine hundred miles,one way,-Rock
Island to Mammoth Cave.

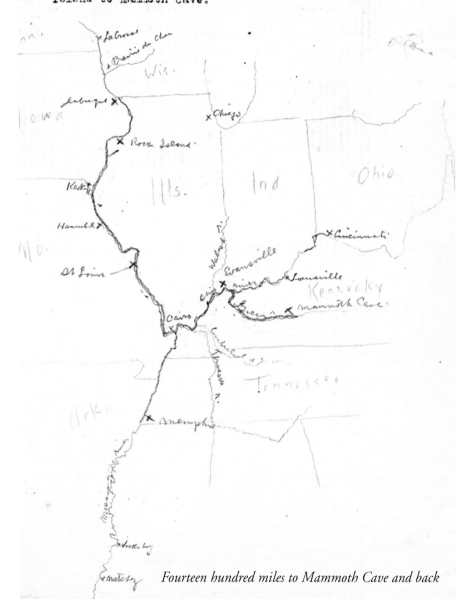

Fourteen hundred miles to Mammoth Cave and back

CHAPTER 8

Boat Trips, Big Hikes, Farming, the Olympics, & Elsewhere

1920s and 1930s

t HE FAMILY TRIPS TO EUROPE IN 1926 AND TO THE HAWAIIAN ISLANDS IN 1928 WERE each ten weeks long and were truly major for us. But no year, including 1926 and 1928, went by without travels in our boat, the *Catherine*, and the "Big Hikes" of the Black Hawk Hiking Club in open trucks. Several "voyages" and truck trips were significant events themselves, but each type was repetitive in its daily routine. Suffice it to say that each event was looked forward to with anticipation and enthusiasm and looked backward on as another accomplishment, a growing up and educational process for Sis and me, and our friends, as well as fun for Dad's associates.

We also began our acquaintance with southern Denkmanns and western Weyerhaeusers, all cousins who made up an extended family for Mother in Rock Island from the 1880s on and who fortunately admired Dad for his energy, common sense, and loyal support. So there began, in the 1920s, Easter-time train trips to Hammond, Louisiana and the mills and woods in Mississippi as well as visits to the woods and mills of the Pacific Northwest.

Oh yes, we were on the move a lot.

The *Catherine*

In February of 1921 Dad ordered a boat of five-foot beam and twenty-five-foot length from Fred Kahlke whose boatyard built, repaired, and stored, in winter, most of the biggest boats in the area including ferryboats and all the fleet of Weyerhaeuser and Denkmann. The goal was a boat to be used for pleasure on inland waterways—a craft that could come right up to a shore which had only a reasonable

approach; it must be roomy so we could on occasion invite our friends for an outing with us; it must be provided with shelter against unpleasant weather; "but it must be so open that the slightest bit of breeze would reach its occupants, and we wanted some speed." (Dad's description recorded later in 1931.) The speed factor was not for watching the shore whiz by, but to make headway upstream on the rivers which had fairly fast currents. The bottom was to be made of two inch oak planks to resist the rocks on the riverbeds and a heavy metal "skeg" to protect the propeller from the same. How many times were we happy with those foresights!!

Dad sprained his ankle badly on January 25 of 1921, a good time to do it, because it kept him from going to Kahlke's boatyard to hurry up the building of the *Catherine*. Fred Kahlke was a man who thought a lot before saying anything, and the construction of our little boat was as slow as his speech. Dad was off his crutches and cane on April 8, but he fails to date the completion of the *Catherine* in his 1921 album, although he did record that I finally learned to whistle on June 26.

However, the first photos of the *Catherine* on the water were taken at Archie Allen Camp just above Port Byron. The boat had been pulled up on the shore in the evening, the river had gone down over night, the photos are of the many people it took to push it into the water, the next page shows the boat with twenty-two of Dad's Band Boys in it, again without date, but a few pages later shows Mother and the YWCA's Archie Allen Camp staff afloat on August 3. Hurrah!! There wasn't any mention of the total cost, but Kahlke had submitted an interim bill on May 20 for $763.03, not including the engine, but including a rowboat.

Sis and I were growing up in the early 1920s and made only a few river outings. In 1924 and 1925 we spent the summers at Hyannisport, Massachusetts, and in 1926 we were in Europe with Mother and Dad for ten weeks. In 1928 we were in Hawaii.

So our first major expedition in the *Catherine* was a very long, eventful voyage of over fourteen hundred miles in length on the Mississippi, the Ohio, and the Green River of Kentucky to visit Mammoth Cave. The year was 1929.

The *Catherine* had extended Dad's ability to explore every corner of Rock Island County. The Hiking Club did it with him by land, and now he could see a lot more of it by "sea."

The years from 1921 to 1929 found him afloat many times each spring, summer, and fall. He rarely went by himself. On odd occasions he took Henry Frank, our houseman, or Andrew Reitz, our chauffeur, to help. But mostly each outing was planned to bring aboard family and/or friends or groups to visit certain areas that were of interest to him and to them. He always had some special mission in mind. His 1923 annual Christmas album has a page of photos and text recording "the 10th trip of the *Catherine* for 1923" before the summer Big Hike began!

My little friend, Joe Meenan, and I went on a lot of these trips, many of which were several days' duration during summer vacation. In 1925 we had a four-day and four-night trip from Archie Allen Camp to Prairie du Chien where Black Hawk lost his last battle against the U.S. army in 1832. By the time we returned, Joe and I had learned everything there is to know about the Black Hawk War. Mission accomplished.

Dad felt we should try a really long trip on the *Catherine*. The nation had been stunned by the deaths of several "spelunkers," cave explorers who had become unable to get out of a cave when wedged in. The rescue attempts were reported in detail. Whether this brought Mammoth Cave, Kentucky, to Dad's mind, I don't know. The Hikers had been to this national park on a two-week-long Big Hike to the Smoky Mountains National Park. At any rate this was to be a test for Joe and me, since we were to do all the piloting and docking. It would involve new rivers, the Ohio, and the Green River of Kentucky—all told, going and coming, some fourteen hundred miles!

To Mammoth Cave and Back

By 1929 Dad and I and Joe Meenan were ready for a really long trip. Mammoth Cave had a ring to its name that suggested adventure. We would be going past Tom Sawyer and Huckleberry Finn country, and with luck might attend a showboat performance.

We left Kahlke's Boat Yard at 6:35 p.m. on July 2, 1929. Joe and I built a deck for sleeping across the forward gunwales, driving nails into the *Catherine's* oak sides! The very next morning we met a showboat! Its theater-auditorium was on a barge that a regular stern-wheeler pushed. Actors and actresses lived on a deck above the auditorium. The crew of the steamboat lived on that. We didn't stay for the show, but at least we knew what to look for.

Shortly below Burlington, Iowa, we entered the open water (Coopers Lake) backed up by the mighty Keokuk Dam. There were big waves and all three of us were soaked. Dad fashioned a "duck back" with oars and canvas and it helped a little. The next problem was the engine which kept heating up. Apparently our water intake was not taking in enough water. Dad fashioned a scoop out of a tin can, got under the boat and nailed the scoop over the intake. Problem solved! I was really impressed with Dad because I had never seen him do anything mechanical before!

Somewhere just above Quincy, Illinois, Dad tried a short cut that looked OK, but we struck a submerged wing dam and bent the skeg and the propeller. We struggled into a boatyard about noon and its owner put his men to work on both problems. For lunch he took us to his "club" where a policeman at the door looked us over and waved us in. It was a "speakeasy," very illegal and the sort of place Dad had spent many years of his life putting out of business. So we were on pins and needles, even at our ages of thirteen and fourteen, to see what Dad would do. He knew we were hungry and weary from the job of getting the *Catherine* ashore. So we all had sandwiches and soft drinks, disappointing our host.

The repairmen straightened the skeg and rebolted it in place, straightened the propeller and remounted it, and put on a new, factory-made scoop. We were much more careful after that about the boat and hidden hazards, but there were more adventures ahead.

The lock at Keokuk was the biggest we had ever seen. It was the Fourth of July and we went down forty feet in the lock with an excursion boat full of very fancy people who seemed quite impressed with our little boat and its crew making it through the rough water. Our canvas "duck back," the condition of our equipment, and the three of us soaked to our skin were quite a contrast to their elegance. I think we swaggered a bit, proud of their scrutiny.

More repairs to our boat in St. Louis gave us time to visit the Jefferson Memorial and the Lindbergh trophies (gifts). Lindy and his *Spirit of St. Louis* had made

Keokuk Lock

his famous solo flight across the Atlantic only three years before and we were excited to see all the gifts from many nations.

How did we eat and sleep? Joe and I slept on the forward deck, Dad put down his bedroll behind the engine. We had a little gas stove to heat up soup, make bacon and eggs, but wherever there was a little town we ate in a café. It was breakfast on the boat most of the time. Dad usually got the boat going around 4:30 every morning and reports that Joe and I slept until 8:00 a.m.!

We bathed in the river. Mother wasn't with us and probably very glad of it. And I suspect Sis was only a little jealous. However, there were lots of mosquitoes, and one night I had eighty bites on an arm left outside my blanket.

The Ohio River flowed into the Mississippi several miles below Cape Girardeau and Cairo, Illinois. It was a yellowish color; very different from the darker Mississippi with a distinct line between the colors which persisted for more than a mile. We were glad to be going upstream again. However, Dad's report pooh-poohs the Ohio. He loved "his" Mississippi.

At Metropolis, Illinois, on the Ohio, we ran into Bryant's Show Boat and attended an evening show. The entire personnel, captain and wife (owners), steamboat crew, actors and actresses paraded the two-block long Main Street of this anything-but-mighty Metropolis with placards and banners announcing the title of the play and show time. The band of perhaps six to eight instruments was blowing and drumming as loud as possible. The whole town had turned out for the parade. The play was about the good guy rescuing the good girl from the bad guy. Everybody hung onto every word of it.

These river towns were too small to have a movie theater, and radio was very new. The Show Boat was the biggest thing. No doubt it played in every small town on the river perhaps three or four times a year. Roads were still dirt, mud in wet weather. The rivers were the roads on which the river people depended for communication with the outside world.

The next day we landed at Cave-in Rock, now an Illinois State Park. In the days from 1800 to 1880 when overland roads were few, if any, the cave was a hideaway for "river pirates" who preyed on people moving downstream on flat boats with produce to

Cave-in Rock

sell in Memphis or New Orleans, and returning home on foot with their money along the Ohio and Mississippi Rivers. Cave-in Rock was notorious for the murders that took place in its vicinity. Dad told us these stories, which were repeated later in an American history course at Princeton, as evidence of the jungle of forests, swamps, small rivers, and creeks that made travel by land impossible and made the big river banks gauntlets of highwaymen to be feared by all travelers. It was not safe to travel alone.

Very soon we turned away from the Ohio into the mouth of the Green River of Kentucky. What a change! It was, by comparison, narrow, but very deep. It was very crooked with many locks, but cozy, friendly, and full of life.

Top left: A baptism; right: The beautiful Green River; Middle left: The incoming water set up a strong current; Bottom left: A steamboat; right: A car ferry

The locks raised us ten to fifteen feet to the water level behind each dam. The lock tender asked for help in turning the wheels that opened and closed the gates, and Joe and I liked to do that. The size of the locks "tailored" the size of the steamboats on the river. The roads that did cross the river came to a narrow place so that the ferryboat had the shortest possible haul across the river.

The Green River was lined with trees. Just where plowed fields began back of the screen of trees we could never see. But the water coming into the Green was clear, so clear that the water churned up back of our propeller sparkled in the sunlight.

On Sunday we went to church and were asked to sit in the choir! It was a courtesy extended to all visitors. Looking out at the congregation, we saw young girls breastfeeding their babies, a first for me. Later, at lunch in a boarding house, the dining room walls were covered with newspaper all upside down so the help didn't (couldn't) stand around reading! All these things were unforgettable.

We arrived in cave country and began to read about Floyd Collins, who lost his life in Sand Cave. Thousands of people came here while a shaft was being dug to rescue him. The national press reported its progress and his condition every day. But all was in vain. A scandal occurred when his brother "stole" his body from its natural tomb. A nearby entrepreneur who owned another cave renamed it the "Floyd Collins Crystal Cave," exhumed the body and placed it in an elaborate casket on exhibition. Wow! There were more shenanigans, but the above will suffice.

Sand Cave where Floyd Collins lost his life

Arrival at Mammoth Cave on July 16, 1929

We finally arrived at Mammoth Cave on July 15, almost two weeks from the start and covering 900 miles. The next day we toured the great cave with a large group. All I remember is that the cave was very big and very sooty from years of the smoke of pitch torches.

Dad had to return to Rock Island to lead the Tenth Annual Big Hike of the Black Hawk Hiking Club scheduled for a July 20 departure. He reports in his 1929 album that our entire family went on the sixteen-day trip and I am in the one photo he took of Mother, Kay and me to prove it, but I haven't a single memory of it. We went to Niagara Falls, "climbed" Mt. Washington, swam in the Atlantic, visited Bunker Hill and drove up Fifth Avenue to the Metropolitan Art Museum. All was lost on me! At least in April 2000 when this is written.

On August 16 Dad and I returned to Mammoth Cave to bring the *Catherine* home. There were no new "highlights," but it gave us a chance to record in photos a few things that are "quaint" today.

We returned 411 miles to Cairo from Mammoth Cave in five days, going past Cairo to the Mississippi to "touch base" before returning to Cairo to turn the *Catherine* over to the Federal Barge Line for shipment to Dubuque, Iowa. Why Dubuque, I don't know, but the last leg from there downstream to Rock Island added a hundred miles to the total to make fourteen hundred.

During the trip, our boat required constant care, repair, cleaning, a bit of painting, makeshift accommodations, decisions about where to land for gas, for meals, and for shopping, and where to spend the night. Joe and I were consulted on all these. At age thirteen I was happy to learn much about responsibility.

Between 1929 and 1931 there were many trips in our boat, most of which were with groups belonging to the seemingly endless organizations that Mother and Dad supported.

Dad's mind kept coming back to another long trip with Joe and me on other inland waterways. By 1931 he described to the family a triangular trip from Rock Island east to Chicago and Lake Michigan, then south, the full length of the Illinois River to the Mississippi, and then upstream to Rock Island. "A Midwestern Triangle" he called it. His twenty-page story of this trip was written for the magazine *Power Boating* and the article was published in its December 1932 issue.

A Midwestern Triangle

We left Rock Island's Kahlke's Boat Yard on July 2, 1931. A few miles south we turned into Rock River. Uncle Tom Davis and Cousin Sam Davis owned the Rock Island Power Company and had built a dam to raise the water level of the river so that the drop of water would turn their turbines and produce electric power. So there had to be a lock and the lock was the entrance to the Hennepin Canal. Another lock soon put us back into the Rock River for a few miles, then another lock back into the canal traversing the prairie. The Hennepin's locks and lock tenders were very friendly, with little to do. The canal was built before either railroads or highways for trucks.

Today, recreation has replaced commerce. Fishermen are frequent, and other watercraft make for variety. At one point a lock tender told us we were two hundred

feet above the Illinois River, with twenty miles and twenty locks to go to get there. This was all pleasant because the lock tenders phoned ahead and the water level in the lock was our level on approach and the gate was always open. All this at no charge to boatmen.

We reached the Illinois River which was, of course, much larger than the canal. Farther up this stream we entered the Chicago "River," actually an open sewer that carried much of the waste of the stockyards, huge blocks of scum and an occasional dead animal. More than a little smelly too. We moored near the bridge that carried car and truck traffic past the Wrigley Tower on Michigan Avenue, not too far from Lake Michigan.

After that it was down the full length of the Illinois River to the Mississippi. And up that great river to Rock Island. Again a lengthy trip of some six hundred miles over a ten-day period. Joe and I fished and swam and fought mosquitoes. We liked going through the locks. Dad loaded us up with history. We enjoyed being with Dad. I was fifteen and ready for experiences with the Big Hikes.

The Big Hikes

Dad became secretary of the Illinois State Sunday School Board through his work in St. John Lutheran Church in Moline. To encourage boys to join and attend Sunday school he created a real winner, the United Sunday School Band in either 1908 or 1909. The boys were ten to eighteen years old and had to have perfect attendance records in a Sunday School of their faith. They learned to play fifes, bugles, and drums and to march in all the patriotic events of Moline and Rock Island, Illinois.

Every other Saturday afternoon from September to June, Dad led his faithful band on hikes on hills, creeks, farms, woods, and along rivers. Each hike ended with a campfire and sandwiches from home plus a devotional period relating events of the hike to scripture.

Every summer, beginning in 1909, Dad organized a Big Hike, a trip in wagons pulled by horses, and lasting ten days to two weeks. The boys were organized into groups according to specific chores, such as drivers, cooks, dishwashers, fire makers, a purchasing committee, and one boy to answer all questions from all the other boys. "When are we going to get there? Where are we going? When do we eat?"

Again, every day ended with a program that became known as "circle." With the campfire in the center, the boys, and Dad, held hands and "counted off" to be sure everyone was present. The day past was discussed in detail with Dad using the events to illustrate biblical teachings and inviting discussion. Then we said the Lord's Prayer and sang the song "Blessed Be the Ties that Bind." (A designated bugler sounded taps and the boys sang it.) "'Day is done, gone the sun, from the hills, from the plains, from the sky. All is well, safely rest, God is nigh.' Thanks for the day, comrades!" And then all went to their bedrolls, a couple of blankets wrapped in canvas, which also held clothes, toilet articles, and maybe a pillow.

I am assuming that the band practiced, at first, in churches. But after Mother and Dad moved into the Great House in 1911, rehearsals were held in the two garage indoor areas across the lawn from the house. The Saturday hikes went on into the 1920s, as did the Big Hikes, and the parading continued until at least 1922 or 1923. I know because I got to carry a flag in one of those years!

All the above was prelude to the Black Hawk Hiking Club and its Big Hikes. Mother and Dad invited several friends one morning in 1920 in wintertime to go for a stroll on the Mississippi. They bundled up and ventured out on ice at least a foot thick and soon were enjoying themselves immensely. Returning to their cars, they exclaimed, "Let's do it again!" They did, and they even had a Big Hike that same summer with a name—The Black Hawk Hiking Club.

In 1921, the hikers were off on July 5 for a trip of eleven or twelve days, all the way to Minneapolis. The tour visited sites related to the Indians of the area and various state parks. Thirty-six people began the trip in these vehicles: a twin-six Packard, a Pierce Arrow truck, a Velie ton-and-a-half truck, and an Oakland five-passenger car. Mother and two other ladies came home at the end of the first day in the Packard driven by our chauffeur, Andrew Reitz.

The first evening "Council was elected...as follows: Miss First, Mrs. Guthrie, Miss Ross, Vernet Johnson and F.W. Adelmann—and then the close of the first day with the joining of hands around the camp fire, the Lord's prayer, and the song 'Blessed Be the Ties That Bind,' and then the sleep under the stars—no tents, no roof—no mosquitoes." So writes Dad in the 1921 album.

Thus, the pattern was set for all the years that followed.

Roads were soon paved, vehicles were improved, the Big Hikes grew longer and longer. One of them went to Mexico in 1937 and another to Nova Scotia, both some three weeks in length. All were very inexpensive. Nobody was paid to drive, to cook, etc. All campsites were in parks where bedrolls were on the ground, the ladies on one side of the parked trucks, men on the other.

The 1939 Big Hike

My job at Mill B in Everett in the late summer of 1939 was about to begin, after I had been with my roommates at their graduation. Mother was joining the Big Hike in

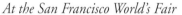
At the San Francisco World's Fair   *Mother and Mr. Courtney*

California in order to take in the San Francisco World's Fair of 1939. Our family had had a fine time together at the Chicago World's Fair in 1933 and wanted to try another.

So, I went west to Everett a week early, and then flew to San Francisco. Mother was sixty-nine and Dad seventy-two. There may have been some evidence of Mother's declining health, but she certainly did enjoy the World's Fair. She and Dad must have hired a car and driver because she did not ride in the back of a truck. Uncle Louis Hauberg was also a Big Hiker whose hearty personality made all of us happier.

A side trip with the 1939 Big Hikers was made to Yosemite National Park and extended to include Sequoia National Park on the return to San Francisco.

The General Sherman Tree with Dad

Some of the best photos I have ever taken were on this trip. Half Dome was splendid, soaring over the entire range and dominating Yosemite Valley. In the evening, Park Rangers pushed a big bonfire over a cliff in a spectacular fire fall. And some of us went to a dance at the lodge.

The next morning, the Hikers drove through Sequoia National Park. Mother, Dad, and I drove in our car and spent a good deal of time among the most giant of the ancient trees. Dad was thrilled by the age as well as the size of these sequoias, especially the General Sherman tree, the largest tree in the world. But I think he secretly felt that the big trees in Rock Island County, that he had photographed over many years, were much more interesting.

Farming

Uncle Louis hated farming. He yearned for the day when he could quit. His older brother John, my father, had escaped the farm at age twenty-five, and his younger sister Ada, also went to college. Uncle Louis and Aunt Anna, in 1894, were left with Grandpa to keep the farm going. And Grandpa wouldn't die until he was ninety in 1929. Anna left shortly thereafter and Louis was only released in 1952, when I bought the farm. He had survived the Great Depression and World War II, still using horses. He was a captive of a run-down farmhouse, barns, equipment, and poorly tilled fields.

Dad had escaped. Two years after his marriage to Mother in 1911, he closed his law office in Moline, and its unproductive practice was turned in for a lifetime of civic and church work at which he excelled. He was now so far removed from the farm that he romanticized his days on that farm. He was sure I would enjoy the fun of feeding the hogs, cultivating the corn, making hay, rising at dawn to harness the horses, and working ten hours through the July heat.

So, I did those things in 1932 for two or three weeks. Uncle Louis did the cooking but Mother knew that I was missing Mrs. Bennett's cooking at the Great House.

Uncle Louis was dreaming of retiring and so had not bought even a John Deere tractor. We went to neighborhood baseball games a couple of times a week, so I got hamburgers and soda pop *and* talk with fellow sixteen-year-old farm boys about all those new green machines from Deere or the red machinery from International Harvester. If I plowed the weeds out of ten acres of corn a day behind my two painfully slow horses, they did forty acres. And so forth.

But I am proud of my stint on an old-fashioned farm. Now I knew what Dad had escaped, and why Uncle Louis had to stay. Because Grandpa lived so long, Aunt Anna could not leave until he died and both she and Uncle Louis could never marry.

The Hauberg, Frels, Stilze, Walther, et al., families were all around as fellow farmers. Uncle Ed Lyford married Nora Hauberg and lived only a few miles away from Grandpa, Aunt Anna, and Uncle Louis. The Lyford girls, Helen and Ada Mary were Kay and my closest (both in miles and ages) cousins. Dad, with Mother, Kay and me in tow, went to all their harvest days. Ten to twenty neighbor farmers joined each other on successive days to husk each other's corn, thrash oats, barley, or wheat. The haystacks grew higher and higher, the men came in at noon for the huge harvest dinner, while their wives assisted Aunt Anna in producing great dishes of meat and vegetables, and pies at the end. No ice cream in those days, at least on the farm.

Here was farm society and neighborliness at its best. Talk and laughter were loud at the table and loud in the kitchen. No politics or religion. These families were of almost every Christian faith. They did follow the Chicago Cubs baseball fortunes. The women had church work, recipes, children, and an occasional trip to Rock Island or Moline.

For once Dad was on the fringe, and Mother was too high up for close association. And Sis and I could, and did, observe those things.

Dad was proud of me for sticking out the several weeks. His albums didn't disclose the length of my stay.

But I got up at 5:00 a.m. in the morning, harnessed horses, plowed up the rapidly growing weeds between the rows of corn, threw last year's corn to the hogs, fed the horses their oats, and cleaned their stalls, pitching down fresh hay. I "shocked" the barley and learned how it felt to have its prickles down my sweaty back. I helped Uncle Louis castrate the little male pigs and then use the same knife to cut open a watermelon for late afternoon refreshment. And I loved Mother and her cook, Mrs. Bennett, a little more when about twice a week Mother and Dad came up to the farm with a supper in a basket to be sure I had enough to eat—and Uncle Louis liked that a lot too.

So I was proud of myself, too. None of my friends in Washington Junior High School, or the Eastern boys at Fessenden and Hotchkiss had any opportunities like mine.

1932 Summer Olympic Games in Los Angeles

It must have been 1929 when we little "athletes" moved from the Washington Junior High basketball program to the Rock Island, YMCA "lightweight" team and our Midwestern Junior Championship. Along with basketball, we learned to tumble and dive in the Y pool and I was high jumping for Washington's track team. We little boys were following the American track and field personalities and "world records."

So we were keen on going to Los Angeles, to watch all the sports: fencing, boxing, wrestling, swimming and diving, but especially the track and field events. Would Jesse Owens break the world record in the hundred-yard dash? He did!

Dad had an old (1923?) Ford open-sided sedan at the House-in-the-Woods. It had not run for some years, but four of us who wanted to get to Los Angeles thought we could get it going. Mother's yard crew brought it down to Rock Island and we four asked them to park it under the huge elm tree across 24th Street. We slung a block and tackle from the tree's great lower branch and pulled the engine out to take it apart. It went back together too, but there were three or four parts left over. That was OK with Dad, but bothered Mother who "wisely" volunteered her two-door green Cadillac coupe for the trip. She did not know, of course, and neither did we, that it went only nine miles on a gallon of gas.

Aunt Anna Hauberg had retired to Los Angeles on her egg, butter, and cream money. She volunteered to house us for a two-week stay.

My first driving problem (at sixteen I had never driven before) was to pull up to a gas pump just outside St. Louis. I was too close and knocked off the pump handle! With that beginning, all my driving improved. I had to telephone home at least twice to beg gasoline money from Mother, even though gas was only fourteen cents a gallon.

We joined Dad's Big Hike group in Rocky Mountain National Park, and with him at the age of sixty-two, we climbed Long's Peak, over fourteen thousand feet high!! The hikers were fun to be with, but we had a far different goal. Headed southwest, we went through Las Vegas with our windows shut tight to keep out the 124-degree heat! And we arrived safely at Aunt Anna's little house for a two-week stay.

So many of the sports were new to us. But we knew about diving and were amazed at the feats from one-meter, three-meter, and ten-meter boards. Since TV had not yet been invented for popular use, we had never seen anything like the variety of Olympic competition. The wrestling and the fencing and the gymnastics, the rope climb, parallel bars, side horse, as well as events of swimming and equestrianism in different parts of Los Angeles, were all new to us.

Buddies: JHH Jr., Harold Fink, Mel "Swede" Seline, Joe Meenan

We still found time to go to the Santa Monica beach to look at the girls, who scared us to death. Although we had seen girls in swimming suits at the Davenport, Iowa natatorium, the California girls on that beach were—well—different!

I made that trip with my old Washington Junior High and Rock Island YMCA friends, and I had a lot to talk about when I returned to Hotchkiss in September, 1932. It was almost the last time with these public school boy friends, although I went to the Illinois High School Basketball regional tournament in the new Moline High gym at least one more time.

With Dad atop Long's Peak

CHAPTER 9
Fessenden & Hotchkiss, 1930–1935

Camp in the Summer of 1930

I WENT TO A SUMMER CAMP ON A LAKE NEAR GRAND RAPIDS, MICHIGAN. THE CAMP, whose name might have been Sheboygan, had a strong athletic program based on swimming and canoeing. I earned a junior lifesaving patch to sew on my swimsuit and also a "middleweight" boxing championship—mostly because my arms were so long that the other boys couldn't touch me.

Perhaps leaving home for one month prepared me to leave home for Fessenden in West Newton, Massachusetts, between Wellesley and Boston, for nine months. How was I fortunate enough to go to Fessenden?

Uncle Ed Denkmann's son Carl graduated in 1929 from Hotchkiss before going on to Yale. A Weyerhaeuser and Denkmann associate, Cliff Musser of Muscatine, Iowa, operated sawmills there, and his son John also went to Hotchkiss. So Mother was determined that I was to go there too, although my father thought Rock Island schools were good enough. My exposure to Latin and to English at Washington Junior High did not impress the Hotchkiss headmaster, George (the Duke) Van Santvoord, who decreed that first I had to catch up in those studies at Fessenden.

Mrs. Harry Good of Moline was escorting her son John, and Dick and Frank Hosford, also from Moline, back to Fessenden for their last year there. She called Mother and invited me to go with them. We took the Rock Island train to Chicago and went to Boston on the overnight Michigan Central train. We spent the next night at the Copley Plaza Hotel. Mrs. Good took a room for herself connected to a bedroom for us four boys. The ensuing pillow fight was a great icebreaker for me. It had dawned on me that these boys were very different from my Audubon and Washington Junior High buddies. They were somehow brighter, they were witty, and they loved Millie Good, joked with her, and she with them. Such a warm, fun relationship with a parent had never happened to me. The next day we all went to Fessenden, a fine green campus with nice buildings, play fields, and trees.

Fessenden 1930–1931

I was assigned to a "cubicle" in a huge, high-ceilinged room with perhaps twenty-four or more cubicles, the sides of which were seven to eight feet high with bed, chair, dresser, and hangers. One could stand on the bed and chat with boys on all sides. No radios were allowed. But obviously not much privacy prevailed. I did not like it.

The same day I was told to go the gym's locker room to put the prescribed clothing in it. I found my locker, and a small boy on the bench between the rows sobbing his heart out. I thought he was homesick and tried to console him. To my astonishment he said, "Nobody likes me!" and

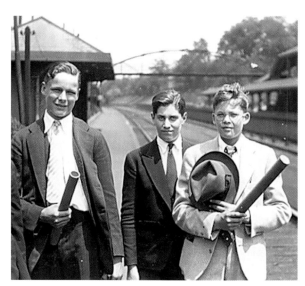

John Good, Dick Hosford, John H. Hauberg, Jr.

both of us had been there less than a day! I pointed that out to him and said that I liked him and asked why he thought the other boys didn't like him. He said, "Because I'm Jewish." It was the first time I had ever encountered anti-Semitism. But he was right. The feeling against Jews was expressed by many of the Eastern boys to the extent that Mr. Fessenden ordered it to stop. We in the smaller communities of the Middle West simply did not discriminate against any race. A young black boy became president of the Senior Class at Rock Island High School a couple of years later. And "our crowd" in the 1930s went together to synagogues on Jewish holidays and they with us for both Catholic and Protestant ceremonies.

Mrs. Good called Mr. Fessenden about moving me out of my cubicle to room with her son John in a cottage nearby the dormitory. It was a great day for me. Our other housemates were Hugh McCracken and William Warren Scranton. Hugh read dictionaries for pleasure! Bill Scranton and I were to go on to Hotchkiss together. Thirty-four years later I chaired the "Scranton for President" committee in the state of Washington before and during the 1964 Republican nominating convention. His candidacy was snowed under by the avalanche of conservatives for Barry Goldwater, a sure loser we thought. He carried only six states. Scranton would have won.

Sister Kay was at Dana Hall nearby. She was not enjoying Dana Hall because she thought the Eastern girls were picking on her because of her German name. I might have had some trouble about that too, but never did. Kay was a bit more timid than I. In addition to a terrible complexion, her childhood diseases of scarlet fever and diphtheria had left her a little awkward. These problems followed her all her life. I was

Kay and I in Boston for Thanksgiving 1931

lucky to have John Good as a mentor since he was one of the most popular boys in our dorm, and I made a lot of friends rather easily.

Mother and Dad came from Rock Island to Boston for Thanksgiving of 1930. They took Kay and me to hear Paul Robeson sing in *Porgy and Bess.* For Thanksgiving dinner we went to Beacon Avenue in Boston to the home of Bessie Lee Howard, a sister of Aunt Rhoda Lee Denkmann, who was married to my mother's brother Uncle Fred. Mr. Howard was the publisher of the *Christian Science Monitor* and quite well off. Cousin Bessie Lee was a huge woman and lots of fun. She had a Jamaican cook who turned out a colossal dinner. While the grown-ups talked, Kay and I finished a jigsaw puzzle.

During the winter semester, a Fessenden master took a bunch of us to a hockey game. Another weekend, probably in the spring of 1931, several of us went to an amusement park to ride the roller coaster, a first for me; we rode it several times. We bought some stink bombs which were scattered about our school study hall successfully without the master in charge being able to find the blame for the ensuing stink. I began to learn to skate, but not very well. I teamed up with another non-skater named Webb Tilton to scrape the hockey rink of snow during games. Later after WWII, I went to see *South Pacific* with the Uihleins in Chicago, and Webb was singing the role of the French planter, created by Ezio Pinza. "Some Enchanted Evening" had a special memory for me and Webb as we called on him in his dressing room after the show.

I enjoyed the studying and the masters after nine years of public schools and almost all lady teachers. The third quarter of the fall semester I was No. 1 in the class. Dad framed the report card. I also enjoyed the boys—we walked to nearby West Newton to buy apple cider, put raisins in the half-gallon glass jar, put the jar on the ledge outside our window and waited for the sun to produce enough action to guarantee a bit of alcohol from the fermentation. The masters had seen all this before and did not object.

Thus the year at "Fezzy" passed by pleasantly. By the time I came back to Rock Island, I knew that the Goods and Hosfords and their friends were going to be my close friends for the rest of my life, and not the boys and girls, with a few exceptions, that I had gone to public school with. It didn't seem to me to be snobbish—I still liked them but that was the way it worked out.

Coming home for the summer of 1931, I looked forward to going to Hotchkiss with eight other boys from Fessenden. John Good was for the Hill School and later to Yale. I saw him during summers in the Tri-Cities and have seen him from time to time in the past fifty years. He was captain of the Yale swim team and later the secretary of John Deere Company.

My father's 1931 album records a visit in the spring by Mother and Dad to Fessenden and Dana Hall, with photos of John Good, Dick Hosford, Harry Whitin, the buildings on both campuses, etc. I appear to be much younger than John Good although we are the same age.

The summer of 1931 passed swiftly with two trips of which I remember only incidents. One was a two-week trip with Dad on the *Catherine*, our sturdy, unglamorous boat that we had all grown to love, up Rock River and the Illinois-Michigan canal to Chicago, then down to the Illinois River over its entire length to its joining the Mississippi, then up that big river back to Rock Island. Joe Meenan, my first best friend, went with us. Dad wrote up the trip for *Power Boating* magazine in an article called " A Midwestern Triangle," a full text of which is in his 1931 album. The second trip was the twelfth Big Hike to the Tetons and Yellowstone National Parks, and I passed my fifteenth birthday.

Hotchkiss 1931–1935

The next four years were to be, essentially, at Hotchkiss School in Lakeville, Connecticut, a beautiful six-hundred acre campus with fine brick buildings, three hundred sixty

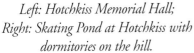
Left: Hotchkiss Memorial Hall;
Right: Skating Pond at Hotchkiss with
dormitories on the hill.

boys in its four classes, Prep, Lower Mid, Upper Mid and Senior. I felt confident about going, and I really don't recall my parents accompanying me there in the fall of 1931. There were eight of us coming from Fessenden of which my best friend was Harry Whitin of Whitinsville, Massachusetts, but also Bill Scranton, Gaspard d'Andelot Belin, Larry Connell, and Ted Beal. I soon added Ed Uihlein and Gus Swift, both of Chicago, to my friendship list. These boys and I were to have a years-long relationship. In 1997 all remain on our Christmas-card list except for Gus, Harry, and Ted all of whom died only a few years ago. Ted Beal became a Boston banker, and as Undersecretary of the Army in the Nixon administration invited me to be Washington State Aide-de-Camp to the Secretary of the Army. Connell's son was murdered by a crazy man with a newly bought pistol and Larry spent most of his life thereafter as a leader in the Handgun Control Association. More about the others later.

Memories of Hotchkiss center on the faculty, however. My great interest in words and language came from several wonderful teachers. My interest in music was kindled by another. The most striking master was Dr. Bickford who taught intermediate Latin and German. He drilled us and he drilled us. Eddie Uihlein could speak German, but

I'm not sure that Dr. Bickford could. His aim was grammar and vocabulary. He never asked simply for the German word for an English word, or vice-versa; he extended our vocabulary by asking for German synonyms or antonyms of German words. Dr. Bickford would walk into the classroom and in his sour voice would say, "Close your books please." And then he'd cover all the blackboards with a test of vocabulary, mute shifts that worked on unknown words in both Latin and English to become a German word or an English word that had to be translated into the other language. I loved it. Eddie hated it. Scranton and Beal coped with it. But Dr. Bickford's Latin class vaulted several of us into an advanced Latin course in our senior year that was unforgettable.

The senior advanced Latin class met in the digs of Mr. Albert George Conway "Aggie" Maitland. We read the Odes of Horace and the speeches of Cicero. As we took turns reading the Latin aloud and translating, Mr. Maitland's silver Persian cat, Xerxes, made the rounds for attention. It was a good class: John Shedd Reed, Larry Connell, Bill Scranton, Ted Beal, myself and a couple of others, all sitting on the floor. About every six weeks Mr. Maitland got a long letter from his brother who was a "high up" British Administrator in an Indian province. Mr. Maitland brought out the letter, Latin was forgotten, as AGCM read about tiger hunts while riding elephants, problems that his brother had to solve, descriptions of the province and its people. Fascinating. Best of all, we didn't have to do any Latin. I decided to continue Latin at Princeton.

By upper midyear at Hotchkiss, I was singing in the choir and the glee club, both directed by Mr. Dennison Fish. Bill Scranton was singing the alto solos, I the tenor solo, and Eddie Uihlein the baritone solos. He was the only one with a really good voice, but Bill and I could at least sing on key. The choir sang parts of the great Masses of Verdi, Haydn, Bach and Brahms, and the works of many other great composers of vocal music. We had two rehearsals a week and then chapel service Sunday morning. Denny Fish was a fine organist and my interest in music was kindled some more.

The Glee Club sang both heavy and light works. It is every glee club boy's dream to become a member of Yale's Whiffenpoofs, so we worked hard. There were sea chanteys, college songs, drinking songs, along with some opera. I sang Walther's "Prize Song" in recital and got through it pretty well.

The Glee Club had an exchange with girls' schools once in the fall and once in the spring. We went by bus to Emma Willard School or Ethel Walker School and each of us was assigned to a girl according mostly to height and then what class we were in. Because my German name sounded suspiciously Jewish to Eastern ears, I invariably was assigned to a Jewish girl as the girl's director got the list of us boys from Hotchkiss with only information about our height and class. My date saw me coming, knew right away I wasn't Jewish, and was terrified that I would stand her up or be mean to her all evening. I tried hard to give her a good time. My reward came when I got to Princeton and was invited

Upper left: Harry Whitin & Tom Sinclair on a springtime holiday hike; Right: Whitin
Lower left: Gus Swift; Right: Reed and Beal

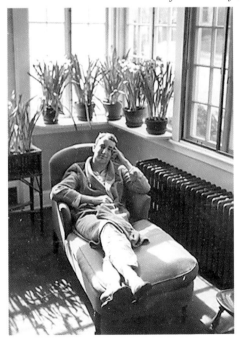

by those girls to proms at Vassar, Smith, etc., with an overnight Saturday in their great houses in New York, dinner at a top café or club, and tickets to plays and operas.

But we are still talking about masters at Hotchkiss and singing. Mr. Davis, the drama coach, and Mr. Fish put on a Gilbert and Sullivan play every year. I was always in the chorus, Scranton was always the girl (Miss Buttercup) and the jilted girl in *Trial by Jury*. Eddie Uihlein was the pirate king in *Pirates of Penzance*, and he and Bill had similar roles in *HMS Pinafore*. These operettas were great fun to do. I can still remember a lot of the patter.

Mr. Fish was a friend of Mrs. August Belmont, the great patron of the Metropolitan Opera. Once a year she let Denny bring enough of us from Hotchkiss to fill the best box seats in the opera house. Gus Swift, of Chicago was six foot-five and more than a bit awkward. Our night at *Die Meistersinger* was highlighted by Gus' tripping on the top step of the grand stairway and then falling headfirst all the way to the bottom. No damage done except to ego. We went to *Tannhauser* one year and to *Parsifal* another. They were great expeditions. We had worked on their librettos and listened to recordings for weeks before going to New York for the performance.

Hence my lasting interest in a wide variety of music.

Although I was elected captain of the track team in my senior year, I was not in any way an athlete. I enjoyed playing on class soccer, baseball, and football teams, but except for track, I was not on any varsity teams. Because few boys turned out for track, I threw the discus, put the shot, did the broad jump, high jumped, and ran the high hurdles. Henry Ford II was the team manager, a rather lethargic chap who had to be prompted constantly to get out all the equipment

I set a new record in the high jump at Hotchkiss, but the coach had forgotten his tape measure

(his job) for practices and track meets with other schools. I relish the memory of being his boss for a couple of months.

Harry Whitin and I made several hikes every year to the village of Salisbury and its fine bookstore, usually on Saturday afternoons. I bought books of poetry by A.E.

Housman that were set in a well-designed print type and were illustrated. Harry and Ed Uihlein and I bought small pocket knives in Lakeville from a couple of old (for us at that time) men who were skilled craftsmen in combining excellent steel parts with apple wood and other woods or deer horn. They rented an old gristmill whose great waterwheel still worked, but was entirely for show. The old stone grinding wheels were lying around—quite a romantic setting and part of Lakeville's two-hundred-year history. The "Ville's" favorite stop for all of us was the dairy where we bought ice cream cones, root beer sodas, etc. The Ville was only a mile and a half from the school. Many of the masters lived in or around Lakeville. They occasionally gave us rides, especially when a sudden rain occurred. They knew the names of every boy who had been in school for two or more years, but always called us all by our last names, never Ed or Gus or Harry or John.

The Duke, headmaster George VanSantvoord, and many of the masters such as Mr. McChesney living around Lakeville, were ardent horsemen. We boys frequently saw them in their riding clothes during classes. The morning foxhunt had ended too late for them to change clothes. I was intrigued. For me, riding a horse was to go somewhere to visit, to fish, to round up cattle, or to mend fences. Both sister Kay and I were good riders, Western style, but we never rode a horse for the sake of riding a horse. Mr. McChesney, the senior English teacher, had a clipped, rather English accent, and a beautiful reading voice. Every Sunday night he read in the school library to thirty to fifty of us who hung on every word of

George Van Santvoord

tales by Edgar Allan Poe, Mark Twain, and James Fenimore Cooper. The Duke rode about the campus accompanied by a Great Dane, naturally named Hamlet.

The hills and creeks, the farms, and forests, and several big lakes around Lakeville were filled with game and fish. The Housatonic River was nearby, rising from the Berkshire

Hotchkiss Holiday Hike

Hills and flowing almost due south through many picturesque towns of Connecticut. There was a famous covered bridge at Cornwall and another private school at Kent. Harry Whitin and I jointly bought a canoe for paddling on Lake Wononskapomack and Wononpakook. On holidays in the spring, the school trucked a dozen canoes including ours to a crossing over the Housatonic where we put into the river. There were some good rapids to get through, one of them just below the Cornwall covered bridge. We wrecked our canoe there senior year. We had, un-awares, a difference of opinion on which side of a big rock we were to take to get around.

The Duke tried to motivate me to study harder. Years later I found a letter from him to my parents saying my work was not up to my abilities. I received no "advice" about it from Mother and Dad. Twice the Duke took me to tea with some of the elegant people who lived near the school. Why me, I don't know. Maybe he hoped some of my rough edges would be smoothed. Maybe it was because I was so pleased, had good manners, and was interested in books not only for their content but for the print, the illustrations, the bindings. I could discuss, for a few moments, the poetry of Housman, Vachel Lindsay, and T.S. Eliot. I don't think he took Harry Whitin or Bill Scranton, Don Belin or Ted Beal, all every bit as interested in these things as I and much more sophisticated. These friends of the Duke were all bookish people, their houses and gardens were very fine, and all had big, comfortable libraries filled to the ceilings.

One of my best memories about Hotchkiss was the "holiday," always in honor of a Hotchkiss graduate who had just won some award. They were spaced about three weeks apart, usually on a Tuesday if good weather cooperated. The Duke, with every boy on the edge of his seat, made the announcement of the holiday and who had "earned" it for us. Then a roar went up. We scurried back to our dorms, and dressed for whatever we were going to do. Autumn holidays found Whitin, Uihlein, Dick Wright, Chester Wiese, Swift and myself hiking up to Lions Head, six to eight miles from the school, amid brilliant foliage. We passed an old stone forge which made cannonballs for the Revolutionary Army. Reaching the top, we ate our sandwiches. On one of these hikes in the late fall we tried cooking hamburgers, only to find that the cold weather offset the Bunsen burner's flame.

I had about fifteen friends I was close to during the four years at Hotchkiss: Gus Swift, John Shedd Reed, Ed Uihlein, Tom Sinclair and Trux Emerson from Indiana, Whitin, Chester Wiese, Dick Wright, John Wardwell, Ted Beal, and Bill Scranton from the East, and Frank Haines from New York. Seventy boys of our graduating class of ninety went to Yale. Two, including Gus Swift, chose Harvard. Nine of us chose Princeton.

In late May, I received an ominous letter from Mother about the death of her first cousin John Philip Weyerhaeuser and the kidnapping of George W., his eight-year-old grandson (see letter on pages 108–109). The letter was to remind me of the table talk at our house during the summers of 1933 and 1934 when Weyerhaeuser Timber Company paid no dividend and the Denkmann Lumber Company had become deeply in debt and was struggling to pay it back. Somehow or other, the letter failed to impress me.

Hotchkiss was a heaven far above earthly matters. Latin and German, Shakespeare and Dickens, astronomy and geometry, the music of Bach, Verdi, Brahms, Beethoven and Tchaikovsky and the operettas of Gilbert and Sullivan were serious and important. We were oblivious to the outside world. World conditions outside our "hallowed halls" were never mentioned in classrooms as in other gatherings. Parents of boys living close enough to the school to attend football games or to invite us to their houses for weekends did not talk about a Depression. Franklin D. Roosevelt was in the White House and not doing anything that our parents agreed with.

MRS. JOHN H. HAUBERG
TWENTY-THIRD STREET HILL
ROCK ISLAND, ILL.

May 26 1935

Dear Johnnie-

We are having a beautiful summer day. This is Sunday but I amm not in Sunday school or church. Neither is Dad. Our hearts are too heavy with all the sad things which have happened to our family and connections in the last few months.

Last Monday John Weyerhaeuser's body was brought here for burial, The funeral was held at the S.S.Davis home. Philip and Elizabeth Titcomb, his daughter and s son brought the body. Many of the other relatives were here too.

Within a week after, Philip's 9 year old son was kidnapped on his way home from school for his lunch.

It seems too terrible to be true. Philip had scarcely returned home. The boy is your second cousin.

The radio and newspapers are exaggerating their family fortunes. Since we are associated with them, you can readily see what outside people might be rating us.

The name Denkmann has been used several times. People dont know the reverses we, as a family have had, and might consequently list us with them. If the kidnappers, who are demanding $200.000 for the boy, and are listening to radios and reading papers,

MRS. JOHN H. HAUBERG
TWENTY-THIRD STREET HILL
ROCK ISLAND, ILL.

and are successful, they will try it another time.

You know what is in our minds and we want you to be extremely careful with strangers whom you meet anywhere.

We had a telegram from Catherine Tuesday the 21st telling us she had been accepted for the California school which begins on the 23rd and ends on the 3rd *June* of August. We phoned her that night and she told us she would come home then unless she got a job.

We feel it is quite a compliment to be chosen one of twenty from all over the country.

I'll add to Mama's--by her request *(for the Summer)*. We have not taken time to figure out anything more than has been made up for us, such as:--Business meeting at Wilmington; Del. June 2 20; your commencement June 24; Prof. Hi's steamboating June 12 to 17; Big Hike July 12--29; Hauberg reunion Aug. 23-25. Then I've promised to take honor campers to Black Hawk's last battlefield--no date set.

Have been at Camp H. almost every day the last couple of weeks. Are building fireplace; addition to Lodge, and some other improvements which we hope will make the place more attractive to campers and to others who use the Camp.

You may want to work something practical into your education instead of loafing from day to day, in which case there would probably be a variety of opportunities. Studying associates in work is probably as valuable, with side reading, as college work with meagre practical contact--i.e theory without practice.

The tennis court is kept clean but not rolled. I have not seen Joe for some time. Jim Burke is looking up trucks for the Big Hike. We may possibly have 2 loads, instead of 3 as before.

Hope you'll lick some more schools in track work.

Love from *Mother & Dad* ,

CHAPTER 10

The Princeton Years, 1935–1939

A Kaleidoscope of Memories

MOTHER'S HOUSEMAN PROVIDED OUR COOK WITH CHICKENS OUT OF OUR chicken coop from time to time. He would bring a couple of the best hens to the courtyard just off the kitchen door and chop their heads off. The headless chickens flopped around until they bled to death. Frank would pick them up by their legs, pluck them, and scald off the pinfeathers before he took them into the kitchen.

The fate of those chickens comes close to describing the years I spent at Princeton. Far less time than my parents even suspected. Without focus and totally free from any direction and motivation from above, I flopped around a courtyard that was mostly New York, girls' colleges, happy friends' rooms at Princeton and scoped from the ski slopes of St. Saveur near Montreal to the nightclubs of Havana—like those headless chickens.

I thoroughly enjoyed it all. I took courses that I knew I would enjoy. I was excited by a dozen superb professors who gave me the best of world history, the best of English literature, and an insight into the greatest composers of the last few hundred years. Sometimes I felt I had more close friends on the faculty than among my classmates.

The late '30s were a marvelous time to be free to do anything, because there were so many wonderful things going on. Toscanini was conducting the New York Philharmonic; Lawrence Melchior and Kirsten Flagstad were singing *Tristan and Isolde* at the Met; Benny Goodman was at the Pennsylvania Hotel; and Tommy Dorsey was at the Commodore. Peter Arno was cartooning for the *New Yorker* along with Whitney Darrow Jr., and Helen Hokinson; Noel Coward and Cole Porter were writing sophisticated, witty lines; the Gershwin brothers produced great musicals, including the serious *Porgy and Bess* that starred Paul Robeson; Dorothy Parker came up with "boys never make passes at girls who wear glasses," and when Calvin Coolidge died, she snapped, "How could you tell?" Ernest Hemingway, John Steinbeck, Dos Passos, Aaron Copland were about.

Franklin D. Roosevelt was president and popular among all but affluent Republicans. Norman Thomas, a former Princetonian, was a Socialist that 100 percent of Princeton's faculty voted for in 1936, despairing of the government's attempts to resolve the terrible Depression. The Republicans muttered and fumed like aimless, toothless mongrel dogs, hating Roosevelt, but devoid of ideas. My first political efforts took place in Boston prior to a Princeton-Harvard football game. I joined a parade in Copley Square passing out big cardboard sunflowers tacked to broomsticks for Alf Landon, who was overwhelmed by Roosevelt in the November 1936 election. I still have my Landon buttons.

Adolf Hitler was attracting much concern over his ambitions, but conservative Americans and Germans praised him for taking charge of the German government after the Reichstag defeated, by a vote of only one, a move to establish communism as Germany's government.

And lastly, a profound Depression had overtaken the world and seemingly no one could find a way out of it, furnishing a fertile field for the seeds of socialism and communism. It was also a great time for wit and vivacity, and anything that would provoke laughter, gaiety, and fun in general. Some of us "gilded youth" didn't even know there *was* a Depression.

Mother and Dad's letter of May 26, 1935 (see pages 108 and 109), expresses concerns that missed their mark completely. I have to believe it was only the beginning of a period of years of which I am not very proud.

The summer of 1935 found me floundering around. I spent a month working at the Rock Island Sash & Door Works for twenty-five cents an hour. Then I moved to the friendlier territory of Harry Good's swimming pool, listening to the radio reporting the Chicago Cubs baseball games, teasing the girls, learning bridge.

The Black Hawk Hiking Club's 1935 summer Big Hike was to the Rocky Mountains of Colorado and western Montana's Glacier Park. Jim Burke, Joe Meenan, and I went to the top of Long's Peak, fourteen-thousand feet high. I took some dancing lessons, private because I was so embarrassed not to know how to dance at age nineteen. So I was ready for Princeton.

In September of 1935, I joined Gus Swift, going to Harvard, and Eddie Uihlein going with me to Princeton, in Chicago and entrained for the East. Eddie was going to room alone freshman year at Princeton and I with Tom Sinclair of Indianapolis, a friend from Hotchkiss days. We came to Princeton a couple of days early to buy much used furniture for our bedroom and sitting room. After a few nights of study we decided to go to the famous Nassau Inn for a beer. Neither of us had ever drunk anything alcoholic. That night, as my bed was whirling around, I learned to put my foot on the floor to stop the whirling. I don't know what Tom learned, if anything, but it turned out to be very useful information for me in the years ahead.

Tom and I lived in Holder Court. Our classmates across the courtyard were Jack Kennedy and two roommates from Choate School. We were invited to a couple of their Saturday after-football-game cocktail parties and were impressed with Kennedy's magnetism, especially with girls.

I suddenly found that I was a very slow reader and did not have enough time for both philosophy and economics. There were no advisors to talk to, no "master" to take an interest in my problems. So economics went down the drain. Later, German and English were no problem except in the sheer volume of reading required. I joined the Glee Club, but should have used the time for studying.

Freshmen and sophomores, all men in those days, ate all meals in "commons." One sat down and instantly met new acquaintances, some for long friendships, others to stay away from. I found myself sitting next to Ed Cone, a Jewish boy from Baltimore, whom no one else wanted to eat with. He was extremely bright, was going to major in music, and was very knowledgeable in many areas. He was going to be our class (of 1939) valedictorian. But the anti-Semitism of the East Coast that I ran into at Fessenden pervaded our class. Soon Cone and I were eating in restaurants downtown. He was never invited to join a club but at least in our senior year, when we all knew he was going to be our brightest classmate, he was invited every evening to dine at the best clubs. Soon we freshmen divided into groups who were to be roommates and later club mates. And, of course, we all ate in commons together as little groups until the end of sophomore year. One pledged a club in the spring of sophomore year, but did not eat there until the next fall of junior year.

In the fall of 1936, I decided to room alone to see if I couldn't find more time for studying. On the third floor of the same entrance were roommates who became life long friends. Gib Harris from Richmond, Rufus King from Seattle, Emlen Roosevelt from New York, and Grandin Wise from upstate New York. We were all over six foot four and made an imposing phalanx walking down Fifth Avenue. Grandin and I turned out for high jumping on the track team. We quickly discovered there were at least four or five boys better than we. I switched to learn and enjoy squash, a game I played for a long time. Emlen invited me to tea in New York at his family's brownstone where Mrs. John K. Roosevelt, on the Theodore Roosevelt side, became a fine friend, counselor, and mother-away-from-home. More of Rufus King later. The five of us went everywhere together and all but Emlen joined the same club, Colonial, at the end of sophomore year.

Meanwhile, trips to New York for symphonies, operas, musicals, nightclubs with Benny Goodman and Tommy Dorsey, plus Glee Club dates with Vassar and Smith were taking more of my time. Amazingly, considering the years since college, I never got interested in art, and none of my friends did either, although the Museum of Modern Art was making large noises, and of course, the Met was the Met.

Eddie and I found Bob Meech of Minneapolis in the glee club and the three of us decided to room together junior year. Bob was a serious student, but fun loving. He and I decided to be history majors. The three of us were joined on the top floor of Patton Tower by four classmates who had come together from Lawrenceville. They called themselves "the Igors"—Dick "Pinkie" Murrie, George "Beastie" Harrington from Wilmington, Jack Miller, already going blind, and Charles "Daeto" Detwiller, from Plainfield. Jack and Pinkie were also history majors, Daeto was to be an architect, Beastie, a member of the DuPont family, was taking, of course, chemistry. He was not working very hard at it. One day a wizened, but obviously powerful, old man showed up to straighten Beastie out. It was Irénée DuPont himself. Beastie instantly hit the books and graduated with honors.

Fall 1937—Junior Year—Both Rewarding and Disastrous

The famous music professor, Mr. Welch, had been stolen from, I think Wellesley, and Ed Cone advised me to take his Music Appreciation course. It was fascinating to hear him at the piano discussing the composition problems the great composers had and the development of the symphonic form and the symphony orchestra almost one instrument at a time. I received my first and only First Group in this course.

The history department was full of well-known professors. I wrote a "junior thesis" on "The German Theater in the Midwest" and got a very good mark on it. Professor Thomas Jefferson Wertenbaker gave famous lectures on colonial America, "Buzzer" Hall lectured on the great personalities of nineteenth century Europe such as Napoleon and Garibaldi. The ferment was very exciting.

But my extra-curricular activities were catching up with me. The Dean of Students called me into his office before the Christmas 1937 break and told me I would not have enough credit hours to graduate with my beloved class of 1939, that I should drop out of the spring semester to "think about things," and that I could return to Princeton in the fall of 1938. I, of course, had to accept that and appreciated the offer of a second chance.

Despite my enjoyment of the camaraderie of the

Meech, John H. Hauberg, Uihlein, and friends–1938

Hotchkiss years, my diaries indicate terrible study habits, tardiness and poor performances, especially in classes I didn't like. I studied just hard enough to get by. I was motivated to be with the boys who were my friends and to be liked by others. Considering that there was a fierce Depression going on, I'm surprised I didn't get letters from Mother and Dad demanding I get better grades or come home. Years later I found a letter from the Duke to my parents saying I was not working up to my potential at Hotchkiss, but that letter was not shared with me. Nor did my parents ever ask me what my classes were about or what grades I was getting. Yet they received that information from the school. These same traits and lack of motivation to do my best followed me to Princeton. Still I was never last in my classes, and thoroughly enjoyed most of them.

My years at Fessenden and Hotchkiss had placed me in a world Mother and Dad wanted none of, but perhaps I was learning what they wanted me to learn. I loved books, my friends, had good relationships with the masters, was learning to get along, and to laugh—yes, I learned to laugh! And to be comfortable in social situations. I was immersed in music, history, poetry, and language. For better or worse, I had become interested in everything that I cherish today. These interests were not of much use to me in Rock Island, Illinois, except that perhaps ten or twelve of us in the "Rez Gang" of the Tri-Cities had "gone East" to school.

Unfortunately, although I brought to Princeton these interests plus some social skills, I also brought with me a lackadaisical attitude toward studying and achievement of good grades. So Princeton was to be déjà vu. Some difference was apparent at the outset, however. Where the masters at Hotchkiss cared about each one of us, the professors at Princeton could not act in loco parentis, and would have had no success if they had wanted to.

Later, I became so regretful about my academic failures that I was greatly motivated to get a Bachelor of Science degree after World War II, which was over for me in 1946. I saw my opportunity to create a forest and by doing so to influence the course of forest policy from devastation to sustainability. And I wound up with gold keys

Eddie had taken up flying and was hedgehopping over the New Jersey landscape.

in three different areas of study. That motivation came straight out of my chagrin over my lack of achievement during the 1930s.

In January 1938, I left Princeton because I wasn't studying very hard and was not too interested in completing college at that point.

I soon learned that finding my place in the real world was not going to be an easy task. The country was still in the grip of the Great Depression and nobody was hiring.

I left Rock Island in early February 1938, driving to St. Paul, Minnesota, to visit "Tall" Fred Weyerhaeuser and Peggy overnight. He and I had met at the annual January reunions of the Weyerhaeusers, Denkmanns, Mussers, Irvines, and Laird-Nortons in St. Paul and were respectively the youngest of the Weyerhaeuser and Denkmann third generation. We had always found it easy to talk to each other. He told me he was going to install a bonus plan for Rock Island Sash & Door Works employees. I was excited about that but the plan got shot down by senior Weyerhaeusers later on.

From St. Paul, I drove to the not-quite-open Sun Valley Ski Resort and found only one guest in the Lodge. It was David Niven, the English movie star who was being filmed for publicity for Sun Valley. We had a couple of evenings together before I left for Seattle. The snow had turned to rain, and only the ice-skating rink and the "hot pool" were in use.

I was determined to get a job in the woods with any company but Weyerhaeuser, because I was ashamed of dropping out of college and didn't want the Weyerhaeusers, except for Fred, to learn about it. But the Great Depression was still going on. I drove to logging camps from British Columbia to northern California and found nothing available. At a Weyerhaeuser logging camp at Vail, Washington, the boss said that he was going to put together a survey crew the first of April and perhaps I'd like that. I had no other choice—and it was one of the best decisions I ever made.

I had been fairly active in sports, but had no experience in traversing the very rough terrain of the wooded foothills to which we were assigned. My young crewmates, on the other hand, were very experienced in walking in the woods. They would leave me behind when we headed out in the morning, and by the time we returned to camp I was definitely dragging along at the rear. The word "tenderfoot" comes to mind as I recall the charley horses and my perpetually stiff and sore condition until I grew accustomed to the terrain and toughened up.

The Big Woods—Spring and Summer 1938

The survey crew was to do two things. One was to establish the boundaries of cuts and fills along lines already staked out to extend the railroad tracks deeper into the woods at Vail, Washington, a huge logging establishment. The other was to make a ten-foot contour map of a very big (more than two hundred thousand acres) virgin forest for designing a network of railroad grades so that logging could commence. Our crew

Top left: Camp Six; Bottom right: The Survey Camp

alternated between Vail and a tent camp in the woods west of Chehalis, Washington, twenty miles or more from Vail.

Camp Six, the logging camp, was reached by a two-hour train ride from Vail every Sunday night. We rode in boxcars filled with wooden benches and full of sleepy and even drunken loggers, and a pot-bellied coal stove. The train held some two hundred fifty loggers, maintenance people, cooks, and waitresses. The trip was through desolate clear-cuts. Huge machinery had been needed to move the huge trees—the sound ones went to log rail cars going to mills and the too small or defective trees were left on the site to burn, a terrible picture. But the Depression made it impossible for mills to take logs smaller than perhaps twenty-four inches in diameter so the "slash" was burned under some controls in order to prevent vast "uncontrolled" fires. Many

Left: The kitchen and dining tent; Right: We had found this fawn alone in the big woods.

such fires had burned entire mountainsides in the late nineteenth and early twentieth centuries and were the most feared hazards. No wonder those mountains looked so devastated.

My roommate at Camp Six, in a bunkroom for two, was a Finn who never spoke a word to me—even a grunt or a smile (and may not have even spoken English). He pulled off his outer logging clothes after dinner and pulled on bright colored pajamas over his black long johns. I could only figure that he was keeping his sheets clean. Women cleaned our rooms and made the beds every morning after we left camp for the woods.

Waitresses at the cookhouse were huge women with biceps like hams. The serving dishes they carried were made of thick ceramic, and they carried four to six at a time. Silence was mandatory. The food was terrific and the variety amazing. At breakfast we had almost thirty choices of fruit, cereal, pancakes, bacon, sausage, eggs, coffee, tea. etc. We picked up our lunch at other tables, usually in paper bags. If you had diarrhea, there was strong tea for "closing" medicine. If you were stopped up, there was "opening" medicine. Fortunately, I had neither.

The Friday-night train came back to Vail after working hours. The first four weeks I worked at Vail, the Friday train took down bodies of men who had accidents that day or the day before.

At Camp Six, I met the road-building contractor, Axel Osberg, who was building the advancing railroad grades and laying the rails. We liked each other right off the bat, though he was maybe fifteen or twenty years older. Thirty years later, his sons and I were building a program for his retarded grandson.

The survey camp was a ten-mile hike into the most beautiful virgin forest I had ever seen. But the first two or three miles were through cutover lands that were as devastated as the same kind of land at Vail. We packed about forty pounds apiece of groceries to camp to take care of the first five days of work. A pack train of mules brought in food for the last five days. We worked ten days in and four days out.

The trees were so big and so close to each other that we had to make offsets to our compass lines across the sections. We took elevation sightings along lines one hundred feet parallel to each other. Marching through the woods, up and down the hills and across steep and deep ravines was tough, especially for an Eastern dude. My Western co-workers were all used to it, and ran across trees fallen over sometimes deep ravines with no fear of falling. They frequently left me to find the way back to our tent camp after the workday was done. Sometimes I didn't find camp until it was dark and dinner was over. A rough life, but exhilarating. The woods had a total silence. There was no food on the deeply shaded ground for birds or squirrels. The odd openings did have sunlight reaching the floor through which alders and vine maple grew under this canopy, and where mice prospered and were the food for some birds and game.

The contour map was never used to design a railroad logging system. None of us knew it then, but that year (1938) the logging truck came to replace the log train, and if a truck could make it into the woods, the loggers could drive to work every day in their cars. Camp Six was closed, as were similar camps throughout Washington and Oregon and elsewhere.

It was also the last year of the double bitted axe and the ten- to twelve-foot "misery whip" saws, pushed and pulled by a pair of "fallers" for hours before a big tree would begin its fall. The loggers' unions had agreed to permit the gas-operated chain saws to be used. Paul Bunyan's days were over.

So I had a good look at the old ways, the old, great, silent virgin forest, and the devastation of clear-cutting practices. Nothing was coming back soon to replace the huge trees, the Douglas fir, western hemlock, western red cedar, and Sitka spruce. Alder, vine maple, a mix of elderberry, blackberry, devil's club, etc., were taking their place. I was concerned about this.

A dividend from this was forthcoming. I took my weary legs to the Washington Athletic Club in Seattle where I had a "visitor's card" every other Saturday and went to a steam bath to sweat out the pain. There was always a portly gentleman there with clipped, almost British speech, who turned out to be Dr. Richard E. Fuller, the august head of the Seattle Art Museum. We became friends until he died many years later and had turned over to me the presidency of the Museum.

New Friends

I had brought my skis west with me and went one weekend in spring to Paradise on the south slope of Mt. Rainier where there was a rope tow. There I met a Harvard man named Brud Nute, a Seattle native, and now my next-door neighbor on Bainbridge Island.

Having no roots in Seattle at that time, I established my weekend headquarters in radio station KVI on the ground floor of the Olympic Hotel, now the Four Seasons Olympic. Six or eight other young men and women "hung out" there with two disc jockeys playing our favorite records. Both "jockeys" became friends for life. There was Jerry Morris, strong-voiced and funny, who turned out to be Morrie Alhadeff. Years later, in 1973, I invited him to help me on the Seattle Art Museum Board of Trustees. The other was Tor Torland, a bon vivant and droll character, who lived in Woodway Park and introduced me to his many young friends there. I was soon to spend every other weekend for the rest of the spring and summer in Woodway as a guest of the Rufus King family (Rufus was a Princeton classmate). Since he was still in school, I slept in his room until he came home in June. I began to get involved in the Seattle social set at the same time I was toughening up my muscles on the survey crew. Most of the people my age were still in college, so my first friends in the Seattle area were slightly older than I—people like Stu Ballinger, Bunny Ambrose, and Howie Richmond. And, of course, I was meeting some attractive young women as well, which, after all, was a major interest at that time!

The summer passed by quickly. The survey crew settled into its assignments. I kept up now with the local lads. And I was called on by the engineers to help make the map, which was done in a special tent after dinner. "Buck" Reichel, who was the camp boss, became a longtime friend. He became Weyerhaeuser's No. 2 forester and I bumped into him many times after I had become a Weyerhaeuser Company director.

In the fall of 1938 I returned to Princeton for my final year. Bob Meech and I roomed together, with Eddy Uihlein next door to us and the Igors—Dick Murrie, George Harrington, Jack Miller, and Charles Detwiller on the same floor. We were a happy group of seven and became very close friends. Pinky Murrie's father was the head of Hershey Chocolate and kept us well supplied with new ideas for new kinds of candy bars. Eddie's father came East after good duck hunting on the Illinois River to give us a banquet of his trophies. "Beastie" Harrington was a member of the DuPont family which kept close watch on his grades. Bob Meech's family was a close, warm friendly tribe in Minneapolis. Bob got me an invitation to Jane Pillsbury's "coming out" party in Minneapolis, which I attended during Christmas 1938 vacation.

Also in the fall of 1938, I was enjoying dates with Virginia Roosevelt, Emlen Roosevelt's sister, even though she was engaged to an impoverished architecture student in Philadelphia who couldn't come to see her in New York. Mr. Roosevelt offered funds for more lavish plays and dinners than we wanted. Virginia had tickets for opera and symphony and I matched the value of the ticket that I used to visit low-cost nightclubs in Greenwich Village. We even "crashed" a farewell party on the famous French liner *Normandy*, to see the Art Deco interiors, as the ship prepared to leave for France.

Virginia's wedding to James Armentrout was scheduled for late May 1939. I was honored and thrilled to be invited to be in the wedding party even though I wasn't an usher. I went to Brooks Brothers and bought the appropriate swallowtail coat, striped trousers, spats, and all for an afternoon wedding. I took a room at the Princeton Club the day before the wedding, donned my black tie and dinner jacket and took the train to Oyster Bay where Emlen "Monk" Roosevelt met me. We were to go to Ginny's wedding dinner at the Oyster Bay home of General Theodore Roosevelt, Jr.

Probably twenty-four of us sat down at his elegant table. The general had invited a British officer with whom he had served in some North African campaign, and both gentlemen were eager to tell us young folk their favorite stories.

After champagne and toasts galore, the ladies went upstairs for coffee in Mrs. Roosevelt's drawing room and we men drank brandy, smoked cigars, and waited for the stories. The British officer began and I don't recall what he said. Then General Roosevelt began, "Kermit, my brother, and I went to India after WWI to visit outposts in Nepal. It was to be a long trek. Shortly after we had begun, I was accosted by a barefoot Indian who begged an audience. I agreed to hear him. He said his older brother was dying in a village well off our journey's path, would probably die before our return, but wanted me to be the executor of his estate, that it was important, but the brother didn't know why. I felt a great curiosity and said I would do it.

When Kermit and I returned, I went to great lengths to get to the village named and was directed to the dead man's house. There was nothing to his belongings except for an old trunk. That had to be his 'estate.'

I saw to it that it was carefully boxed-up and added it to our baggage for England. When Kermit and I arrived there, we went through the old dilapidated trunk layer by layer of old clothes and papers. Nothing there. But at the very bottom of the trunk was a bundle wrapped in layers of waterproof paper. When opened, it turned out to be a first folio edition of the plays of William Shakespeare!" We guests exploded with applause for a great story and asked many questions but the general was content and added no more to his story.

I wore my striped trousers and spats to the subsequent wedding, but it was anticlimactic.

I was still floundering about. My roommates were now seniors, while I was repeating my junior year, or at least most of it. I turned in a junior history department thesis on "The German Theater in the Midwest," which got a good mark. I took a marvelous course in music appreciation and history, in which I received a "first," the only one I had except for Latin classes.

The history department was fascinating and I did very well. A social psychology class examined the techniques used by such crowd movers as Aimee Semple McPherson, the evangelist; Father Divine, a black preacher who had established a series of "heavens" for developing black self respect; Adolph Hitler, etc. It was a course, really, in how to manipulate people, and it was spooky to follow Hitler's staging of parades, thousands of youth in uniform as well as the growing military machine, especially its air force. The "Heil Hitler" salute given in unison by fifty thousand boys was pictured repeatedly in our newspapers and movie news programs. Our professor made no prognostications, but it was obvious to us what was coming in Europe. I didn't remember that there was any talk of the U.S. getting into it, but there was ardent talk by conservative German-Americans, including Dad and Eddie Uihlein's father, that Americans must not interfere. During the 1937 Christmas holiday, I stayed in Chicago with Eddie to go to some debutante parties. His father insisted that we attend, for just a few minutes, a banquet given by the German-American Society for German foreign minister Von Ribbentrop. Everyone was speaking German. Ed Seipp, a cousin of Eddie's, was with us. After a short time, we left for a Princeton Triangle Club performance and a debutante party at the Blackstone Hotel.

Knowing I wasn't going to graduate gave me the freedom to spend weekends in New York and several weekends in the Berkshires trying to learn how to ski. Most of my New York dates were Rez Gang girls from Moline and Rock Island who were at Vassar or Smith, or were working in New York. We went in groups to the theater, music halls for symphony and opera, and on to nightclubs where we danced to the swing music of Benny Goodman, Tommy Dorsey, Guy Lombardo, and small combos. We took a room for our dates at the Biltmore Hotel and a room for ourselves on a different floor—all under the beady eyes of the lady supervisors. It was a good arrangement. On one weekend, we arrived back at the Biltmore at dawn and decided to play baseball in Central Park before collapsing for most of the rest of Sunday and then going back to school. The Saturday afternoon Metropolitan Operas were attended by a full house of college students.

So I had a fling, stood among my class of 1939 roommates, my club mates, and others at their graduation ceremonies, burned our books in a colossal fire somehow tolerated by the proctors, and parted with a few tears and many promises to keep in touch.

Left to right: Pinky Murrie, Daeto Detwiller, Jack Miller, Bob Meech, Beastie Harrington

*Top left: On the left,
Art Reis; on the
right, Bob Meech;
Right: Art Keyes &
Pinky Murrie*

*Middle left: Jack
Osborne, Newell
Brown & Charlie
Dennison; Right:
Jim Clements &
Benny Coates*

*JHH (middle far left corner) at the
Princeton 35th year reunion in 1974*

Downtown Seattle in 1940, the Smith Tower is the tallest building in Seattle!

CHAPTER 11

Wandering, 1939–1943

I N THE FALL OF 1938, WHEN I HAD RETURNED TO PRINCETON, RUFUS KING AND I were on our way to visit friends at Smith College when he suggested we stop off at Vassar to see an old friend of his from Seattle, Annie Gould. Our visit was brief, and although I spoke to her for only a few minutes, her lovely smile remained in my memory. I knew by Christmas of 1938 that I was not going to have sufficient credits to graduate from Princeton in 1939. But I decided to stay with my roommates and cheer for them in June of 1939. Eddie Uihlein had already left our group so Bob Meech of Minneapolis and I roomed in the same suite together. On the same floor of Patton Hall were the "Igors" from Lawrenceville School—"Pinkie" Murrie from Hershey, Pennsylvania, George "Beastie" Harrington from Wilmington, Charles "Daeto" Detwiller and Jack "Jake the Rake" Miller already knowing he was going blind. Bob had joined Cloister Club, the Igors were members of Charter, and I ate at Colonial Club. All of us had friends in different clubs, friends within our clubs, and I had Jewish friends who had been snubbed by all the clubs. Just as we roomed together but had joined, in sophomore year, our individual clubs, so our other friends lived in a variety of dormitories scattered about the campus and ate at different clubs, (there were twenty or more).

After my roommates graduated, I headed for Rock Island, stayed for two months with Mother and Dad, and in late August of 1939 left for Everett, Washington to begin work in the Weyerhaeuser Sales Trainee Program. I had already worked in the woods in 1938 and this was the next step.

What, if any, was the legacy of my on-again, off-again Princeton years? I felt comfortable with all kinds of people, confident of my manners and grammar. I was gregarious, and I was concerned about people who had fewer advantages than I had. I had become a "social liberal" and a "moderate Republican." I was in good shape physically, curious about the world I was going to enter, and eager to get on with it.

Mill B in Everett was a huge sawmill with fourteen hundred employees, mostly men, working around the clock in two shifts. The mill cut mostly Douglas fir, but also western hemlock and western red cedar. The logs ranged up to forty feet in length and eight feet in diameter! They were turned into products almost entirely for construction. Premiums were paid for products without knots or other blemishes for strength

Acres of 2"+ thick lumber "air drying"

or aesthetic reasons. We were to learn all about end uses of the three major tree species.

There were several interesting "special" differences in the routine during my years in Everett. Grand Coulee Dam was being built and demanded lumber for concrete forms with very narrow specifications. I can't remember just what they were, but most were to be Douglas fir—two inches thick, eight to ten inches wide, and eight to ten feet long. And the job required hundreds of thousands of them. A train of boxcars filled with these left for Eastern Washington every day.

Hitler marched his German troops into Poland in September 1939 and the American military buildup began. And in 1941 British Spitfire fighter planes were engaged in a fight to the death with well-armed German bombers. The Germans concentrated on the English airports in hopes of preventing the Spitfires from taking off. Each bomb created a crater in the runway. Although the crater was quickly filled with gravel, the planes took off one behind the other in several parallel columns and each plane kicked up gravel which pitted the aluminum propeller of the plane behind, causing a loss of speed. Some genius discovered that western spruce could be laminated into blocks from which propellers could be made that resisted pitting. My last three months' work at Everett was to grade spruce timbers for shipment to England. Mill B must have been very profitable during this time.

But of course the "family" had its eyes on me too, and this made my sales trainee life a bit awkward. I wanted to work as a fellow employee in each mill, a trainee, of course, but still one of the guys in the mill. But cousin Rudolph Weyerhaeuser, probably in his late sixties or perhaps seventies, visited every western mill annually to meet with the managers and inspect the mills. I don't believe he had any official assignment any more in the family hierarchy. He just didn't want to lose touch. Most managers had worked for the Weyerhaeusers for years and Rudolph wanted to "keep in touch."

My "cover" was, of course, not having the name Weyerhaeuser. But whenever Rudolph spotted me there was a brief "family reunion" that took me off my job for a few minutes while he gave me a pep talk, put his arm around my shoulders, and finally walked on. The guys I worked with had had to do my job as well as theirs for a short period and I don't think they liked it much, although I got teased about it during the lunch break or later.

I lived in the Windsor Apartments in Everett, rising at 5:15 a.m. and going to Clara Senter's boarding house a few blocks away for breakfast. My lunch box was prepared for me there by Mrs. Senter. Two other Weyerhaeuser sales trainees lived there, and also Duke Watson, a lifelong friend, who worked for Soundview Pulp Company as a forester. Ken Boyd and I worked in the mill and shipping sheds and were moved about the mill—the sawmill, planing mill, shipping shed, drying yard, the timber yard for me. Four or five other men boarded at Clara Senter's, and also Miss Agnes Feeney, a prim veteran Everett High School English teacher, who put up with our jokes and pranks. It was a ten- or fifteen-minute drive to the mill.

Anne Gould and Janet Paulson were partners in a decorating business and furnished my apartment (one room and kitchenette) with a leather chair and a deep red rug. I played my Magnavox phonograph a good deal, with symphony and concert records as well as the "big band" records. When my neighbors objected to the "noise," the management moved me into the Mayfair Apartment next door where I stayed until my neighbors there complained. Then back to the Windsor.

The day shift at Mill B began at 7:00 a.m. and ended at 3:30 p.m. That gave me time to change clothes and head for Seattle. No one was as yet in uniform in the fall of 1939. I really don't remember that we young blades paid any attention to the war "over there," and yet more than a million men died in battle before that year's Christmas. The Germans had begun by invading Poland, surrounding Warsaw, and bogging down there for the winter. For the French and the English it was a lull. In America it was known as the "phony war."

The social front in Seattle (and elsewhere, of course) was going full blast.

A group of us "Easterners" hung out at radio station KVI, then located on the ground floor of the Olympic Hotel in Seattle. The two disc jockeys, Jerry Morris and Tor Torland, became our close friends. (Jerry Morris turned out to be Morrie Alhadeff after the war.) There were also Bill Bernhardt, who was Northwest public relations manager for Pan American Airways; the Dutch and Italian consuls; Dorothy Ferguson of Bainbridge Island; Audrey, who became Dr. Ole Jensen's wife; the cousins David Whitcomb and Emily Whitcomb, who later married; and others with foreign business connections. We called ourselves "Seattle's International Set." Annie Gould, Janet McDonald and Betty Wright were also involved. It was a gay (when that word did not mean what it does today) and happy crowd.

When World War II began in 1939, there was a sense among us young people that while America seemed isolated and insulated from this war, ultimately we were going to be involved in it. Several Seattle-based friends in our set were connected with

European homes or businesses. The Italian consul returned to Italy in November. Dorothy Ferguson left to join the British Women's Corps. Some went to Europe to drive ambulances. Seattle declared a practice blackout the night our group was partying at Emily Whitcomb's apartment. We forgot to close our curtains and received a sharp telephone call from a block captain. Since Aldo Mazio, the Italian consul, was at the party we complied instantly and hoped nobody would be sent to investigate us.

In 1940 or perhaps late 1939, I began to take Anne Gould to musical events—a violin recital by Fritz Kreisler at the Music Hall and a symphony concert or two. As most of us were settling into jobs, the International Set gradually broke up into smaller groups according to our new interests. Dr. and Mrs. Maimon Samuels hosted a junior symphony group in their home on Queen Anne Hill. "Sammy" Samuels, their daughter, brought together Janey Matthews (later Mrs. Joseph L. McCarthy), Janet McDonald (later Mrs. Chester Paulson), Anne Parry, Bill Bernhardt and me and a few other young men and women. We listened to the august Miss Louise Van Ogle discuss the next concert program and play the music on the Samuels' phonograph.

I took flying lessons at Boeing Field and received a solo license, short of one permitting me to take anyone else with me. It was fun for a while, but I was not flying enough to justify the expense. I did take a few photos.

Most of us tried skiing on Mt. Rainier at Paradise and on Mt. Baker. Both had short rope tows that were also short on excitement. With skins on the bottom of our skis we climbed the slopes to fairly high altitudes where we settled down in the snow for a happy hour of sunbathing, sandwiches, and beer, then skied down to the lodges in long traverses. Only a few of us knew how to turn so the rest of us stopped, did a

My Piper Cub

The Fleet's In

A pass on the slopes of Mt. Baker

kick turn, and made another quarter mile traverse, eventually getting back to the lodge about 3:30 p.m. for dancing to jukebox music and much happy dating.

Young men with ROTC experience were being called up into Army and Navy units. I had not signed up for Field Artillery ROTC at Princeton, but I began to realize that I would be drafted sooner or later.

Anne Gould

On Lincoln's Birthday in 1941, coming down from Mt. Baker to Seattle, I proposed to Anne Westbrook Gould. It was sealed with a kiss. Her mother was not pleased. Apparently I had portrayed for her the picture of a small house in Rock Island and myself as an ambitious young man hoping for a future with Weyerhaeuser. It was not what she had in mind for Annie. She flew back to Rock Island to visit Mother and Dad and discovered for herself that I did have some prospects.

I was intrigued by the Goulds and the Fays. Annie's mother was such a dynamic woman, very interested in the arts, and particularly in the history of the Pacific

Northwest. I had never met a woman who was intellectually so worked up about things. My mother wasn't intellectual at all. She had great compassion for her fellow man, the underdogs of life. Annie was pretty dynamic herself, and very pretty. It was four years from the first time I met her until we got married.

In April 1941 Ken Boyd and I were moved to the Weyerhaeuser Company mill in Klamath Falls, Oregon, to get experience with the use of western sugar pine and Ponderosa pine in making doors and window frames. Klamath was a rip-roaring town with bars, cafes, and even stores with no doors, and ranchers and Indians drinking, hollering and fighting. Every Friday night I drove over a Cascade pass to attend parties in Seattle for Annie and me, and on Sunday night back to work. The trip to Seattle always seemed short.

We were married June 9, 1941 at the Florence Henry Memorial Chapel in The Highlands. The marriage service was

Top: Dad, Mrs. Gould, Annie and John, Carl Gould
Bottom: The Bridesmaids

conducted by Dr. H. H. Gowen, who had married Annie's mother and father. Her bridesmaids were Janet MacDonald, Fay Frederick Padelford, Betty Wright, and Anne Parry. My ushers were Bill Bernhardt, Bob Colwell, Hugh Pickel, and Carl Gould. The best man was my Hotchkiss and Princeton roommate, Edgar J. Uihlein of Lake Bluff, Illinois, at whose wedding I had ushered a month earlier.

We took a month's honeymoon to the Hawaiian Islands, staying first at the Moana Hotel on Waikiki Beach. To our great pleasure, we met a bunch of my Princeton pals who were Navy ensigns assigned to live at the Moana. Both the Moana and the Royal Hawaiian Hotels were sparsely occupied, as everyone except Annie and me felt that war with Japan was imminent. To keep hotel occupants happy, the management treated us to a yachting party in Pearl Harbor, where we observed battleships moored together in pairs, cruisers in fours, destroyers in eights, or more—all supposedly safe because at night a chain was raised across the entrance to the harbor against submarines. Apparently the military did not foresee the possibility that the Japanese could sink almost the entire fleet in Pearl Harbor by an air attack, which they did on December 7, 1941.

After the honeymoon, we returned to Klamath Falls for one month, probably the longest of Annie's life. There was no art, or music, no museums. Few gardens. No one to talk to. And then we were transferred to Coeur d'Alene, Idaho. This

Top: Leaving the Florence Henry Memorial Chapel;
Bottom: Cutting the wedding cake at the Sunset Club

was a lot better because of wonderful friends in nearby Spokane. But Annie was terrified that this was to be her life, with Coos Bay next, etc.

My mother had a stroke in March of 1941, just as our marriage was imminent. Dad's letters told of his loneliness and misery. So we moved to Rock Island, Illinois, and lived in the Great House with Dad. I was assigned to Weyerhaeuser's Rock Island Lumber Company. After Pearl Harbor, I realized that a parting with Weyerhaeuser was inevitable because I would be called for military service. Annie wanted a house of our own so we remodeled Dad's House-in-the-Woods, along the Mississippi River just

The House-in-the-Woods. Our remodeling let in the sunshine. The woods were filled with opossum, raccoon, and squirrel. The trees held five different kinds of woodpeckers, flying squirrels, bluebirds, orioles, etc. The ground was covered with hepatica, jack-in-the-pulpits, and Johnny jump-ups. Throw in some poison ivy and wild blackberries.

upstream from Port Byron. We moved in shortly after Mother died in February of 1942. The commute to work was about thirty minutes. We had a happy time with our Tri-City friends, but the thinning out of the men who had undergone ROTC training at their colleges began. Annie had a sad miscarriage late in 1942. I entered the Field Artillery's Volunteer Officers Candidate program, and reported for duty at Camp Grant, near Dixon, Illinois, in March of 1943. Wartime travels began for both of us.

A lot of learning about all sorts of things helped me feel pretty good about those four years from 1939 to 1943. I got a good look at sawmills and the lumberyard retail business, the immediate extension of the mills I worked in. I fell in love and married and fathered a daughter. Annie and I took a good look at a medium-sized community in which Mother and Dad were very important people and where we knew very well what would happen to us if we stayed there. And there were trips to Louisiana and Mississippi and to Arkansas where Davenport and Moline, associates of the Denkmanns and the Weyerhaeusers, were struggling to rebuild a forest (Southern Lumber Company) cut over long before. I was committed to the forest industry in every aspect. The war was an apparent interlude, but a big surprise was waiting for us at war's end.

My first cellular, 1944, with a quarter
mile radius. We called it a "walkie-talkie."

CHAPTER 12

The Army in the U.S.A.

1943–1945

I N 1941, MOTHER SUFFERED A SEVERE STROKE, AND I FELT I SHOULD RETURN TO Rock Island to help Dad. I asked the Weyerhaeuser Sales Company to move me to Rock Island, where there was a lumberyard that would be good training for me, and I would be at home. Annie and I arrived in Rock Island in November 1941. It was a dismal day. The trees were bare and there was snow on the ground, blackened by the soot of the town. It was a pretty bleak experience and Annie never really warmed up to Rock Island.

Charlie and Suzy Shuler, my cousins, invited the young people in my old Tri Cities crowd to a party to help everyone get acquainted with Annie. It was Sunday, December 7. Annie and I arrived at the Shulers' about noon and the radio was blaring out the news of the Japanese attack on Pearl Harbor. The party was off. Our country was going to war.

Not exactly a Brooks Brothers tailoring job

Mother died in February 1942, the day before Valentine's Day. I continued to work at the lumberyard in Rock Island, wondering just where all this would lead. World War II began December 8, 1941, for the United States, but I had a very high draft number. I did not want to enlist in the army as a private, and when the army offered a Volunteer Officers Candidate program (known as VOC), I went down and enlisted in May 1943. I was sent to Camp Grant in northeastern Illinois to be inoculated with a variety of shots and pick up my uniform. I returned home to await the decision as to where I was to go, but I was to wear my uniform, which was very baggy and ill fitting.

I went to Broadway Presbyterian Church the following Sunday with Annie and Dad. The Commandant of the Rock Island Arsenal, Brigadier General Ramsay, and his wife sat in the pew just in front of us. Here I was in uniform, I knew nothing about the army, and when the general joined us at the steps leaving the church I saluted him with my left hand. He roared with laughter, stuck out his hand and we shook hands. I realized I had made my first great military blunder of the war.

I went back to Camp Grant to join quite a few other VOC candidates. We were separated into a bunkhouse, and then put on a train for the field artillery section of Camp Roberts, at Paso Robles, California. Camp Roberts was divided into an infantry camp and a field artillery camp. The training period of both was four months. We learned to march and went on long hikes, sometimes as long as twenty miles with packs on our backs. I was twenty-seven and already pretty old, even to become a second lieutenant. Some of the other draftees who had high draft numbers were in their mid-thirties. They were businessmen or clerks or what have you, all of us very soft. The first ten-mile hike we went on found these chaps limping back into camp two hours late with tremendous blisters on their feet. The sergeant in charge was not very sympathetic, which I thought was being pretty tough on these men who probably were in no better shape than me, and were perhaps seven or eight years older. I survived the hikes because I knew how to take care of my boots and had done a lot of walking with my father's Black Hawk Hiking Club.

Annie came to Paso Robles so she could be near me while I was at Camp Roberts. She found they were charging two-hundred dollars a month for chicken coops for families who wanted to be together. Annie sat in a USO office sobbing, but she had taken a book out of the library. A lady came by and asked her why she was crying. She said, "I can't find a place to live. We've only been married a year and a half, and I just don't want to go home." The lady said, "What are you reading?" It turned out to be a book which dealt with the Bible. The woman said, "I happen to be a minister's wife, and I think we could put you up in our son's room." The room turned out to contain a double-decker bunk. The Reverend Thomas was a delightful Episcopalian minister in this small town of Paso Robles, California. Annie and I of course went to church, and sat with Mrs. Thomas.

In the pew in front of us was a uniformed officer with two general's stars on his shoulders and a bit of white hair—a very nice looking gentleman. At some point he turned around and said, "Well soldier, you have a fine singing voice, where are you stationed?" I said, "Sir, I am at Camp Roberts in the Field Artillery." "Well," he said, "I happen to be Commandant of the Field Artillery section of Camp Roberts. Where are you from?" "Rock Island, Illinois," I replied. He said, "I have a wonderful old friend I roomed with at West Point who is now the Commandant of the Rock Island Arsenal. Do you know a Colonel Ramsay?" "Yes sir," I said. "He and his wife sit in front of us at the Broadway Presbyterian Church in Rock Island." I thought to myself that if anything ever happened to me I could really depend on the general for support. It was a nice feeling. Annie and I spent weekends at the Thomas parsonage until October of 1943, and we saw the Field Artillery commandant almost every Sunday.

My Gun Crew

At the end of the four months' session, our fellow trainees were shipped to places to be further trained for active duty. The captain of the field artillery battery in which I had trained asked me and two other VOC candidates to stay over and join the staff as instructors, even though we were privates at that point. We were then made privates first class with a single chevron on each sleeve. I remember what a thrill it was when Annie sewed on the chevron for what was the first promotion of anything I had had in my life so far. I stayed on as a member of the "cadre." The camp was short of teaching people. The Army needed men overseas. We men who had been asked to stay were six or seven years older than these chaps who were being drafted at age eighteen, and were better educated than the other older trainees in their late twenties.

In December 1943 a group of three officers visited Camp Roberts looking for officer candidates for Fort Sill, the officer candidate school (OCS) in Oklahoma for the field artillery. The three of us who were VOCs were then invited to appear before this three-man board. I was eager to become an officer. I stood at rigid attention while they read my resume. One of the officers said, "Hauberg, I see you went to Princeton, class of '39." I said, "Yes sir." He said, "Were you at the Princeton/Yale game in the fall of 1938?" I said, "Yes sir. I deeply regret that Princeton lost to Yale in the last five minutes." This officer said, "And I am happy that they did. By the way, Hauberg, at ease." That meant I could stop standing at rigid attention and put my feet apart a little bit with my hands clasped behind me—still a rather uncomfortable position.

The officer said, "I want you to meet my other committee members. This is Major so and so, Dartmouth class of so and so, and on my left is Captain so and so, Harvard class of so and so. By the way Hauberg, pull up a chair and let's talk about those football games." Pretty soon we were all laughing about things. When I left the room after giving them a very snappy salute and feeling much more at ease, the captain of the field artillery battery who had recommended me to this committee said, "Well, judging from all the chatter and laughter I heard in there, I'd say that you are going to be accepted." Both the other VOC candidates were also accepted. Annie, very pregnant, went back to Seattle.

We candidates were assigned to the class of 99, which in field artillery parlance was known as niner-niner. We all went down to Fort Sill together, I believe in mid-December. That was to be another four-month course. On February 4, 1944 my daughter Fay arrived in this world. Annie and Fay found a home with Mrs. Mansel Griffiths at 38th East and East Prospect, and that is where I first saw Fay some six weeks after her birth, when I had graduated from Fort Sill. I was assigned back to Camp Roberts and Annie again came back to Paso Robles with Fay.

We were happily doing our job as "training officers" when D-Day took place in 1944. It had a profound effect upon the entire country. Thousands of second lieutenants were killed in the invasion on Omaha and Utah beaches, and in the days immediately after. It was apparent that the field artillery and other artillery branches such as antitank artillery and antiaircraft artillery stationed in the U.S.A. were very overstaffed with officers who were undoubtedly never

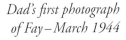

Dad's first photograph of Fay – March 1944

going to see action. By a stroke of his pen, President and Commander in Chief Franklin D. Roosevelt took all of us out of whatever artillery groups we were in and assigned us, some eleven thousand lieutenants, to the infantry. We were to learn immediately all about infantry weapons and tactics.

My orders permitted Annie, baby Fay, and me to drive across the continent from California to Georgia's Fort Benning, a military training station for officers, in our big four-door Buick which used up a gallon of gas every nine miles. Fay was "changed" at gas station rest rooms as Annie coped with the long trip. Again, Annie found a "home" to rent while we were in this "infantry retread" program for a couple of months. Fort Benning became the "retraining center" for us artillery officers in six-week waves.

The Tire Story

Although my orders to move from Camp Roberts in California to Fort Benning in Georgia covered gas requirements, they covered nothing else. Our spare tire had little tread left and the four tires on the wheels were not much better. Sure enough, as we approached Jackson, Mississippi, we had a blowout and limped into the state capital on four poor tires and a useless spare.

A gas station manager looked at my papers and shook his head. "There is nothing in them that will enable me to replace a tire I might sell to you with another tire to sell." But he took a closer look at my papers and noticed my name, Hauberg. He said the Mississippi state attorney general had that name which was so unusual. I was able to get Robert Hauberg on the phone, he was amazed to hear from another family with the same name. He came down to the gas station with documents that made it possible for the station manager to sell me a brand new tire! He also told me of his unmarried sister, a nurse, in the hospital at Camp Hood. Little did I know that after Fort Benning I would be assigned to the infantry-training center at Camp Hood, Texas. And of course, I looked her up as soon as we got there.

From Fort Benning, Georgia, where I took the infantry officers' short course training, the same three of us, Charlie Goggi, Jim Failey, and I, who had been together from basic training in the field artillery, were assigned to Camp Hood, about fifty miles from Austin, Texas to be infantry instructors. It was a huge spread of dusty terrain, very dry, very hot. The town nearest the camp, Killeen, was not very attractive but Annie came down and bought a house for an enormous sum of money, something like seventy-five hundred dollars. We lived there with baby Fay for quite a long time.

The house was downwind from a rendering plant and the odor was almost unbearable when the wind blew in the wrong direction. We worked over a hundred hours a week. I would take a bus from camp to Killeen and maybe have five or six hours to have a meal and sleep in a good bed. Then I'd get up at four or five in the morning to get back to camp to resume training. Whereas field artillery officers and men carried a carbine and a light rifle, infantrymen carried the brand new M-1 rifle with a bayonet attachment and a far heavier load of ammunition. Field artillery "guns" were howitzers from one hundred fifty millimeters and larger. Infantry "pieces" were forty and sixty millimeter mortars for firing close into an enemy line, on up to only a seventy-five millimeter howitzer. And, of course, an infantryman carried a half-dozen hand grenades for really close-in fighting—and then the ultimate bayonet. Infantry tactics were new to us as well as the signaling process. Walkie-talkies were new. The antitank "bazooka" had just been invented. We had to learn all this at Benning and teach it at Hood.

The training was tough. The boys who had been assigned to field artillery were, on the average, superior in intelligence to the chaps who were assigned to the infantry. About fifty percent of the latter were from the slums of the big cities—Detroit, Chicago, New York—and working with them made for frustration and also provided many interesting experiences. They resented being ordered to do anything, and we new officers gave commands gingerly and hoped there would be no objection. The remaining fifty percent, however, were from small towns and these were boys of great character, determination, loyalty and patriotism. Without these chaps, we never would have won the war.

They were very homesick and lonely. Every Sunday I invited a couple of these boys to come to our little house near the camp. They played with Fay on the lawn, but mostly they just lay in the sun and slept because they were so exhausted. No one suffered any bites from the tiny scorpions and black widow spiders in the grass.

At the end of the first period when there was a training company farewell party, the master sergeant who was the ranking noncom in the infantry battalion, hosted the party and the officers were all introduced. One officer had told a lot of jokes during his classes and had been very lax in his training. At the end of the party he got lots of laughs and loud applause. When the sergeant introduced me the whole house stood up, recognizing the fact that I had done my best to give them tough training which would bring about their survival in battle. After these boys had been overseas, some for not even a couple of months, I would get a letter from the wife saying that Bill had been killed in action—that he told her if anything happened to him she was to write Lieutenant Hauberg and tell him how much his training was appreciated, in spite of his death.

In 1944 I took two trainloads of five hundred to one thousand troops each from Texas to Boston for transshipment overseas. My title was "train commander," and I had literally nothing to do. I had some noncommissioned officers to help. None of the boys left the train, although there were opportunities for them to have done so. They all got off in Boston and were sent overseas to Europe. The second trainload included myself as one of those to be shipped overseas. We went over on the USS *Washington*, a beautiful ocean liner that normally carried about two thousand passengers and a crew of one thousand. By this time I had become a first lieutenant. There were eleven of us first lieutenants in a stateroom designed for a couple of people in peaceful times, and six thousand troops. I suppose there were second lieutenants by quite a few hundreds.

There were more than one hundred twenty-five ships in this flotilla. As we moved slowly across the Atlantic, each ship was at least a mile apart from the others, spread from horizon to horizon. The submarine danger had been substantially reduced by the Allies' constant bombing of submarine bases in Germany, but it still existed. So we had little destroyer escorts that were like mosquitoes, just flitting through this vast fleet, "pinging" to discover submarines, if any. There were none. I'm sure my feelings of excitement and trepidation over what was yet to come were shared by most of my shipmates.

John Hauberg with Charles Goggi, soon to become Captain Goggi, adjutant of the 41st Reinforcement Battalion at Amberg, Germany

CHAPTER 13
The War Years in Europe

The Follies Bergere

t HE USS *WASHINGTON* DOCKED AT LE HAVRE, AND FROM THERE SOME TROOPS WERE sent to a camp near Paris. It was a beautiful country home which had been commandeered from a member of the Rothschild family. We were five hundred enlisted men and about six officers. The officers lived in the old stone house. The troops lived in tents in the courtyard. The property was surrounded by a beautiful beech forest. All the trees had been planted according to a transit, so they were in perfect lines north, south, east and west. No matter which way you looked you were always looking down a row of these beautiful trees, which probably were two hundred years old. It was a memory I never forgot, and was one of the reasons I chose to study forestry later on.

We were there only one week. We officers went to Paris, attended the Follies Bergere, climbed the hill to Montmartre, visited Notre Dame Cathedral, and did some shopping for a good bottle of wine or two. Then we boarded a train with five hundred GIs, and were headed for the front in Germany. There was just a single track that had been repaired by French railroad workers. On either side of this were twisted tracks and heaps of wrecked locomotives and boxcars. We passed barbed wire enclosures that were perhaps a mile square in which hundreds of thousands of German prisoners were held. They were administering their own prison camp because the Allies were too busy fighting the war, and these Germans were glad to be out of it. Most of the prisoners we could see from our boxcars were old men and young boys, who had been conscripted, but not trained, for Hitler's last gasp, the Battle of the Bulge. They had all soon surrendered.

The railroad workers were working hard to clear the wreckage and lay a second track to the German border. If anybody ever tells me the French don't like to work I can testify that if the conditions are of a certain kind, the French will work as hard as anybody else. As we approached the Rhine, the size of the camps dwindled because the Allies were advancing so rapidly that they shipped the prisoners only as far back as would get them out of the way. When we pulled into the railway station at Frankfurt-am-Main, a tributary to the Rhine, the newsboys were hawking the *Stars & Stripes*, the army newspaper. The headline was GERMANY SURRENDERS. So our timing was perfect; we arrived in Germany the day that Germany surrendered. One of the boys said the Germans surrendered because they knew we were coming and there was no hope for them.

I don't know where the five hundred young men went who were under my command on the train, but I was sent to an officer's replacement depot. Shortly thereafter, I was joined by my old friends Goggi and Failey. There were six or eight of us first lieutenants who were unwanted by any division because the battle divisions had second lieutenants who had been through all kinds of action and deserved promotion. If we had been assigned to any particular part of the army, we would occupy the first lieutenant positions and therefore deny these battle-hardened second lieutenants a chance to be promoted.

We were held for quite a long time in Bavaria, during which we developed a volleyball team. We played a lot of games and got pretty good at it. We also toured the countryside. We couldn't get to Berlin because the Russians were having a standoff with our Army at that time, but we visited places such as Munich and Oberammergau and Innsbruck in Austria. Finally, I was assigned to a cannon company in a little town called Lembach along the Danube River in the Oberdanau district of Austria. We were not aware that this area had al-

Lembach

ready been scheduled for transfer to the Russians. Austria was carved up into zones for the British, French, and Americans, and now the Russians demanded a "zone."

It was an area of prosperous farmers who had big barns, most of which were occupied by displaced non-military persons. These were people who were taken prisoner by the Germans and who had been abandoned as the Germans retreated. They were from almost every country in Eastern Europe. There were Hungarians, Bulgarians, Rumanians, even Austrians, Ukrainians, and some French people. Some of them had taken wives among the Austrian girls. They were stacked up in these barns in bunks that were sometimes four or five levels on top of one another. They slept, made love, and ate in terribly crowded conditions; and generally waited for something to happen to them, hopefully being sent home.

The U.S. Army wanted to get these people back to their countries. I spoke schoolboy German, and it was a pleasure to go into a small community, talk to the mayors, known as burgermeisters, and announce that I would have trucks coming to their village to pick up Hungarians, for example. Well, the Hungarians were delighted and they all showed up with their small amount of possessions. They cheerfully boarded the trucks and were sent back to Hungary—others to France, Italy, etc.

The Ukrainians, however, were terrified of going back to the Ukraine. They were sure they would be shot as traitors because they had been captured and put to slave labor. I made a big mistake. I ordered a group of Ukrainians onto the trucks and they wouldn't go, so I had my boys fix bayonets and we pushed them on the trucks. I considered this action with a very troubled mind, because I knew I had to go back to get the rest of them. So I conceived the idea of calling up the burgermeister first and telling him we were coming to get the Ukrainians. By the time we arrived at his village, there were no Ukrainians. They had shifted to barns in other parts, and when we got to those barns, they had shifted back. I don't know what happened to those people, but I felt very good that at least the remaining Ukrainians probably never saw Russia again as long as they lived, and that's the way they wanted it.

Our infantry cannon company had some very coarse officers. There were about six of us. The captain could never be sexually satisfied, and whenever a farmer wanted to go from our Oberdanau district to Linz or on down to Vienna, the captain insisted on sleeping with the farmer's daughter before giving the family permission to reach its destination. Other officers and men were simply out for everything they could get. They did a lot of so-called looting, which was nothing more or less than finding something you wanted and putting it in your duffle bag. I wasn't happy with them at all.

Suddenly we were joined by Ninth Infantry Division officers, who had been in battle against Rommel's tanks all across North Africa and all up the Italian boot. Psychologically, they were wrecks and they frequently fired their 45-caliber pistols into the ceiling above us. This usually took place at the dinner table, and it of course wrecked the house. Finally, they were assigned to the Sixty-fifth Division which was to be sent home. We became the Ninth Infantry Division. It was a great honor to replace these psychologically exhausted men. Lord knows what happened to them when they got home, but I'm certain they all needed a lot of hospitalization.

Near Lembach, but on the edge of the high cliffs along the Danube, were two castles built and owned by chieftains who once demanded tribute from boats passing by far below. They were now owned by a wealthy Austrian and a former German secretary of treasury. The wives of these men were most cordial to another officer and me, who went to tea with them and talked about the future of Austria and Germany. They surprised us with the news that the Russians were about to take over our territory of the Oberdonau, and that they were quietly packing up to leave. The German treasurer's castle had a fantastic collection of old sleighs and buggies, and also room heaters known as *offens*. They had already sent their art collections to what would become the American zone and another house for them.

The sergeants of our company, whom I liked very much, went hunting twice a week for tiny deer, called roebucks, eight of which would feed our hundred-man cannon

Boy holding a roebuck fawn   *The Danube from the castle window*

company for one meal. The German invaders had taken away all guns from everyone including the farmers, and the roebuck had multiplied greatly, feeding on the crops. The fields were small, but beautiful openings in this forested area, creating a wonderful landscape. The farmers would call us that their field was full of deer and off we would go in two or three jeeps armed with our carbines.

Our two mess sergeants (cooks) were from the western United States and knew all about cooking "fists" of deer meat. So the twice-a-week deer dinners were highly prized by one and all. And the farmers were pleased the most.

The day arrived when I was ordered to a frontier gate to meet my Russian counterpart, also a lieutenant, and to show him around. He was in rags but armed to the teeth with a pair of tommy guns and ammunition belts over his shoulders. He was driving a dilapidated wagon drawn by horses on the verge of starvation. If he was a representative of the whole Russian army, the U.S. Army could have probably gone into Berlin.

I kept him away from the Danube where hundreds of boats were taking Oberdonau residents and their most treasured possessions, including their daughters, across the river.

I have not been back to the Oberdonau since the war years. The Russians have moved out, and perhaps all is as it was before Hitler's "Anschluss."

I had my job and I enjoyed the enlisted men a lot more than the officers. We next were moved into Germany, to a little town called Hebertshausen, which was about to celebrate its nine-hundredth anniversary. The town had no water system. Everybody in Hebertshausen had a well, and God knows the water was polluted from all of the animal and human fertilizer, which got sprayed on the farms all around town, with a tremendous stench. So we gave them, as an American birthday present, a water system. About a mile and two hundred feet in elevation above the town there was a self-filling lake, probably from an artesian well. With German help, but under the direction of our American officers, we dug a trench all the way into the heart of town and brought this water to town through a pipe furnished by the U.S. Army. We had to drain the pond in the middle of this little town in order to put up a common water tank.

To our surprise and to the amazement of all of the Germans, whose families had lived there for centuries, the pond was full of giant carp, some of which were three feet long and weighed fifty or sixty pounds. The Germans had been denied meat and fish all during the war because everything they produced was requisitioned by the German army. When we drained the pond, all of these fish were left high and dry, gasping for air. The Germans pounced on them and had a square meal for the first time in four or five years, I guess. The town was overjoyed, but people must have wondered why none of them had ever discovered the fish before.

*Over 90 percent of Wurzberg
looked like this.*

I didn't enjoy the officers of my company, but the colonel who was in command of our regiment was from West Point, Class of '37. It turned out that he had actually attended a cocktail party my Princeton roommates and I gave for some army cadets after an Army-Princeton football game. So he and I became friends. I asked him one day if he could change my assignment around so that I could be with officers that I liked a lot better. He accommodated me by saying "You are going to become a postal officer." I was immediately sent to Wurzburg, which had been 95 percent destroyed by either American or British bombing. Some of it looked as bad as, if not worse, than Dresden.

I spent a month in Wurzburg. We were bivouacked in one of the few houses that remained intact. Every morning for a month I went to school to learn American post office regulations, and how to cope with postal problems. Well, it was a ridiculous school, but it was a lot of fun. I discovered that almost all the Army post offices were manned by experienced American postal people so I really was learning what I didn't need to know. But that's the army for you.

A great thing happened for me in Wurzburg. It was the beginning of my interest in art, and the beginning of my art education. The Prince Bishop's palace in the middle of the city had been damaged in the bombing. The bombers tried to keep away from historic buildings to preserve national treasures, but this one had been bombed. The

Top: The palace in the city; Bottom: The Prince Bishop's fortified castle above the city, fourteenth century

grand stairway had a fresco ceiling by Tiepolo, and German artists were restoring it. The title of the ceiling was The Continents. There were four of them, because in Tiepolo's time (1696–1770), nothing was known of Australia.

Tiepolo had worked from stories brought back by explorers. The animals, of course, were quite fanciful, but were the artist's idea of what kinds of things were living on those continents. It was a beautiful work—very colorful, very extensive.

At Wurzburg, the Prince Bishop's fortress castle, abandoned after the turmoil of the Middle Ages, was up on the hill. It produced the only loot that I brought home to Seattle—a small chunk of carved stone with a Bavarian bear holding a shield. It was pretty beaten up but I picked it up on top of the hill where the Prince Bishop's castle was lying pretty much in rubble.

In the period immediately after hostilities ceased, the Americans could do no wrong. The civilians absolutely loved the Americans. They were destitute. Many

Left: My only "loot" from the war. A stone Bavarian bear from a rubble pile at the Prince Bishop's castle on the high hill overlooking Wurzburg.

people had been living on whatever they could find, for example, fish heads for protein. The GIs came in and began to share their wealth with their hosts.

At the end of the month, I was transferred from Wurzburg to Bad Tolz, south of Munich and not too far from Oberammergau and the Alps. One of the officers who lived with me in the hotel at Bad Tolz was a Catholic priest, and, of course, in Bavaria, being a Catholic country, we were treated to some fresh eggs and milk.

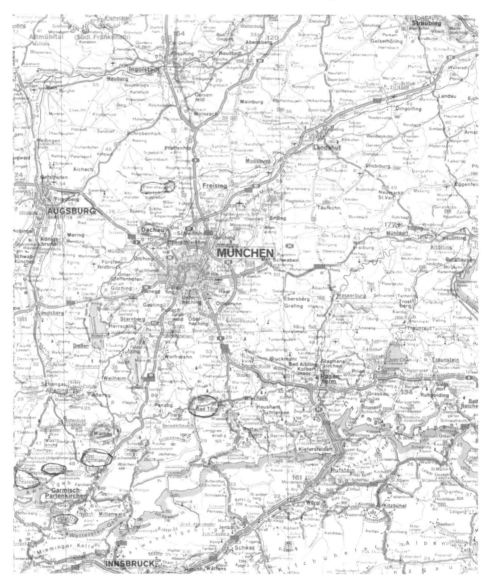

My "command" was the city's post office in downtown Bad Tolz. Our little group of twelve men included a staff sergeant who was a trained postal employee and had been a clerk in the post office in Washington D.C. He had personally handed a couple of important letters to President Roosevelt, he said. He was quite a guy, and I could see that if I attempted to exercise any command over the eleven enlisted men plus the sergeant, I would be making a big mistake. So every day I put in an appearance at the post office for a couple of hours, and then went sightseeing while he ran the post office. Finally we got so confident in each other that he would say, "Lieutenant, why don't you take two weeks off and go down to Italy or Paris. You can sign about two weeks of morning reports ahead, and I will see that they get filled in with whatever happened." We had a wonderful working relationship.

Each of the twelve had a local young lady living with him in the post office. The girls were members of families in Bad Tolz or the surrounding countryside. We had a two-and-a-half-ton truck with which we took the mail to Munich once or twice a week. Our truck was made available to the fathers of some of these young ladies. We hauled their cows to other farms to be bred to a bull, or vice versa, and we did all kinds of favors for townspeople as well as the farmers and their families. The farmers would reciprocate the favors we did for them by giving us fresh eggs and milk, and maybe a chicken every now and then that wasn't canned someplace in Missouri. So we lived quite well, and, of course, their standard of living increased markedly right off the bat.

We also had a small jeep that went with my rank. The young man who drove it was a champion skier from Minnesota so we spent a lot of time skiing in the spring of 1946. The Zugspitz, the mountain where we skied, was about an hour's drive away. It had a cable-car train that went up inside the mountain and emerged very close to the ski area level. I believe the top of the Zugspitz was at about eleven or twelve thousand feet elevation. We took the train up, got out at the station inside the mountain, walked out on the deck nearby, and here were all the Alps spread before us. The Zugspitz was the boundary at the corner of Italy, Austria, and Germany, so one could glide down into any of these countries from the summit. We had a lot of fun doing that. I was a terrible skier, but the T5 who was my driver gave me a few lessons and I got along fine.

Our post office platoon was an auxiliary organization which handled the mail of all of the troops in support of the headquarters regiment of the Third Army, which General Truscott had inherited from General Patton. He became America's representative all over Bavaria and, I believe, in certain parts of Italy and Austria. Because the men and the trucks didn't have much to do, I made at least one trip down to Italy when General Truscott had run out of Scotch and wine. As a courier, I was given a list and the money to drive all the way to Rome and pick it up. I never met the general.

That was a very happy time. My friend Charlie Goggi had been stationed finally at the German town of Regensburg, and had been in charge of a prison camp. All the prisoners were German generals. Goggi was supposed to run a clean camp, and he turned the management over to some of the generals. That gave him plenty of time off, so he and I went through Mad King Ludwig's three castles in Austria: Herren-Chiemsee, Neuschwanstein, and Linderhof. Goggi and I enjoyed each other's company and we've been pals ever since. Jim Failey was the other member of our group of three who had been together from the start. After the war, Jim and his wife moved to Honolulu where Annie and I met them several times.

There was a Lt. Robert Dietz in the officers' hotel at Bad Tolz, with whom I became good friends. We were almost the only two young men who were not furiously in pursuit of women. We played endless games of ping-pong to pass the time.

In November of 1945, Dietz and I took two weeks off and went down to Cannes on the Riviera. We swam in the Mediterranean. Dietz knew how to sail, so we rented a small sailboat and generally enjoyed ourselves. The high point of the visit to Cannes was meeting a very famous artist. We were walking along a street one day and the door to an art gallery was open. The store was having no business whatsoever. There was a pretty young woman behind the counter so we went in and began to try out our French on her. I bought two bronze art deco figures of Mary and the Babe in a cradle, and a separate figure of Joseph with his hands over a beam of the stable. Those two figures are on Bainbridge Island, and give me a great deal of pleasure every time I look at them.

The young woman said, "Please come back tomorrow. The boss will be in and I want you to meet him." The boss turned out to be Aime Maeght, who later became Europe's most prominent art dealer. He was odd-looking. When I said I was from Seattle, Washington, he apparently confused that with Washington D.C. He had a scheme in mind, so he invited Dietz and me to go up the hill to meet "Le Maître." We jumped in his little Renault and went up to a villa overlooking Cannes. It was a beautiful pink stucco house in a setting of palm trees and shrubbery. We parked above the house, and walked down the steps to a huge studio room. On the way down there were a lot of objects such as leaves pinned to the wall. At the foot of the steps was a tiny little man with a monk's tonsure. It was Pierre Bonnard, whom I had never heard of. A lady came toward us and asked if we would like to speak to "Le Maître."

I asked him about the objects pinned to the wall and he said "Everything is from nature, and they have natural colors. I use them as inspiration." On the studio wall was a huge picture, maybe six by ten feet. It was a canvas commissioned by a church that Maeght represented. Maeght took a look at it and went up and simply ripped it off the wall. Pierre Bonnard said, "No, no, no. It's not finished, Ce n'est pas fini." Maeght turned to me and said in English, "Damned artists never know when a picture is done." He put it under his arm and we marched out.

It was time to go home, and Dietz and I were going to get on the train for Munich where I would be met by my driver and returned to Bad Tolz. But Maeght said to me, "I want you to ride with me to Paris in my Renault." I went to his apartment and studio on St. Honore. He was just getting established as an art dealer, and on the walls of his family room were six paintings by Matisse. I had never heard of Matisse, but I said to him, "Those are the most beautiful paintings I've ever seen. I think I'd like to buy one. How much are they?" He said they were ten thousand dollars. I said to him, "In my office in Bad Tolz I have a picture on the wall of a Lincoln Continental Mark I convertible. I'm dying to own one of those when I get home but I don't think I can afford it, so I certainly can't afford ten thousand dollars for a Matisse painting." That was the biggest mistake I ever made in my life, although I really don't know where I would have gotten the ten thousand dollars. I never got the convertible either.

Maeght's scheme was to send his son to Washington, D.C., to stay with me and my family, learn about the U.S.A., and make "connections." He remained friendly even after realizing that Seattle, Washington, was a long way from Washington, D.C.

During my stay in Germany, my ability to understand what others were saying in German improved a lot, but my ability to converse was only fair because I simply didn't have the vocabulary. Since we were to be sent home very shortly, I didn't make much of an effort to learn more German. I was overseas fourteen months, and it went by very quickly. The scenic part of Germany was wonderful and in a way I hated to leave; but I also was anxious to get home to my family. When my orders came to travel to Le Havre for shipment home, I was overjoyed.

By this time Fay was two and a half years old. Although my wife and I had exchanged lots of letters, they were no substitute for going home and being with them.

Getting home was interesting. There were, of course, no submarines to worry about, so our ship made a swift crossing, I think in about six days. It was an ocean liner that had been a passenger ship in its palmier days and probably would become one again. There were a hundred officers and nine hundred enlisted men aboard. The ship carried big stainless tanks, which contained about twenty thousand gallons of fresh milk. The GIs went through the twenty thousand gallons in about two days. The decks were crawling with purebred cats and dogs, and even a few monkeys. The captain said, "I hope none of you young men are stupid enough to try to bring back any birds, especially parrots, because, if you are, we will be quarantined offshore while the birds are checked for psittacosis."

Finally some guy confessed that he did indeed have a parrot. The captain realized that this GI might be murdered for delaying our arrival and the parrot done away with, so the captain took the bird into his own quarters. The crossing was considered a part of the bird's incubation period, and since there was no evidence of psittacosis we sailed into New York harbor. We all stood on deck as we passed the Statue of Liberty, feeling wonderful. The captain gave the bird back to its owner, I imagine with a stern lecture about his folly.

I was made the debarkation commander. I don't know why I got selected for such a terrible job, because here was my wife at the foot of the gangplank, and I could see that I was going to be the last person off the boat. I was in a terrible hurry to greet her, and I wanted these guys to throw their duffle bags onto the dock and then run down the gangplank as I checked them off my list. But they would say, "Oh no, Lieutenant, I can't throw it off—I've got dogs in there (or monkeys, or cats)." So it took more than two hours to unload the ship.

Home Again

I finally got down the gangplank to a very warm reception from my wife. Hotel rooms were very hard to come by, but Annie had found a very small room, almost a service room, in the Drake Hotel at 56th and Park. It was going to take three or four days to travel to Fort Dix, New Jersey and go through the process of becoming a civilian again. There was one thing I was dying to do, which was surprising to me. I had never been terribly fascinated by baseball, but I had an overwhelming desire to see an American baseball game. I think the doorman at the hotel had some connection, and we got in to see the New York Yankees in Yankee Stadium playing the Boston Red Sox at the end of a red-hot season. This was August of 1946. We had seats way out in the bleachers. The players looked like miniature people, but we stayed until the last out, and then I was satisfied. I don't think I've seen more than four or five baseball games since.

We saw Annie's uncles and aunts on Long Island and elsewhere in the New York area, and finally we headed back to Seattle.

All of the officers were given a promotion to one level above, so I was mustered out as a captain in the infantry. Each of us was asked if we would join the army reserve. I felt confident that I didn't need the money that came from being in the reserve. It required two weeks every summer, and then two evenings per month of reserve training. I said no. I wanted to go back to college. But all of my officer friends said yes because they were uncertain about getting a job and what it would pay, so they felt they could use all of the income they could get. Every one of these men lost a lot, because they were all called back for the Korean War. Marriages, new homes, new careers, went down the drain. Goggi and Failey were caught by this, but both emerged all right. Jim Failey died about 1990, and Charlie Goggi and I are still exchanging Christmas cards in 2001. He is a very happy chap, an excellent businessman. He lives in Charlotte, North Carolina. His wife is named Ann too. Delightful people. We've gotten together at least twice since the war.

To my father's house for a first welcome home
from the army in Europe

CHAPTER 14
Families & Friends Postwar

Families

COMING HOME FROM EUROPE IN AUGUST 1946, AND NOW CAPTAIN JOHN H. HAUBERG, Jr., I was enrolled in the University of Washington College of Forestry. There was nothing fuzzy in my mind about what I wanted to do with my new education. I wanted to create new forests and regenerate old ones. I would have my own forest in order to find out how to do these things. Princeton and the army were ancient history. My uniform went into mothballs.

But, of course, there was life outside the walls of Anderson Hall where the Forestry College demanded academic excellence. That life had to be devoted to other learning. Annie Gould and I had not lived in Seattle since our marriage in 1941, and I had not had any chance to get much more than an acquaintance with her family, and she with mine, although we had lived in Rock Island with Haubergs and Denkmanns from the fall of 1941 to the spring of 1943 when I entered the army,

What was our extended family? Who were the Goulds and the Fays? Friends or foes? Annie had some pretty starchy Gould uncles and aunts and cousins in the East from New York to Massachusetts and a famous uncle, Dr. Temple Fay, in Philadelphia. She had a lot of Fay family right in Seattle! Most of them were startled when Annie decided to marry someone with an odd German name who came from the Middle West—Illinois, or something like that. And he had gone to Princeton, not Harvard. These were all handicaps. I had to prove that I wasn't all that bad to a lot of Annie's relatives.

Annie's mother, Mrs. Carl F. Gould, or Dorothy Fay Gould, had engaged the University of Washington regents in a losing battle over architect's fees, which she thought they owed her. To keep Annie out of this suit became my first effort in family relations from which we all emerged rather quickly without scars. Annie's Granny Fay came back from retirement in Tucson, Arizona, to live with us at 1031 McGilvra Boulevard in Seattle in 1947. She had been an emotional firebrand, as was her husband, John P. Fay, but the fires were banked, and she was now a most lovable lady, enjoying her grandchildren and great-grandchildren, Fay and Sue Hauberg. I learned from her the highly emotional nature of most of the Fays.

Granny Fay was Alice Ober, born in 1863 into a very intellectual family that produced professors, writers, even actors. Granny married John Purinton Fay in 1889

*Granny Fay with
Sue in her arms
and Fay Westbrook
Hauberg looking on*

in San Francisco. Mr. Fay was a lawyer also with a New England upbringing and a Harvard education. Both had moved West as did many of their contemporaries. In March 1889 Mr. Fay opened a law office in Seattle's Boston Block, now the core of Pioneer Square, and in June came the great fire that destroyed all of Seattle's downtown area, except the building he was in. He had the only law library in Seattle, so he found himself with many lawsuits that resulted from the fire. Mr. Fay ran for the Washington State Senate and served at least two terms. He asked the State Senate to elect him as a United States Senator, when that was the procedure in the early twentieth century, but he was defeated. He invested in land between the south end of Capitol Hill and the north end of Beacon Hill, betting that this would be the route of a canal joining Lake Washington to Elliott Bay, and again he lost. His living ultimately came from owner-ship of at least one apartment building. His children Dorothy, Alice, Temple, and Jean were born in Seattle between 1890 and 1904. Granny joined the Browning Society to read and enjoy the poetry of Robert and Elizabeth Barrett Browning.

Harvard men swarmed to Seattle in the 1880s and 1890s to practice law, and to acquire professorships and banking positions. Followed by Yale men, they and their wives provided what cultural level there was in the otherwise raw town of Seattle, whose economic underpinnings were fishing, timber, construction, shipping, and later the gold rush to Alaska. The men founded the University Club and the Seattle Golf Club.

The Fays were involved in many of these ventures. It seemed only natural then that Dorothy Fay, a Vassar graduate, would become a teacher at the University of Washington. Fascinated by the history of the Pacific Northwest, she wrote *Beyond the Shining Mountains, Thirty-Six Northwest Adventures* in 1932. Possessed of a fine voice,

Dorothy Fay Gould, Alice Fay Case, Granny Alice Ober Fay, Fay Carol Case, Fay Westbrook Hauberg, Anne Gould Hauberg, Sylvia Case

just right for radio, she had her own program on the air about this region's history, with many fascinating anecdotes.

She also charmed Carl Frelinghuysen Gould, a tall, lanky, sophisticated professor of architecture, and founder of that department at the University of Washington. Born in 1873, he was a Harvard graduate who then went to Paris to study architecture at the École des Beaux-Arts of the University of Paris. He returned to New York to join the famous architecture partnership of McKim, Meade, and White, which had already done the Metropolitan Museum of Art and many other such grand establishments. Afflicted with a breathing problem, he went to a health resort at Lake Saranac, New York, and from there came to the milder, cleaner airs of Seattle, quickly affiliating with an established architect, Charles Bebb. The firm of Bebb and Gould designed many University of Washington campus buildings, especially the Suzallo Library, the Seattle Art Museum in Volunteer Park, and many homes of Seattle leaders. In 1915 he married Dorothy Wheaton Fay.

Socially, Carl and Dorothy Gould seemed to be the center of Seattle's activities. Although I never met Carl Gould, Sr., who died in January of 1939, I went to Mrs. Gould's Sunday afternoon teas where she held forth as a grande dame over us younger swains. She was, no doubt, judging us for a possible husband for her daughter Anne. Mrs. G. as we called her, was fascinating and domineering. She suggested books to read about her history specialty. On one occasion when our "set" wanted to visit Seattle City Light's Ross Dam and lake, she agreed to be our chaperone for the weekend. We, of course, behaved ourselves, but would have anyway if she hadn't been along. But certainly Annie would not have been permitted to go.

The impact on Annie and me of these three, Granny Fay, "Mrs. G." and their recollections of Mr. Carl F. Gould, was profound. Annie and I were in the spotlight as soon as we came back to Seattle to live. It was much harder on Annie than it was on me, since I had a firm commitment to a forest research/management career.

These pressures to excel were different and obvious, but the social pressures on Annie were difficult to define. We gave as many parties as we were invited to, and Annie's parties were always the best.

Carl Gould, Jr., learned to avoid the spotlight, and so did John V. Gould, known as Wyck to many of us. They kept their heads down and developed their own careers as architect and engineer. Annie and I really did not see a lot of them and I think they liked it better that way.

Aunt Alice Fay Case was the ear into which we all poured our problems, our sorrows, and our joys. She lived in Washington Park not far from our house. She was sensible, unflappable, loving, and wise. We were close to her and her family, Ronald,

Thanksgiving on Bainbridge–the Fay family
Standing: Dorothy Fay Gould, Dick Given, Marion (Mrs. Temple) Fay, Carol Case Given, D.M. Case, Win Case holding Deidre Case, Myra Ober More, Marion (Jr.) Fay, Aunt Jean Fay, Anne Westbrook Gould Hauberg, Fay Westbrook Hauberg, John Jones, Margaret Gould, John V. Gould holding John G., Jr., Alva Ober, Carl F. Gould, Jr. Seated: Bradford Jones, Uncle Bunty (Dr. Temple) Fay, Gretchen Gould holding Kim Gould, Sylvia Case Jones behind Kathleen Jones, Sue Bradford Hauberg, Danny Case, Bryce Given, Cathy Gould, David Given.

Aubrey Gould, Jr., Uncle Aubrey Gould   *Elsie Swan and Rosie Clark*

her husband, and their children, Sylvia, Winthrop (or Win), and Fay Carol all through the years. She kept me from exploding quite a few times.

And then there was Dr. Temple (Bunty) Fay, a world famous neurologist, head strong, opinionated, and very creative. He didn't care about any form of criticism or efforts to force him to accept rules and regulations. He did outrageous things for the good of mankind, and either loved (or cared less about) the impact he made on everyone. No one could be neutral about Uncle Bunty.

I have a copy of a witty book he wrote about his experiences as a hospital intern. It was called *My First Baby and Other Ambulance Anecdotes, by The Intern,* (Temple Fay) in 1933. I watched him turn a young couple with a brain-damaged child from despair to hope after his own examination of the child. I watched him reduce a radio-preacher from arrogance to falling on his knees in front of all of us, to beg God's forgiveness for his lack of attention to his son with muscular dystrophy. And from afar I followed the American Medical Association's efforts to revoke his license because he did not follow the rules in waiting for approval to practice some of the results of his research.

At Camp Hood, the huge Texas infantry-training center where Annie, Fay, and I spent a year, I bumped into a doctor at the camp's infirmary who had studied at Temple University Medical Center under Dr. Fay. I asked him what he thought of his teacher. His eyes widened and in almost a hushed voice he said, "He was the greatest man I will ever meet."

So the Fays were powerful people, one could almost say "loose cannons." And with our visits to the starchy Goulds in the East, I began to realize I had married into two most unusual clans.

The Haubergs and the Denkmanns liked Annie very much but we were in Rock Island only sixteen months. Annie's milieu was Seattle, with old friends, lots of arts and crafts, her own house and garden, and her family. We joined the Arboretum Foundation, went to flower shows, planted our own garden, and learned the names of shrubs and trees. The "Arb" was under the supervision of a wonderful director, Brian Mulligan, an Englishman trained at Wisley Gardens. He brought professionalism to the Arb, which had been pretty much controlled by the Seattle Garden Club, Mrs. Alexander Fraser McEwan, a great friend of the Goulds, in particular. Working with the Arboretum Foundation brought more contacts with Gordon Marckworth, Dean of the College of Forestry, to whom Brian Mulligan reported and who was following my forestry school progress rather closely. So Annie and I met lots of arboretum enthusiasts and for five years were very active. We especially liked Mrs. William Blackford and her daughter and son-in-law, Ginny and Newt Morris and their children, Fay's age.

And of course, our friends who were in our wedding party formed a close circle – Fay Padelford, Janet MacDonald (soon to marry Chester Paulson), Annie Parry, Hugh and Dorothy Pickel.

Our Fay was the center of our world. Her little friends and their parents made up most of that world.

1031 McGilvra Boulevard East

Before I arrived from Europe, Annie had bought a tiny house for us just above the entrance to the Arboretum. It was just too small. We quickly moved to 1031 McGilvra Boulevard., when it suddenly became available, and for the next nine years

John Jones, who married Sylvia Case,
and Uncle Ronald Case

The country club pool

bounced between it and the Gould family's Topsfield on Bainbridge Island, which added to the focus on family ties.

Summers on Bainbridge brought Annie, Fay, and me, and our wonderful helper in every way, Crissy Hargreaves, into lots of days with Aunt Alice and Uncle Ronald Case and Win, Sylvia, Fay Carol, and later on with Carl and Wyck Gould. Uncle Ronald was a bow and arrow expert and set up his targets in the Country Club's meadow beyond the Gould's fence. No one complained. These were all happy days with Granny Fay and Mrs. G. as the grande dames. Wyck and I stole our way onto the Country Club tennis court, an ancient place with a huge bigleaf maple growing in one corner. A well-placed shot could send one of us scrambling up the trunk to return it. We were frequently rather sternly ordered off the court by Messrs. Ketchum, Pelly and Fisken, who were club members.

The Country Club pool was an invitational right and, of course, Mrs. Gould had been invited. I think there was a small privilege fee which Annie and I cheerfully paid. It didn't extend to the tennis court however. The pool was, in the 1940s, neither filtered nor heated. Mr. Cebert Baillargeon, a club member and speaker, insisted on new fresh Puget Sound water to fill the pool at high tide. The fifty-eight degree temperature was what made men of us boys. By the time the sun had warmed up the pool to sixty-eight degrees, it was time to refill it with new water. We got used to it, but it made for more sitting and child watching for us grown-ups, and greater use of the "wading pool" by our children. It could be filled with a garden hose using precious Country Club reservoir water, which was much warmer.

Carl Gould, Jr., had a wherry, a wider version of a rowing scull. Win Case brought over a shotgun and I had a clay-target throwing machine. Cases and Givens boys made good use of the joint opportunities presented. All these good reasons for Fays and

163

Left: Fay Westbrook Hauberg and Jayme Clise; Above right: Wyck and Carl Gould with Carl's wherry

Goulds to get together on Bainbridge were augmented by the special occasions of July Fourth, Labor Day, Thanksgiving, and birthdays.

My daughters, Fay Page and Sue Hauberg, carry on close connections with Aunt Alice Fay Case's children and grandchildren as well as Uncle Temple (Bunty) Fay's descendants who live out here in the West. We keep in touch with the Carl and Wyck Gould families, although not the Eastern Goulds. And, of course, we out here are involved closely with my sister's children, the Sweeneys.

So we felt a very close association with our families in Seattle for over thirty years following the war. We had contacts at intervals with the Goulds in the East, and we had many visits with my sister and all the Sweeneys, both in Wash-

Carl Gould with Fay, Gretchen Gould, Win Case, D.M. Case, Fay Carol Case with Jane Adams, Anne Gould Hauberg, Jack Adams

Sweeneys and Haubergs–1948

Dave Shuler, Mabis Chase,
and Al Rawson

ington, D.C., and in Miami. We kept close to my father until his death in 1955 and have had interchangeable visits with Midwestern Hauberg relatives up to the present.

Meanwhile, the older Denkmann generations had decided that the family should not manage its lumber operations any longer, and had therefore leased almost all our lands in Louisiana and Mississippi to International Paper Company for several million dollars. We could then settle down to a handsome income from leasing mineral rights, which had been kept in the family. So income from oil and gas poured in. But a rift in the family over those changes had set in between the Reimers and the other family members beginning about 1943. I felt it was not my generation's fight and that we should get the family back together.

Accordingly, in 1953, I telephoned my favorite cousin, Marietta Reimers Schneider in Hammond, Louisiana, to suggest we make that effort because there were many assets left to manage even if our seniors had decided to give up the responsibility. She concurred. We proceeded to invite cousins from all the four branches of the Denkmanns descended from the four Denkmann sisters, Marietta, Lonie Tom, Elise, and Sue. The Lee family, descended from Tom Lee, Aunt Rhoda Denkmann's heir, joined the group.

Our Weyerhaeuser cousins were notified of our intentions to visit woods and mills while getting better acquainted among ourselves and talking business. We were royally "entertained" with parties that gave way to many trips through woods operations, sawmills, and pulp mills that finally wore out our ladies.

Below left: Denkmanns in the woods

Right: A spectacular tree topping

Bottom of page: Our two yachts, the Onawa and the Deerleap. Denkmann family get-together in 1953.

The final two days and nights were aboard two 80-foot yachts, the *Deerleap* and the *Onawa*, where fun and frolic, Weyerhaeuser and Denkmann family traits, returned. But now that was tempered by information about our assets that were at stake and how we were going to move into their management as the seniors retired.

We were now a united Denkmann family and we had reestablished our connections with the Weyerhaeusers of our generation. This led to two Weyerhaeuser–Denkmann reunions in 1960 and 1965. Each clan then became too numerous for further joint gatherings. In 2000, the Denkmanns have had another every-fifth-year reunion in Woodstock, Vermont with over ninety in attendance. There seems to be no reason why this happy, growing family will not have many more.

Left: Barry Shuler, Dave Shuler, Sumner Macomber, Jean Shuler Rawson, Mabis Chase, Dick Stibolt, Ann Shuler Chase, Courtney Stibolt. Right: Franny Blunt, Ann Shuler Chase, Ethleen Taggart. We invited Franny to join us. Her father, Carleton Blunt of Chicago, was a Weyerhaeuser Board member, representing the Laird-Norton family interests and heard about our family visits to woods and mills. We were glad to include Franny.

The 1953 Denkmann family trip to the Northwest operations of the Weyerhaeuser Company brought renewed relations with the many Weyerhaeusers who lived there, Phil Weyerhaeuser was the president of the company, and he and his family entertained us and helped escort us through woods and assorted mill operations. "F.K." Weyerhaeuser, Phil's brother, and F.K.'s wife Vivian were very warm hosts. My favorite Weyerhaeuser cousin, Ed Titcomb, and Julie were also on hand. All these felt a renewal of old Weyerhaeuser and Denkmann ties. I am sure it had much to do with my election to the Weyerhaeuser Board of Directors following Fred Reimers' death in August of 1958, a position I held for thirty years.

The later success of Pilchuck Tree Farm in discovering the way to regenerate Douglas fir on high-site lands kept me close to Weyerhaeuser forestry people, especially C. Davis Weyerhaeuser who was Vice President for Land and Timber operations. Dave was an ardent aviator. He invited me one day in the late '50s or '60s to join him in a flight over the Snoqualmie Tree Farm. I could tell that he was searching for a special place from which one could see something special. At last, he turned to me with a great smile of satisfaction as we settled down into a sort of pocket among the hills. "Now," he said, "everything you can see from this

Home from Alert Bay. United Airlines? No, a united family

point belongs to us!" We could see some two or three hundred thousand acres! Very satisfactory. I wondered how many hours he must have spent figuring it all out.

Today, in the year 2000, there are few Denkmanns in the Northwest. But I maintain close relationships with George and Wendy Weyerhaeuser, and Howie Meadowcroft, married to George's sister, Wizzie. Ed and Julie Titcomb's sons, Bruce and Rick, and their wives live in Seattle, where Bruce teaches school and his wife Katie is a member of the Seattle Art Museum Board.

The Weyerhaeusers and the Denkmanns have been associated since 1860. Although both families have proliferated, there are now no business operations to bring us together, sad to relate. But our association with the Weyerhaeusers is part of our Denkmann heritage. Three generations of Denkmanns served on the many company Boards, our founder F.C.A. Denkmann, his son Frederick (my Uncle Fred), and his nephews, Fred Reimers and myself. Now there are eight generations of Denkmanns on the family tree. Wow!

Friends in the Postwar Years

Phil and Fay Frederick Padelford married a month before Annie Gould and I married in June 1941. Then came our move to Rock Island, Illinois and three years of the army. Those years seemed no more than a day or two after our return to Seattle to catch up on what happened to our friends in the same time. Nothing! Almost all the men had served in the military longer than I did. Were the girls waiting for us? You bet!

There was an explosion of marriages, then an explosion of babies, birthday parties, school days, and graduations over the next sixteen years or so. Living on McGilvra

Boulevard, across from the Seattle Tennis Club, close to Epiphany Church, Helen Bush School, the University of Washington, and even closer to Washington Park, the hill above our house, there were daily contacts with a lot of friends and their children. By 1950 we were spending summers on Bainbridge Island at the Gould's Topsfield, and by 1957 we had built our own house on Bainbridge near the Country Club and Topsfield.

Nevertheless, there were friends that we saw much more often than others. There were Annie's old friends from her "growing up" days, such as Fay Frederick, Anne Parry, Janet McDonald, Betty Wright. All these were her bridesmaids and all to marry except "Parry." With Fay's marriage to Phil Padelford, and Janet's to Chester Paulson we were off and running. Then we sold our 1031 McGilvra house in 1955 to Sheff and Patty Phelps as we moved into our new home at 1101 McGilvra next door. Sheff became my best friend and has remained so ever since. Don and Nonie Taft Hall and the Padelfords and we were invited to annual Easter egg hunts at Fay Frederick Padelford's mother's huge house in The Highlands. Our pals on 36th Avenue East, in Washington Park were the Willard Skeels, Josie and Wetherill Collins, Whitney and Dorothy Howland, the Hedderly-Smiths, and the Padelfords—just on one street! There was no dearth of birthday parties for our kids and buffets, with dancing afterwards in the basements, for parents.

Left: Fay's third birthday; Right: Fay & Sue at Easter egg hunt at 1031 McGilvra backyard

Left to right: ?, Liz Fisken, Evans Wyckoff, ?, John Robinson, Janet McDonald Paulson, John H. Hauberg, John H. Davis, Joseph McCarthy, Harriet Davis, Dan Henderson, Carol Henderson, Mary Lou Kravik, Chester Paulson, Gerry Kravik. Lurking behind Janet Paulson and John H. Hauberg are Phil Padelford and Jane McCarthy.

There were several "special" groups. There were men I played tennis and squash with, and an Alberta game bird shooter's group. I was active at the University Club both as a trustee as well as in the cast of four Christmas shows. There were stints on the Helen Bush Board (nineteen years!) and the Epiphany Church vestry. Annie and I attended sessions of the World Affairs Council with Herb and Tattie Little. Annie was in the Junior League Follies, but mostly seeking out and befriending young (and old) artists in our region. We were busy, busy.

Above: Phil Padelford & John Hauberg; Below: Anne Gould Hauberg & Fay Padelford

But we had good help and noble companions. Mabel came to 1031 to cook and do many other things. She was with us for years. So was Crissy, a saucy, funny lady. And Marty who took care of both Sue and Fay, making trips to Rock Island to show off Fay to my Dad, her grandfather, who was not very interested.

And then we had Jazz, a standard-bred, white poodle dog. He was a ferocious fighter. He was also very funny, with a great sense of humor. He visited every house for blocks on the west side of McGilvra

University Club Christmas Show "Dearie." Among the cast: George Perry as Dearie, Bill Bowden, John H. Hauberg, Dick Doran, Dick Moser, Ned Skinner, Peter Garrett, Howard Lease.

Above left: Sue & JHH in 1951; Right: Sweeneys, Burkes, Edward Simpson, & Fay with Bertha Winterhalter, "Nussie," in Rock Island in 1948?

Boulevard every day, finally leaving a trail that was as visible as a sidewalk. And a yellow cat, Cleo, who brought mice and moles up onto our bed on Bainbridge Island to show off her prowess as a hunter. One night one of her trophies escaped between the sheets, and Cleo went into hot pursuit as Annie and I leapt out of bed!

Well, enough of families, friends, and the many, many "little" things we did in the postwar years from the '40s into the '60s. Larger enterprises will have their own chapters.

John H. Hauberg, Jr., Anne Gould Hauberg, Fay and Sue in 1949

CHAPTER 15

My Family

I HAVE A WONDERFUL FAMILY. ANNE GOULD HAUBERG AND I HAD MANY WONDERFUL years together, enjoying our families and friends, our travels, our houses, and most of all our children, Fay and Sue.

I always thought of Annie as a far better mother than I was a Dad. She spent more time with them while I was involved with many organizations. Be that as it may, we certainly were with them through joys and sorrows, schools and horses, travels and parties, life and death. While Fay and Sue were happy, our little boy Mark, born in 1950, lived only a little more than four

Left: Mark Denkmann Hauberg & Annie in 1954; Right: Fay with Jazz, 1947

years. His brain cells never developed and we had to find foster parents for him. They loved him as we did, but nothing could be done to save him.

We felt tremendously fortunate to have Fay and Sue as healthy babies. They entered our lives as much-wanted and much-loved children.

Returning from Germany to Seattle in August of 1946, I discovered a happy, energetic, little two-year-old girl. Fay, and her mother and I, moved quickly to 1031

McGilvra Boulevard across the street from the Seattle Tennis Club, not far from Bush School and Epiphany Church, and only ten minutes away from the University of Washington campus. It was to be the neighborhood Fay grew up and lived in until her marriage to Nathaniel Page in 1967, never far from Fay and Gould aunts, uncles, and cousins.

Although Fay says I was always with her when she needed me, I became deeply involved with studies at the University of Washington College of Forestry, the activities of the Arboretum Foundation, and all the later frantic organization work to turn the Seattle Symphony around, ten years as a frustrated Republican state leader, then creating the tree farm, and heading the Bush School Board.

After Fay's birth we hired a great nurse, Marty, to take care of her. Marty went with us to Rock Island to show Fay to her grandfather during an army leave. Fay was primped up for each formal presentation, but my father was not enthusiastic. We got the idea that he would take more interest in her when she was perhaps eight years old and he could tell her about Chief Black Hawk and Rock Island County history.

Fay and Red at Topsfield

Fay was first, however, to take to horses. I don't remember when or from whom we acquired Big Red, but probably Phyllis Crooks had something to do with it. The sight of little Fay on this huge horse was very heartwarming. Soon Fay graduated to a superior horse, Rayhak's Rahwan, a fine jumper. She became a pupil of Evelyn Huff along with Carol Padelford. Fay Padelford, Annie, and I became chauffeurs taking these friends over to Dorothy Avery's stables just north of Bellevue, on the edge of Bridle Trails State Park.

Fay became a top jumper in Washington State and came in second at the Oregon State meet in Salem. I was glad when she found boys more interesting than horses when she was about sixteen. While she was in the eighth grade she won the Washington State Equitation Championship medal, qualifying her to compete for the National Equitation Championship in Madison Square Garden.

At that point, we gave Rayhak's Rahwan to Marge Parrington (now Mrs. Philip Padelford) and her family near Indianola, where he spent many happy years.

Fay on Rayhak's Rahwan, 1957

It was Sue's turn next. We were living at Topsfield in the fall of 1954 waiting for our new house at 1101 McGilvra to be finished. The architects, Roland Terry and Phil Moore, would only say "soon" as the pleasant weather of October turned to a cold, wet November, and Topsfield was without insulation of any sort. Dorothy (Mrs. Leo) Black, our Bainbridge neighbor, saw our plight, pulled some strings and "soon" became "now" as we headed for a mysterious place in the Arizona desert called Castle Hot Springs. This ten-acre oasis was, in the old days, an Apache watering hole turned

TB sanatorium by some eastern doctors in the 1890s, and ultimately sold to four-teen wealthy American families for their winter hideaway. Difficult to get to and therefore little known to the public, it had perfect weather, a friendly staff of long standing, and pleasant, laid-back facilities.

We had the whole place to ourselves from mid-December into January. No members were expected until the end of January. Certainly, our new house in Se-attle would be ready by then. Ha!

The hot water of Castle Creek gushed from an underground hot spring meandering at 124 degrees. Much of it went to the resort's laundry room, kitchen, guest rooms, and cottages with no further heating. The rest went into several pools, the first too hot to swim in, the next to soak in, the third for swimming. And then the creek went beyond to irrigate lawns,

Middle: The pool and hotel
Bottom: Riding horses in the desert

Sue on Bainbridge Island

gardens, and the handsome royal palm trees along the roads and paths. Along this external route were physical therapy uses such as indoor hot tubs, and saunas, and the main swimming pool of the hotel.

We all, Fay, Sue, Annie, and I, quickly made friends with the hotel staff, cowboys, Johnny the golf pro, the resident doctor and bird song expert, and soon the family from Montesano, Washington who always came in January. We had a palm tree for a Christmas tree and relished letters from Seattle about the rain and cold.

Over the next four years, we enjoyed the routine of the place. After dinner in the lodge there was bingo and/or singing western songs with the cowboys leading and playing guitars. Corny, perhaps, to overly sophisticated people, but great fun for us. And there were special times. Jascha Heifetz, a guest, was practicing his violin for hours every day. I beat Gene Tunney, former heavyweight boxing champion who had dethroned

Jack Dempsey, in a putting contest, only to lose the next round to a ninety-year-old.

The cowboys loved Sue who vanished almost every day after breakfast. Every staff person would know where she was, perhaps at the laundry and sometimes in the kitchen, but mostly at the stables. The cowboys put her on a horse named Fox and led her around to start. She then went very quickly from riding with me, either in front or behind, to handling the reins herself with Fox. Sue was hooked for life!

Sue on Fox

From this early beginning, Sue now rides in Arabian western horse shows all over the West and has reached the finals in national shows in Louisville, Kentucky and Albuquerque, New Mexico. Her specialty is herding cows, a game between a frisky cow and the horse and rider. She has had to enlarge her trophy cases several times to display all her trophies and ribbons.

Fay had "her own" horse at Castle Hot Springs and needed no special attention on any of the rides.

The resort had a strong family atmosphere. There were no "rules," no fences. We were all pleased to be there and with our friends. Our children learned many things. I relaxed and enjoyed every aspect of our annual visits from 1954 to 1959.

Sue winning a trophy with her first horse, Hooligan

Sue later on attended high school at Devereux School near Santa Barbara, California. It was Arab horse country. Her riding instructor was a Miss Arvil Crawford, who introduced Sue to this remarkable breed of horses that seems to enjoy friendships with humans. Sue spent a year with Mrs. Moore, who had a forty-acre pasture near Arlington, Washington, full of young Arab horses who galloped to the fence whenever we appeared, perhaps for a tidbit, but seemingly just to say "Hello, pal."

Sue & Ann Homer Hauberg at Sue's ranch with her horse, Lisa, at Victoria Hill, 1980s

In 1970 Sue moved to her own ranch on Victoria Hill surrounded on three sides by Pilchuck Tree Farm property. The fourth side was 316th Street. With a fine house designed by Roland Terry, and with Dea Stroebel as her first housemother, she enjoyed the barn with twenty horses, pastures for cows and horses, and a covered riding area. Since Annie and I had a little prefab house, known as Instant in a meadow nearby, and Pilchuck Glass School was just a mile up the hill, we saw a lot of Sue.

Today she lives in Kirkland with Ted and Gloria Snook as houseparents and commutes to Oregon to train with Russ Brown at his Diamond B Stables. She has appeared almost every year in national tournaments, both American and Canadian.

School Days

While horses seem to have dominated each girl's early life, school was more important and took even more of our family's time.

Sue's schooling began in Grandma Marsh's house under the guidance of a very brilliant young scholar from the University of Washington's experimental preschool, Myrene Kennedy. Myrene was exploring the new concept called "structuring" to open

Left: Aril Crawford helps hold all Sue's official achievements; Right: June, 1968, Devereux graduation; Anne Gould and Granny Gould came to celebrate

the mind to the learning process. It certainly worked with Sue. She continued through the Helen Bush pre-school to the Pilot School at the University of Washington, a program I funded through its final inclusion in the CDMRC or Child Development and Mental Retardation Center. More about those organizations in another chapter.

Sue completed the Pilot School's program, went to the Devereux School near Santa Barbara, and graduated in 1968 with a California high school diploma and a lifetime passion for Arab horses. All her family and all the teachers and professors who had taught Sue were immensely proud

Sue in California; Below left: The Christmas Ball, 1962; Below right: Bush School Graduation, 1962

of her. It was clear to one and all that Sue would have a lifetime of horsemanship. She certainly has done that!

Fay attended Helen Bush, for almost a lifetime, it seemed, beginning in a preschool class and graduating in 1962. She survived my presidency of the school and my nineteen years as a board member. It was a good girls' prep school education with good teachers and lots of neighbor-friends. Her senior year she was the editor of the school literary magazine, *Flight*. Birthday parties, vacations, and travels punctuated the passing years. Some of these will be recorded later on in separate chapters.

There was also the Christmas Ball of 1962, and Fay was asked to be one of the debu-

tantes. It was an exciting evening for the whole family, a rite of passage into the larger world beyond the family.

From Bush to Middlebury was a big step for Fay. I was never sure that her high school years at Bush adequately prepared her. But Fay survived and graduated in 1966 with a BA in English and a motivation to enter the Peace Corps. She went into Peace Corps training in Los Angeles that summer, initially for teaching English in Ethiopia. During that summer, she met Nathaniel Blodgett Page of Massachusetts and wrote us that she "had met the man she intended to marry." Nat did not have a chance, or even a say, in the matter! He had come down with mononucleosis and had to return home to Braintree, Massachusetts, to recover. We all flew to Washington, D.C., for Susie Sweeney's marriage to Abdul-Wahhab Kayyali, in September 1966, and then went to New York and Boston. Fay decided to stay in Cambridge to keep her eye on Nat and landed a job at Harvard's Freshmen Dean's office. By April 1967, the Peace Corps asked them to rejoin as teachers in Ghana, West Africa.

Fay and Nat were married June 17, 1967 in St. Barnabas Episcopal Church on Bainbridge Island, with a big wedding reception at our house there. A big tent covered the tennis court, the first of such events over the years, including my eightieth birthday party in 1996.

Fay and Nat in 1967

Ten days later, after a week's honeymoon at Harrison Hot Springs, the married couple were on their way to Ghana, West Africa, and a village, Berekum, close to the boundary with the Ivory Coast for a two-year assignment in a teacher training institute. Fay taught TESL, Teaching English as a Second Language, and Nat taught math. It was a joyous beginning of their married life. Annie and I visited them in Ghana the spring of 1969 to observe the affection for them shown by their students and the residents of Berekum.

Back in the U.S.A. in 1969, they took jobs teaching school in Wilmington, Massachusetts which kept them in the East until 1980. Fay taught high school English and Nat, eighth-grade math. Nat attended Babson College of Business in Wellesley from 1978 to 1980, graduating first in his class with honors and an MBA in Finance, while also serving as Assistant Dean.

With two little children, Carey born in 1974 and Benjamin born in 1977, Fay and Nat left Bedford, Massachusetts and moved to Mercer Island, near Seattle in 1980. School was now to begin out West for my grandchildren with Carey in first grade and Ben in preschool.

More Incidents in the Lives of My Family

In 1960, we decided to switch our winter breaks to Hawaii's Hana Maui resort, recommended by Bill and Alice Wright. Equally remote by a terrible road from the rest of Maui, the resort was a family experience like Castle Hot Springs. The staff was pure Hawaiian. Johnny was the bellman, also waiter, also lifeguard, and a superb ukulele player, singer, and dancer. He taught Fay Hawaiian songs and dances, while we grown-ups learned the words. A bus took all of us to a black-sand beach maybe five miles from the resort. One year Chet and Janet Paulson joined us. There was a nine-hole golf course around the hotel and tennis courts to keep us busy, and the usual after-dinner singing and participatory hulas with Santa even dressed in a grass skirt! We went to Hana for four years.

Patriotic Tours

Remembering my family's ten-week trip to Europe when I was ten, I decided on a "patriotic" tour for Fay when she was ten. In 1954 Annie, Fay, and I began a spring vaca-

Above left: Old North Church & Paul Revere; Above right: Our Christmas card, 1963;
Below left: Nat Page, John Hauberg, & Ben Hauberg Page;
Below right: Fay & Carey at Carey's graduation from Colby College, 1996

tion, with a trip to Williamsburg and its early colonial significance, the difficulties with the British governors, the handsome homes and the capitol building.

The homes and crafts of its eighteenth century days of glory were beautifully displayed in the reconstructed village. We loved it.

On to Washington, D.C., the Capitol building, the White House, the Smithsonian and the Sweeneys! Then to Mt. Vernon, the Washington Monument, the Lincoln and Jefferson Memorials. "All men are created equal," has stayed in my mind ever since.

Then to Philadelphia, the Liberty Bell with its famous crack, and Independence Hall. On to New York with the Statue of Liberty, and the new United Nations buildings. On to Boston and Bunker Hill, the Old North Church, Paul Revere's house, Faneuil Hall,

and the old warship, the *Constitution*, famous as *Old Ironsides* of the War of 1812 fame. We exited this tour with a visit to Concord Bridge where "the shot heard 'round the world" was fired.

We were to do almost all this trip again with Sue in 1963. She loved Williamsburg with its horse-drawn cannons and colonial uniforms. She bought a tri-corn hat there and wore it the rest of the trip. The Old North Church steeple had been blown away by a hurricane and I contributed twenty-five dollars and a letter of appreciation for its reconstruction, mentioning our "patriotic tour." The church's public relations people published the letter all over the U.S.A.

Later, Annie took Sue to Holland because Sue had become infatuated with her Dutch (Gould side) ancestry and the tulips which did so well at her ranch in upper Snohomish County. And Fay joined Helen Bush classmates for a summer trip to Europe in 1960 with Bush high school English teacher, Joan Wheeler.

So, in the year 2000, I look back on almost sixty years of "My Family." I have shared those years with a great sister, two remarkable wives, two wonderful children, two fine grandchildren, four stepchildren and their spouses, and step-grandchildren. From the Haubergs and Denkmanns, Fays, Goulds, Pages, Homers and Brinkleys, Mohlers, Rosanes, and Kingsleys, My Family has been a joyous, loving, learning experience.

Gaudeamus igitur!

Bainbridge

1942 Pine timber near Canton, Mississippi,
Marietta Lumber Company

CHAPTER 16

Forestry: Early Influences

PILCHUCK TREE FARM WAS CERTAINLY NOT THE BEGINNING OF FORESTRY AS WE think of it today, and it is certainly not the end. The founding of the Society of American Foresters was not the beginning either.

Probably the Vanderbilt estate in North Carolina with the German forester Schenck as manager was the first North American woods to be managed with sustainability in mind, and Schenck was the first white man on this continent to create the new job of forester. We now know that various Indian tribes were quite capable land and forest managers with very definite goals to achieve.

I don't know when our Society was founded, but in this chapter I'm going to write about my interest in forestry, how and when that interest came about, and this goes back to a beginning almost one hundred fifty years ago!

Midwestern sawmill owners began business along the upper Mississippi in the 1850s. They competed for pine logs from lands drained by many rivers into the great Mississippi. They never heard of forestry and would have told you that these forests were "inexhaustible," no need for "management." Getting the logs out in the fall and winter in time for spring thaws, and as cheaply as possible, obsessed the mill owners, one of whom was my grandfather, Frederick Denkmann, who ran five sawmills for his brother-in-law and partner, Frederick Weyerhaeuser.

"Inexhaustibility" lasted fifty years until the northern white pine had been cut out. With a consortium of upper Mississippi River mill owners to keep in business, Mr. Weyerhaeuser took an option on nine hundred thousand acres of Northern Pacific Railroad land in western Washington for six dollars per acre in 1900 to create the Weyerhaeuser Timber Company. The Boeings followed suit in 1908, sending Bill Boeing out to run the land and the mill. Instead he became interested in airplanes. The Eddys came west from Maine and Michigan. The Merrill-Ring family arrived in the nineteenth century. They all harvested and then kept their lands. The Anderson-Simpson-Reeds did the same.

The profits, yesterday as today, are greatest in the owning and harvesting of timber. The timber is sawed into wood products and sold with far lower operating margins than the production of logs. The demand for products sets the demand for logs, but the margin of profits from logs remains the larger.

1943 St. Helena Parish, Louisiana pine pulpwood stand to be traded for saw logs;
Facing page, top: 1934 log train in Mississippi hardwood forest;
Bottom: 1934 Pearl River, Mississippi—a steam skidder-loader

"Give me timber or give me death," was the cry.

The Denkmanns went west with Mr. Weyerhaeuser's group in 1900, but we also went south to Mississippi, Louisiana, and Arkansas. Mr. Weyerhaeuser came down south for a look, did not like to see so many black people, got a pants full of ticks and chiggers, and went out on his own to northern Idaho to the western white pine country. The Denkmanns liked the southern pines and hardwoods and the proximity of major markets.

When was forestry as a profession invented? The Pacific coast was the boundary beyond which no more forests could grow. In the country east of the Rockies and north of Tennessee and the Carolinas, the pine lands were growing as yet unmerchantable second- and third-growth trees. The Deep South was logging hardwoods and long leaf and loblolly pine for local consumption. A Yale conservationist named Gifford Pinchot was stirring up the country on the value of timberlands, and by 1900, a Yale forestry Professor, H.H. Chapman, was taking his classes to Urania, Louisiana to study

southern pine of various species and try out methods of managing it. Another Yale graduate named Crossett observed the Urania classes and set aside two thousand acres near Crossett, Arkansas for the development of harvesting and regenerating ideas as well as a species improvement program. As southern pine old growth disappeared, the demand for knowledge about reforestation became greater. The need for learning about forests increased as the forests began to disappear.

By the 1920s, the Denkmanns were harvesting at a great rate, both hardwoods and pine. The photos I have here for you are the result of my father, an early amateur photographer, who married into the family and went south to see the business. He was amazed and distressed at what he saw. By the time I was ten, I had visited these same operations and had come away with a sense of the enormous energy that went into the woods and mill operations and the general destruction that ensued.

By the mid-1940s, I had visited operations in Arkansas, owned by another consortium of Rock Island and Moline, Illinois and Davenport, Iowa "lumbermen" including my family and the Weyerhaeusers. I had also visited great timberlands in the Stillaguamish River drainage owned by the Sound Timber Company, the same group of Davenport, Rock Island, and Moline families.

1934 Louisiana loblolly pine. My mother is walking the ties in the background.

Top: 1934 Mississippi oak on way to the mill in Canton; Bottom: 1934 Louisiana pine

Somewhere in this period (1941-1943), I learned that the Denkmanns and the Weyerhaeusers were in the forest business with others, the Mussers, the Laird- Nortons, the Ingrams, and other families in the Weyerhaeuser Timber Company. They were families from Moline and Davenport! I had not known about our business relations with these fine people, although some of them were Black Hawk Hiking Club members and knew Dad well.

Living now in Rock Island, I could not very well dodge the Rock Island Rotary Club and the Rock Island Chamber of Commerce, nor the Community Chest (now United Way). Dad was past president of all of these, and now they all saw in me the future leader that would take all the responsibilities for civic projects out of their hands and off their shoulders. I could see it in their eyes.

Dad was still involved in Weyerhaeuser and Denkmann board memberships of the Rock Island Lumber Company (more than eighty retail lumber yards), president of the Rock Island Sash & Door and St. Louis Sash & Door companies, and recent president of the Rock Island Bank and Trust. Where were his Denkmann brothers-in-law? All dead. Dad was not a businessman and he knew it. He opened meetings of the Boards and turned the reporting and discussion leading over to some member of the Weyerhaeuser family and the managers of the companies. Everybody loved these arrangements. It was a path I was slated to follow.

Something else got in the way.

The Weyerhaeusers and Denkmanns were also partners with the Ainsworths of Moline, the Shulers, Lindsays, Phelps, Richardsons, and Morrisons of Davenport, Iowa, in companies in Arkansas and Washington State. I had never heard of them!!

I know my first trips to Louisiana to visit the Reimers must have begun in the 1920s. I certainly was aware that the Weyerhaeusers were not with us in Louisiana and Mississippi even at the age of fourteen. The Haubergs and the Reimers were very loving cousins. The annual spring trip via the Illinois Central train to Hammond, Louisiana at strawberry festival time brought our Hauberg family, the Marshalls, the T.B. Davises, and Uncle Fred Reimers (but not Christian Scientist wife Aunt Rhoda) to a great reunion with the Reimers in Louisiana and the Richardsons from St. Paul.

Sunday School and church were on the minds of the ladies; the woods and mills, logging operations of all kinds, and new timberland purchases on the minds of the men. It all lasted about a week each year.

And it was entirely a Denkmann family business.

Dad's photo albums are full of pictures of smoke-belching mills, railroad operations on crooked tracks with wood-burning locomotives, and huge oak and pine logs on flat cars. Left behind was a shattered swamp. It was a dismal scene.

I compared all these images of Denkmann lands of the 1920s with those of the Southern Lumber Company in Arkansas in 1942 and 1943. I have no knowledge as to how long the Tri-City associates operated in Arkansas, but the results were about the same. The two trips I made there were to assess any value left in the two hundred thousand acres and the principal sawmill in Warren, Arkansas. I would say their judgment was to sell.

But one old man stopped them. Old Mr. M.N. Richardson, ninety years old, had persuaded the group to listen to one of the first southern professional foresters, and one of the best I ever met, to make a cruise of what old timber was left, if any, and what young timber may have grown back since the 1910s and 1920s.

Kenneth Pomeroy was the man. He found enough trees of every age, mostly loblolly and short leaf pine, growing all over this huge acreage to keep busy six or seven very small, portable sawmills scattered over the property. They would only be sawmills producing rough boards, without drying and planing facilities.

The big mill at Warren would do the latter two operations plus the marketing of the lumber. So, these little mills sawed the logs into one-inch boards and perhaps four by fours and sent them to Warren.

Rodney Ainsworth of Moline's Dimock Gould and Company, a retail lumber yard. 1949-1952, Southern Lumber Company, Warren, Arkansas. He is standing in a hole left by the root of a pine tree after a very hot forest fire on more than two thousand acres of Southern's lands.

There might not be much profit, but we would still be in business, continuing to own the land and with the young timber growing at rates we hadn't expected.

So the Tri-City investors followed Pomeroy's advice and kept the land. I saw the results—a bad one of which was a twenty-five-hundred-acre fire in the new young pine that burned right down to the tree roots. So that was the risk. But the directors kept the faith and had the burned area replanted.

And at that point I went off to war, bearing with me many memories of this "new" idea—forestry.

In 1938, I spent six months on a Weyerhaeuser survey crew in Thurston and Lewis counties with the principal task of making a ten-foot contour map of the McDonald Tree Farm west of Chehalis, WA. The map was to provide the company engineers with the information needed to lay out a railroad system for the logging of this magnificent stand of fir,

1952: Thousands of trees per acre. Loblolly and short leaf pine left standing after the burn, Southern Lumber Company, Warren, Arkansas

1952: A dead stand in Arkansas, same fire.

cedar, and hemlock. The trees were so big and so thick that we rarely got to the end of our two-hundred-foot chains aiming at targets on north/south or east/west lines without making offsets and hoping to correct them farther along on the line. Our crew consisted of twelve men: eight surveyors, two map makers, the cook, and the boss. We worked ten days in, and four days off—a great schedule! And what a contrast with southern pine!

The railroad tracks were never laid, and 1938 was the last year for railroad logging. Some engineer figured out that truck roads would be shorter and cheaper to build. And if you got trucks into the woods, loggers could drive to work. It was the last year of "logging camps" deep in the woods. It was also the last year for twelve-foot-long saws, double-bitted axes, and springboards. Logger unions okayed the use of chain saws.

The first couple of miles of our hike in were through a clear cut that, to my eyes in 1938, was utter destruction. I remember seeing alder, vine maple, lots of ocean spray, and elderberry. The land was waiting for seed from nearby seed blocks. No doubt the slash had been burned, but the fir, hemlock, and cedar seed had lost the race to alder and vine maple seeds. No matter the logs had been efficiently milled in Everett and Longview, the Depression of 1929-1939 persisted in spite of Roosevelt's cheering up the public, and no log below a given dimension could be profitably turned into wood products. There was thus a tremendous waste of woody material that was not acceptable at the mills and left in the woods after logging.

The old growth stand where we were surveying was going to be next. Huge trees made up a forest so dense that no sunlight made it to the forest floor. Sword fern was everywhere. In the occasional swales were devil's club and enough alder to provide browse for a few deer and let in enough sunlight for grass for mice and mountain beaver to hide in. These openings were where the owls hung out.

The memory of the great fires that burned from 1890 to 1910 or so was very keen. They left a few seed trees for miles in every direction. There were no "seedling plantation trees" available for many years for replanting.

Seven years later, in 1945, I was visiting forests in France, Germany, and Austria. Their "inexhaustible" forests had been managed for over two hundred years. Those old countries found a need to maintain their forests for many reasons: deer chasing for the nobility, homes and fuel for everybody else, peace and quiet, beauty and mystique and hiking for one and all. Most forests in Europe are mixtures of pines and hardwoods.

A forest service of professional, educated foresters had developed during those years and was highly regarded. A forester in Germany wore a uniform and worked for a nobleman. I don't know how much science underlay their plans but sustainability of the forests took precedence over everything. I saw only one forest devoted to a single species. Just ten miles outside Paris, a member of the Rothschild family had a Euro-

*Above: 1946–1949,
Weyerhaeuser Timber Company:
After a huge but careful burn,
seed blocks that were left standing
were supposed to reforest the
land. Years have to pass before
the wind scatters their seed over
such a huge area. Chances are
that alder, vine maple, and
grasses will beat them to it.
Left: 1946–1949, College of
Forestry trip to Wind River; this
is the Tolt River burn.*

pean beech stand laid out with a transit, each tree spaced about twenty feet in perfect rows in every direction, perhaps three hundred to four hundred acres with a stone wall around it. About a dozen infantry officers and one hundred fifty men just off the USS *Washington* were stationed there for a happy ten days or so. We had landed at Le Havre and were headed for Patton's Third Army. That forest was quite a shock to me. It was beautiful, but it was impractical. No one could harvest a single tree without destroying the forest. But it was also seventy-five to one hundred years old!

With the war over a year or so later, I was moved into Austria, then Bavaria, and had a chance to get acquainted with their forests and their foresters. At that time the men were either too old to go to war or they were wounded veterans, without an arm or a leg, who were recruited to do forest work.

Those forests were also almost gardens. If a tree died at a young age, it was replaced at once by a fairly sizeable one- to two-inch-caliper tree and fenced against deer.

I knew then that I wanted to go to forestry college and develop a Pacific Northwest forest through research into harvesting techniques and regeneration methods that would result in a sustainable AND profitable forest. I wanted to learn how to regenerate Douglas fir on high-site lands.

On to the University of Washington College of Forestry!!

John H. Hauberg, Jr., John H. Hauberg, Sr.,
Fay, Anne with Sue, & my sister Kay

CHAPTER 17

The University of Washington College of Forestry

*a*LL DURING THE OCCUPATION TIME IN BOTH AUSTRIA AND BAVARIA, I HAD BEEN very impressed with the forestry practices I observed. On the day we arrived in France, four hundred or more of us officers and men were billeted in a Rothschild estate surrounded by a beautiful beech forest. Then in Austria I saw the foresters busy restoring the forests, because they had been cut to meet wartime demands. I traveled in Bavaria visiting my pals Goggi and Failey and watched German foresters in action. Their forestry was almost horticulture. Trees were planted in holes dug with a spade by local farmers. Then they put wire fences around each little tree to keep the deer away. All of these were things we were to do with substantial differences later on ourselves. Then if a tree didn't live, the Germans replaced it with another tree, usually of a different genus. So it was very much on a tree-by-tree basis. The foresters were intelligent and well trained, and I liked them. I could see a career in forestry in connection with my Weyerhaeuser Company involvement and the need to restore Douglas fir forests after clear-cutting.

I had written my father from overseas saying I wanted to go to forestry school. I applied at Yale and they turned me down because of my wretched academic record at Princeton. I wrote to the dean of the forestry college at the University of Washington from overseas. He said pretty much the same thing, except that they could make an exception if I had letters of recommendation from the right people. I wrote Dad and he said, "Well, I'll write a letter and I'll get Phil Weyerhaeuser to write." That was all the clout that it took. Dad also said graduating from college at age thirty-three was OK. "Three years of college will seem like only three weeks." He was so right.

So, when I came home in 1946, I was accepted at the University of Washington and my forestry education began. I was to graduate in 1949. I got one year of credit for all of my three-plus, on-again, off-again years at Princeton. I didn't have to repeat English or economics or philosophy, or Latin or German. All of the credits I needed were in those disciplines that were needed to become a graduate forester such as biology, chemistry, physics, and some engineering—all studies that I avoided or did poorly on at Princeton.

My studies at the College of Forestry went amazingly well. I was motivated in the highest degree to do my best and to learn everything I could possibly learn. I never studied harder than I did for those courses. There were areas that I never thought I could possibly be good at such as physics, chemistry, engineering, and a certain amount of mathematics. It gave me a lot of pleasure to discover that I could get top marks in all of those disciplines.

I was the third oldest student in the forestry class of '49. I realized right then that I was going to have my own forest and prepared myself to make the right decisions and get started on it, and so it turned out. The dean came up to me at the end of my first quarter when I had all A's. He said, "John, I'm simply astounded." Having seen my Princeton record he expected the worst.

We were a class of sixty men. All of us were veterans. Fifty-six of us were married. Many of us had a child. We were a highly motivated group. We were appalled at the old age and lack of contemporary knowledge of our professors. The class appointed me to go to Dean Gordon Marckworth and ask if he couldn't find some younger, better-trained persons to become our professors. The implication was that he might retire himself, since I think he was as old as any of the rest of them. We had a professor called Pappy Pierce, and then there were Scotty Robertson, professor of forest management or silviculture, and Bror Grondahl in wood products. I think all of them were in their sixties. But all of a sudden, the College of Forestry had more students than it had had for years. The Dean could not let these teachers go before finding their replacements. That took most of the years we were there.

Almost all of us in the forestry school were headed for private enterprise, and we all got jobs. Few of us wanted to work for the U.S. Forest Service. We were not interested in an examination called the Junior Forester, which would prepare us for service in the United States Forest Service. I've kept up with a lot of the classmates and almost everyone has had a very happy career in some aspect of forestry. The years of school went by very quickly and pleasantly.

In 1947 as sophomores, we spent eight summer weeks at Pack Forest, a five thousand acre University of Washington working and teaching forest on the slopes of Mt. Rainier. It was

The Group

Left: Mazamas' Trail; Below left: Harrigan in the sack; Below right: Camp at Glacier Basin

during that summer that six of us decided we wanted to climb Mount Rainier. One of us had a brother-in-law who was a member of the Mountaineers. He had been at the top twice and never even seen it because of the fog, so he was eager to go up again. He became our trainer and leader. We spent four weekends practicing falling, the use of crampons, the use of ropes, what to do in emergencies, and generally getting in shape. Every evening we ran up the trails of Pack Forest as far as the road extended, getting prepared to climb Mt. Rainier. Our wives went with us on a Friday afternoon to a camp below Steamboat Prow, an intermediate stop. We packed in a great amount of food for dinner that night from steaks to apple pies. We had a huge feast and spent Friday night in sleeping bags at Camp Stevens. The next morning, Saturday, the girls went home and we went up to approximately the ten thousand foot mark under Steamboat Prow, a traditional starting point for the climb itself. There were little bathtubs carved out of the loose gravel so that you could be out of the wind. There must have been twenty or thirty of them, all made by years and years of climbers. The chinks between rocks were loaded with old candy bars. Two of the boys ate the stuff and paid for it the next morning.

At about three in the morning on a perfect Sunday, we started our climb. There were four of us on the first rope including our leader and his brother-in-law.

Left: Steamboat Prow; Below left: Having lunch in a "bathtub" under Steamboat Prow; Above: The Prow again with John H. Hauberg

Left: Second rope;
Center: At the foot of
the bergschrund;
Bottom: Looking back

Then there was a rope of three. We started up a broad trail from Steamboat Prow left by the Mazamas, two hundred people who had climbed the mountain the day before us. We didn't even have to put out willow wands the afternoon of our arrival at Steamboat Prow, which was traditional, because if it was foggy you could find your way up the hill following the wands. But it wasn't going to be foggy. This trail just marched straight up the mountain toward the top. We didn't put on our crampons, but we were roped up. We skirted some crevasses, and suddenly we came to the foot of a cliff. The glacier had broken in half

Right: Crater at the top of Mt. Rainier. Looking along the rim from Columbia Crest; Below: JHH & Harrigan at the summit

in the middle of the night, and there was about a sixty-foot ice wall. Our nice broad trail led right up to the wall, and would begin again sixty feet higher at the top of the wall.

We didn't want to go up it because it was dangerous, so we sent a scouting party in each direction and agreed to be back in an hour to see if we could find a way around this thing called a bergschrund. We couldn't, so we had to climb it. We put on our crampons and started up the steep ice wall, with the leader cutting footholds into the wall with his ice axe. We all proceeded to follow him very carefully. We got up about twenty feet from the top and the No. 2 man leaned into the wall, which was a no-no. Of course, his crampon chipped out the foothold and down he went, pulling his brother-in-law, the leader, with him. Jack Nattinger and I quickly pushed our ice axes into the wall, quickly took a couple of turns of the rope around them, and prepared to break their fall, which we did. It was very scary. The leader was unhurt, but the guy who had chipped out his foothold had dug a crampon into his leg, which bled profusely. We had to engage in some first aid right there on the wall. He had learned his lesson, and he didn't chip out any more steps. We got to the top of the wall, and spent maybe half an hour recovering. We still had a couple thousand feet to go to reach the summit. But we didn't have any more ice walls to contend with.

We finally got to the rim of the crater, about a mile from Columbia Crest. The men who had fallen and the two who had eaten the candy were just absolutely worn out, so three of us made the hike to Columbia Crest. We signed in all seven of us. If you had reached the rim of the crater, you had reached the summit, according to our guide. Jerry Harrigan was one on the rope of three and he was a very amusing chap. He drove a cab to raise the money to put himself through forestry school. At his suggestion we all had worn our forestry tin pants and tin coats, which are very hard fabrics. Jerry thought it would be a great idea to toboggan down Mount Rainier. When we got down to snow level from the rocks at the rim, we made two teams of four and three. The man in front would lift his legs up and the man behind would put his feet in the lap of the man ahead of him. Then everybody held the feet up of the man behind him. So off we went scooting down the mountain. I suppose we went down a thousand or fifteen hundred feet in this manner before it became obvious that this was not quite the thing to do. We also found out that the seat of Jerry's tin pants had worn away and so had a good deal of skin off his bottom. He was in some pain, but we got down successfully and were met by our wives at Camp Stevens. We had a late lunch at North Bend and everyone went home.

We had to report to the school the next day for a five-day engineering trip that Pappy Pierce, the professor of logging engineering, had organized. We were going to learn all about diesel engines and watch various types of logging equipment in action, so that we would know something about what it took to log the old-fashioned way. But I wanted to learn about logging in second-growth fir, especially thinning, requiring entirely different equipment although diesel-powered.

We did learn about diesel engines. We went to an equipment fair, and also visited some logging sites where they were logging gigantic trees, six or eight feet in diameter, two hundred feet tall. That's what we were supposed to know all about by the time we graduated and went looking for work. I don't know how many of us students took jobs in the big woods. Certainly not at the hard labor level, and there were no jobs different from tradi-

tional ones. Every graduate found a job, however, in such diverse areas as selling equipment, public relations, as well as working in the woods surveying, cruising timber, and supervising the logging.

At that time not many people were interested in reforestation, leaving the job to the wind blowing seeds from clumps of low quality trees. I had a vision, but the other boys were just looking for jobs—whatever they could get. In December of my senior year, 1948, I made the first purchase of land from Bill Eastman, who was a professional forester. He and his brother had acquired the so-called Parker Ranch, about twenty-five-hundred acres on both sides of Pilchuck Creek, which drained Lake Cavanaugh and flowed into the Stillaguamish River between Arlington and Sylvana.

I went out with Bill Eastman and I bought the acreage on the east side of the creek. The west side seemed to me to be better for farming than it was for forestry. I acquired

Above and left: Very heavy, steam powered machinery

about eleven hundred acres and paid about eleven dollars an acre. A lot of it had been used by the previous owner for pastureland. Most of it was alder, but there were a good many acres of second-growth fir and cedar. My father sent me a check from a trust for my benefit and that paid for the land. Some fellow students and even professors thought this was a foolish price to pay. The Eastmans had bought the land at a tax sale for $2.50 per acre and there wasn't much timber on it. But it was just exactly what I wanted. Professor Robertson had invited Axel Brandstrom, an early expert about young Douglas fir, to speak to our forest management class during the course of which he mentioned the qualities of timberland he would buy. First were "high-site" lands that would grow trees the fastest. Second was gentle topography (no mountainsides) to reduce road building and logging costs. And third, timberland should be close to tidewater markets for logs from which to make lumber, pulp and paper, and plywood. The Pilchuck Ranch fitted those requirements to a T.

In June 1949, I graduated from the school of forestry with honors in forestry and biology, and a Phi Beta Kappa key as well. Then I had time to go up and appraise what I had bought from the Eastman brothers.

The Sunde Road extension

CHAPTER 18

A Forest Takes Shape

tO BUILD A ROAD TO REACH MY PROPERTY, THE EASY WAY IN WAS TO EXTEND WHAT THE county called the Sunde Road. I heard there was a very knowledgeable man, an owner of the Associated Sand & Gravel Company of Everett named George Duecy, so I went to see him. I met with him in his kitchen and he said in order to use the road I would have to build it to county specifications. He told me what those were. I asked if I could keep it as a private road, and he said yes, but because sooner or later there might be a great deal of use of it, it should be built to county specifications.

In going about locating the road, I used a staff compass so I could look down on this and find true north, which was the direction I wanted to go from the end of the Sunde Road. The paving of the county road stopped just before the road itself stopped. I dug a hole just beyond the end of the paving and cut down a small cedar pole, about three inches in diameter and maybe ten feet high, which I put in place in the middle of the road. Then I went ahead about two hundred yards, just over the hill, and put in another pole due north of the first one. Then I went far enough toward the entrance of my own property and looked back, and lined up all the poles by eye until I had a perfectly straight line.

George Deucy told me about a county man I could hire to operate a grader on weekends, to whom I paid a fee to push the road through with ditches on each side. Then I paid Associated Sand & Gravel to gravel it, and the grader operator simply spread it around and put a crown on the road. By the end of 1949, I had access to the trees, and it was time to see what I could harvest and get started with the process of buying more lands for my research.

The first logger I hired was Gunder Gilbert. I said, "I think there are a few cedar poles there in the hills just beyond the road. Probably you could work in there for a month or so and bring out several thousand dollars worth of cedar poles." Gunder went in with some very primitive logging equipment, mostly homemade. I went up there in two or three weeks to see how he was doing. I said, "I suppose you'll be finishing up soon," but he said, "Oh, there are so many cedar poles there I could be here for the rest of my life." I was very encouraged by that. So, Gunder concentrated on poles.

As the Sunde Road crossed under the power lines and went northward down the hill and up the next, a hillside with no trees appeared. It was covered with a profusion of daisies, ferns, and a good deal of grass. The local family at the south end of my property had been grazing cattle there for years. They had simply put a gate in their fence and kept it open. I closed it to make this beautiful hill my first plantation in the spring of 1949. It was part of the Parker Ranch I had purchased the previous December. I hired some of my classmates to do the planting with me. The trees were Douglas fir one-year-old seedlings, so-called 1-0 stock. Most of the five friends had planted for the Forest Service and the State Department of Natural Resources during vacations. I was about to find out what hard work this could be.

We laid out lines eight feet apart going straight up the hill with eight feet between the trees in a row. It was walk a step, walk a step, swing the hoedag into the ground ahead and raise up the handle to expose a hole. Then reach over your head to pull a little tree out of the sack on your back, carefully spread the roots into the open cut so they didn't curl up at the bottom, stamp the cut closed around the seedling and repeat. Each of us carried a hundred little trees in our sacks. A thousand trees a day was supposed to be the standard for professional planters, but *we* were not out there to make a living so we planted maybe five hundred and enjoyed the daisies, the companionship, and the knowledge that we were creating a forest.

Classmate planters: Denis Lavender & Jack Eskanazi at right

Two summers, quite dry, followed. I returned to the hill often, and the seedlings seemed to have vanished! In 1952, knowing a bit more, we replanted the hill with 2-1 stocks from our own brand-new transplant bed. Nineteen fifty-three was a very wet year and by fall both 1949 and 1952 plantings had sprung into vigorous growth! The hill was way overplanted!

Meanwhile, Annie and I had had several picnics on that hill with splendid views of hundreds of acres of our new tree farm. We decided to build a little structure there for overnight and friends on weekends. I laid out a six-percent grade eastward to a

Left: Sunde Road
& Cabin Spur;
Center: Our
A-frame cabin;
Bottom: My
horse logger

saddle about a half-mile off the Sunde Road and then came back along the hill's ridge to a fine lookout. We built an A-frame bunkhouse, dug a successful well, and enjoyed it for many years.

At the beginning of 1950, I hired a man named Earl Wood. He and his son Jim, also using some homemade equipment, began to take out all kinds of logs—alder, cedar, hemlock, and fir. At that point there seemed to be quite a ready market. I didn't really know what we had, and I also didn't know much about the problems of logging and marketing logs. Earl and Jim couldn't get in to some stands because the trees were so thick. They suggested I get a horse logger. Pretty soon we had Gunder logging cedar poles, and the Woods, father and son, logging larger stuff, and then a horse logger bringing small but marketable trees out of the dense woods. It was an odd combination of harvesters, but some money was coming in and I was buying more land.

My secretary, Grace Bartlett, became a licensed realtor so we could produce earnest money agreements and actually complete all of the real estate forms in our office. When I went to buy some land and the owners would agree to sell it, I would say, "There won't be any charge for all the legal problems associated with a real estate transaction. We'll do it all in my office, and we'll be willing to pay the title insurance. And you can continue to live here in the house for as long as you want."

It was a good deal for them, but actually most of them wanted to sell in order to move to town, nearer grocery stores, doctors, etc. Most of these Scandinavians had bought their land sight unseen in the 1920s, after much advertising by logging companies who wanted to sell their logged-off stump ranches for farms. The purchasers found gigantic stumps on the property that had to be removed. However, it cost so much to blow up stumps they never were able to turn their land into farms. They had committed their resources in the '20s, and now it was the early '50s and they really wanted to get out and have enough money to buy a little place in town. So it was very timely for me, and for them.

By 1960 we had as much as ten thousand acres. The early parcels of land were not contiguous, so the second thrust was to begin to buy the intervening properties and block out the stands.

The harvesting techniques improved as we learned more about how to do it. We also learned that we could develop markets for alder. Up to that point the only markets for alder logs were furniture plants in Seattle and California and they were cheating the farmers by telling them that they wanted alder logs, but if the farmer showed up with alder logs they would say they didn't really need them. The farmer couldn't take them back so the farmer would leave the logs there. The same thing was happening with furniture manufacturers on the East Coast and down in California. They could offer to buy alder logs and then say they weren't "on grade" and not pay for them. They could get away with it because there was no grading system in place for hardwood logs on the West Coast.

I got together with local people with stands of alder, who were very interested in setting up grade standards for alder, and we created the Northwest Hardwoods Association. A man from Seattle was the president. I was on the board with some other people. One was John Spada, for whom the lake which furnishes Everett's water supply is named. John was from Granite Falls and had alder to sell. We finally got the Pacific Lumber Inspection Bureau (PLIB) to develop standard grades for alder. They sent us men who taught us how to grade logs. Then we got the furniture plants in California, the Midwest and the East Coast to agree to the standards. That meant that when we sent a boxcar or flatcar of alder logs, the grade of the logs was guaranteed by the new standards we had set up. Then, of course, we had to teach men how to use these standards and grade the logs.

Above: Visiting foresters look over our transplant beds;
Below: Henry Campbell & truck with our name on door

That was my first effort to get into the marketing of a species of tree that I had always considered the enemy and worth absolutely nothing. Gradually, the value of alder has increased until today, in the 1990s, alder has, on occasion, been worth more than Douglas fir. We also sold cottonwood and bigleaf maple. We had a lot of activity going on in the harvesting of the growing tree farm. My wonderful long time secretary, Grace Bartlett, did all the bookwork in my office, with Henry Campbell telephoning expenses and mill receipts to Seattle.

In 1954 the Scott Paper Company research department learned how to bleach alder chips which could then be used for a rather low-grade pulp used in shipping containers, boxes, etc. Scott immediately sent out buyers to acquire alder land. Since I didn't live up there I found myself unable to compete, so I hired a forester named Henry Campbell. He was soon out in the woods among the Scandinavians, wheeling, dealing, and getting properties lined up for me to buy. We did pretty well. I also found out that Port Blakely Mills was looking for lands that had young fir and cedar on them. At that point I didn't think I could buy that type of land because it was pretty expensive, and I never did compete successfully with Port Blakely. They had lots of money and knew exactly what they wanted, while I was scrambling around trying to find land on which I could practice some of my ideas about reforestation and had begun to realize that I needed land with young timber to learn about thinning. Henry Campbell was an excellent land buyer and road builder.

Before long, we discovered that grass and other herbaceous material were smothering the little seedlings. Almost everything was growing faster than the little one- or two-year-old Douglas fir seedlings. So, we built our own transplant nursery to produce taller, stronger trees to plant. It was inefficient, but we started to transplant two-year seedlings and grew them for one more year, and sometimes two more years in a transplant bed. These transplants had a bigger diameter and were taller, so the ferns, nettles, and grass just couldn't smother them. We had learned how to manage the first problem in reforestation, but it was costly.

Why did Douglas fir grow more slowly than other species, especially herbaceous trees such as alder and maple as well as grass, nettles, wild blackberry, and ferns? Douglas fir puts its roots down into the ground before it begins to grow above ground for up to five years! A little Douglas fir only two inches high will have a five- to eight-inch root! And this tiny tree will not persist in the shade. It requires sunlight to grow. A very tender baby before it becomes a giant.

We hired a nursery man to keep the transplant bed weeded. Then when the transplants were dug up, we hired boys from the Monroe Reform School to do the planting. We wanted to replant the logged-off land with Douglas fir, which was worth fifteen or twenty dollars per thousand board feet, whereas you had to sell alder by the ton. Alder sales were not profitable but at least paid for the cost of getting alder off the

Crown Zellerbach first thinning in an eighty- to one-hundred-year-old heavily stocked, naturally seeded (vs. planted) forest. Our forestry class of '49 is looking at this land in northwestern Oregon

land so we could replant it. Our plantations, although not extensive at that point, really weren't very good because Henry, having planted them, almost immediately forgot them and the little trees lacked strength against the regrowth of alder. I finally had to dismiss Henry because of his lack of follow-through.

I talked to the UW College of Forestry's silviculture professor, Scotty Robertson, and asked him if he had a good young man coming along. He said, "I certainly do. His name is Duane Weston." But Duane was only a junior at that point. He not only had another year to go in college, but after that he had to put in a year in the Marines, having joined ROTC during college years. We made an agreement that we would hire him after his stint with the Marines. He came on board in mid-December, 1962.

I had hired a land man named Glenn Greener to learn where all the section corners were and to work with Henry Campbell. After Henry Campbell left and Duane came on board, Greener agreed to stay on as land manager and show Duane where all the section corners were. Duane turned out to be just a marvelous young man to work with. He and I began to see that we had to develop herbicides that could be sprayed on our plantations. These were formulas that had been collected in Europe after the war by American chemical companies like Monsanto, Dow, and DuPont. They were 245-T, and 2-4D. The mixture, which later became known as Agent Orange, was lethal to broad-leaved angioplast trees and herbaceous plants, but it did not affect gymnoplast

A "sawmill" in the woods—solely to trim long logs to a length suitable for truck hauling. Crown Zellerbach Operation.

coniferous trees. Broad-leaved and coniferous trees have different internal systems. We found these sprays very effective.

Duane and I had to develop an efficient system of spraying. The chemical people thought we should put on more of these expensive chemicals than we finally realized was needed, but it was an interesting process. To begin with, we thought that trees had to have all their leaves on. We're talking about alder trees, maple trees, any kind of broad-leaved tree or shrub, ferns and all sorts of grass. We thought that summer time, when all the leaves were on the trees, would be the best time to apply this so we started spraying in late July to mid-August. We did not kill the biggest trees because the spray didn't get on enough leaves.

We finally learned that early in the spring, when the leaves were just barely out but the trunks were exposed, was the best time to put on this herbicide and it really didn't take very much. This was very crude and amateurish research, but it worked. All of a sudden, our three-year-old plantations were surviving, although we had to spray again at about age seven or eight because some herbaceous plants had reseeded.

Another question we had to contend with was how far apart to plant the little trees. The school solution in the 1950s was to plant trees eight feet apart, which re-sulted in about seven hundred trees per acre and was for that reason expensive. It took money to acquire the seedlings and transplants, and money to plant them. Then, when they grew up, we had to thin them because they began to compete with each other at an early time, and *that* cost money with no return.

The spacing problem was very interesting. The above-described conventional practice was called a pre-commercial thinning (PCT) and was done when the stand was about ten to fifteen years old. It took every other tree and perhaps had to be done again when the stand was several years older. We played around with spacing of trees, and went from eight by eight to eight by ten and finally ten by ten although we also did some planting with a twelve by twelve spacing. Duane was very concerned about this wider spacing, and thought it just wasn't enough trees. Also, the branches of trees spaced that far apart got to be very big and resulted in poor quality trees. Wider spac-ing also encouraged the broad-leafed trees and shrubs to invade the plantation requir-ing an additional chemical application. We finally settled on ten by ten, and that's where we still are today.

For a short period of about six weeks, Ray Baum set up a portable "American Mill" in the woods near Samish. The idea was to cut out the high cost of yarding, loading, and hauling small logs to mills ten to twenty miles away. We would create much more valuable boards and small timbers on the site of the ongoing thinning, yarding the thinned trees right to the little mill which itself could be moved as the thinning progressed. Great idea! But at the end of the six weeks, I assessed the size of the sawdust pile as equal to the pile of lumber, and decided that although the idea sounded good, safety factors, costs of moving the mill, and the poor quality of the milled lumber and timbers outweighed any savings.

I was just full of ideas that I wanted Duane to follow through on. The trustees of my trust were worried about these expenses. Duane gradually began to take over the business management of the tree farm and we soon ran a very tight ship.

In 1952 Gordon Harper, our family accountant, suggested that we incorporate the tree farm. At that point, it wasn't worth very much, and Gordon suggested we put all of the stock into a trust, because it clearly would be very valuable in thirty to forty years. That was probably the most important financial decision that our family ever made, because today the tree farm is worth thirty or forty million dollars. It is the basis of a trust that can be passed on to my children and grandchildren. By 1964 land was selling for four hundred dollars an acre. That made the earlier purchases of ten dollars an acre look pretty good.

When I began to pay $40 an acre, the trustees complained that was excessive. Then, of course, the price went up to $80 an acre and all the $40 purchases looked very good. When the land values went up to $120 an acre, then the $80 purchases looked good. By 1964, we had acquired land in four areas quite well blocked out. Land prices, including alder stands, had risen to $400 per acre. "Open land," that is, without any trees, was far more costly at $1000 per acre!! We settled down to a gradual filling in of the "holes" in our ownership to shorten property lines, make road building possible, and reduce objections to such operations as herbicide spraying.

Today, year 2000, we hold more than fifteen thousand acres and are hoping to fill in the "holes" in our ownership. Our land and timber improvements are on the books at about $380 per acre. And we are still trying out new ideas for managing our lands as environmental goals and markets change, and as we learn more from our own experience in multiple species planting, spacing studies, and changing technologies for harvesting.

Vogelsang Forest — Forerunner of Pilchuck Tree Farm

CHAPTER 19
Pilchuck Tree Farm Today

Part I

PILCHUCK CREEK TREE FARM, OUR FIRST NAME, HAS EMERGED FROM ITS GEOGRAPHICAL topographical, historical, and economical backgrounds. It was born and grew in an interesting time frame—the vigorous, optimistic years following the Great Depression and World War II. The economies of the U.S.A. and the rest of the world had slowed to a crawl and then focused on the military needs of the most important countries with democracies lining up against dictatorships both Fascist and Communist.

The post-World War II period was filled with opportunities to try out new ideas—rock 'n' roll, abstract art, exploration of space, public air travel, huge farm machines, road building equipment, great housing developments (Levittowns), nationwide networks for radio and TV, banks, hotels, and stores other than the A&P and Montgomery Ward. Women became business executives and education branched out to minorities.

I felt that there was great room for new ideas in forest management. Even ideas of reforestation were in dark closets. Dad must have sensed the need for *something* to replace the Denkmann cutover lands that he photographed in the '20s and '30s. Those pictures show the utter destruction of the vast southern pine and hardwood forests. The Denkmanns were, of course, just doing what everyone else was doing. Weyerhaeuser Company was doing the same on the West Coast, showing disdain for the problem by creating the Weyerhaeuser Cutover Land Company to dispose of such lands to real-estate developers. Well, why not? Douglas fir was worth less than twenty dollars per thousand board feet and anyhow no one as yet knew how to reforest the lands or how long it would take to grow into a useful log, say, thirty inches in diameter. Nature was left to do the job and generally did it in ten to fifteen years with more alder than Douglas fir.

So, in short, the time had come to bring new ideas to the woods. It took optimism, a lot of it, to change the American attitude towards the forest, but Weyerhaeuser had taken the earliest stand by creating America's first tree farm to be managed on a sustainable basis at Clemons in 1940.

My idea was to have a small acreage of forest lands that had been cut over in order to try out ways of reforestation, management, and harvesting that would be economical enough to lure others into trying them out also.

Axel Brandstrom had pointed the way for good land purchases—high-site land that would grow trees the fastest, easy topography to hold down road building and logging costs, and proximity to tidewater mills. The eleven hundred acres on the left (east) bank of Pilchuck Creek (hence our first title) that Bill Eastman offered in November of 1948 met all three ideals.

Part II

Geographically: Pilchuck Tree Farm lies between Interstate 5 (I-5) on the west to the North Fork of the Stillaguamish River on the east, and from the city of Arlington on the southeast to Conway at its northwest corner. Washington State Highway 9 bisects and divides our two western blocks, Victoria and Middle, from our two eastern blocks, Pilchuck and Armstrong. County roads touch many of our tracts of land. In spite of our more than fifteen thousand acres, we own only one 640-acre section entirely. So, we are not "blocked in." But we are only twenty-five miles north of Everett and about the same northwest to Mt. Vernon. The Pilchuck Tree Farm office can be reached easily in an hour from Seattle.

Topographically: Pilchuck lands lie in the first range of the foothills of the Cascade Mountains. Our highest elevation, fourteen hundred feet, lies between I-5 and State Highway 9 and only three to four miles from the Skagit Flats. The eastern slopes of this hill drain toward Lake McMurray, again just a few miles away. Thus, in our western Pilchuck and Middle blocks, there is little chance for rivulets to become creeks of any significant size. Nevertheless, there are chum and coho fingerlings in these tiny streams, and one or two families of black bear. There are also many species of warblers, summer residences for cedar waxwings, red-winged blackbirds, hawks and horned owls.

Pilchuck Creek is our major internal stream, draining Lake Cavanaugh in Skagit County southwesterly and flowing into the Stillaguamish River just west of the I-5 bridge over that river. Pilchuck Creek flows through our lands for several miles. But the lands drained by Pilchuck Creek are not higher than four hundred to seven hundred feet, and do not produce more than rivulets.

As the Pilchuck and Armstrong blocks stretch eastward, there are higher and higher hills above them, mostly owned by the state and the national forest. This results in two major creeks, Rock and Harvey, that are spawning streams and hence have problems to manage. Much of the Armstrong tract is a terminal glacial moraine, a lower site for trees.

By and large, we have few problems with our physical lands. However, the gentle nature of these areas and their proximity to towns via county and state roads has caused property owners to remain on their lands. We have not been able to create many solid blocks of ownership. We have many neighbors with many different attitudes to our management and we are determined to have good relationships with them.

Historically: Ours was a land of gigantic trees of many tree species running heavily to western red cedar and Douglas fir. Indian tribes seem not to have had a presence except along the Stillaguamish River. Vast lightning fires of the kind that created great contiguous forests on the Cascade slopes did not occur here, hence the larger size of our area's trees. Darius Kinsey, the famous photographer of the forest scene and early settlers and loggers, lived in Sedro Woolley, not very far north of our tree farm. His photos show the evolution of logging giant trees using oxen and horses, and then the first steam machines and railroads. Many were taken on our present property. Today we make use of the web of railroad grades everywhere for our own internal automobile and truck roads, reducing road-building costs.

Many aerial photos taken by the Snohomish County Assessor's office showed, in 1949, a solid gray sea of alder with dark lines of old railroad grades across it. As the locomotives traversed these hills they gave out sparks, starting minor fires in the duff on either side of the tracks and creating a fine seed bed for the red cedar to regrow. I used these photos to keep track of where I was as I crossed otherwise solid alder lands owned by people I was buying from. And they were useful for us well into the 1960s because the walking was easy and one knew the direction being taken.

Economically: Most owners in the 1920s to the 1950s were Finns, Swedes, and Norwegians who bought, sight unseen, logged off lands for "stump ranches" in the 1920s. These were sold in 40-, 80-, 120-, and 160-acre tracts through newspaper ads in those countries where land ownership had been denied to farmers for centuries. By the 1940s, some people wanted to move to town—Arlington, Stanwood, Marysville, etc.—closer to doctors and grocery stores. They were glad to see me come by. Most had cleared only an acre or two for a house and garden, and pasture for a cow or two. The stumps were so numerous and so huge that the new owners could not afford to clear them and had to rely on jobs in the logging camps, the mills, and fishing boats. Darius Kinsey photographed many families in the undercut of a giant tree or on top of a huge stump. My early purchases left many ownerships in between. It has taken many years and many dollars to develop such "blocks" as we have.

Part III

Now it was time to put all these lands to use as a research forest, finding out how to recreate a Douglas fir forest and then to manage it for a profit sometime in the (hopefully) near future. Hah! But my goal was simple and plain. If European forests could survive two or three centuries of warfare, why could we not rebuild forests in America that had been so badly harvested that they looked like battlefields?

Pilchuck Tree Farm today has more than fifteen thousand acres, almost every one of which has had the attention of foresters over our fifty years of management. We were not confronted with the battlefield look because all of our lands had been finished with such logging by 1922. For the most part, the land had then been taken over by red alder. So, alder was the enemy that had to be destroyed in order to get to that dream Douglas fir forest. And there was very little demand for alder in 1949. We survived on whatever fir and cedar were mixed with alder in many stands. Strong fir seedlings and transplants solved the planting problem. Spraying became a useful tool in permitting our seedlings to survive competing vegetation. Spacing of the little trees was resolved to reduce the need for pre-commercial thinning and resolve quality problems, and at the same time reduce the need for pruning. We have thinned our stands at a variety of ages, from sixteen to forty. And we recently clear cut eight and a half acres of thirty-six-year-old fir plantation with amazing results.

We have battled Swiss needle cast blight in Douglas fir plantations, and from that learned not to plant only one species of tree that might be attacked by some disease or other. Today our plantations are usually a mix of Douglas fir, western hemlock, and western red cedar. Our road system is excellent. Most miles have been maintained for ongoing management.

So, what about today? What have we accomplished in fifty years?

Economically: Our venture is struggling in 2001 to produce enough income to satisfy investment goals. Our timber inventory is growing every year. But markets for logs could be better. There is competition from every corner of the globe. Also, new rules and regulations to preserve habitat reduce the volume of timber we would like to harvest.

Analysis of Plantation Size by Decade
Dec-00

Decade	Acres	# of Units	Ave Size	Max Size
50's	238.4	29	8.2	57.1
60's	1519.7	151	10.1	65.6
70's	3614.4	187	19.3	136.4
80's	4489.7	247	18.2	110.6
90's	1498.6	100	15.0	86.0
Total	11360.8			

Total Acres of Established Plantation by Decade

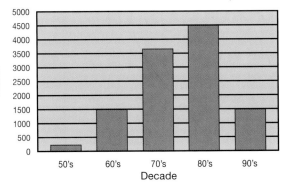

Average Size of Plantation by Decade

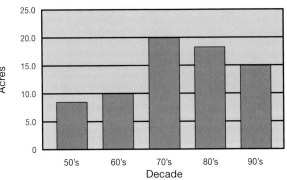

Part IV

We certainly are pleased to have accomplished our very first goal, which was to regenerate fast-growing Douglas fir on high-site lands. Above three thousand feet, everything grows more slowly, making it much easier for always slow-growing young Douglas fir to stay ahead of competing species. But the lower altitude, deeper soils, and longer growing season found alder, vine maple, grass, nettles, ferns, wild blackberry, and other shrubs smothering the fir. Over thousands of years, Douglas fir had learned to endure our dry summer months by putting its roots down first before using all the nutrients to put its head up. A five-year-old Douglas fir can be only knee-high, giving its competition a chance to dominate.

So we now plant two- or three-year-old trees with larger, stronger stems and reduce competing grasses, ferns, and shrubs with sprays laid on them in early fall before planting when there is little runoff.

By 1960, our road system gave us access to all our properties and was extended as we began to block in our ownership. Of course, by design, we are close to county roads in every block.

Spacing between trees and between rows of trees has been varied as we learned how fast our seedlings grew both in height and in branching. In 1983 Wally Michalec established a ten-acre spacing trial for Douglas fir and six different spacings from eight by eight feet to ten by twenty feet. We are learning how spacing affects height growth, diameter growth, and how soon branch tips close with neighboring trees. The latter determines how large lower branches will become and how soon they will die, a huge effect on log quality and, hopefully, a substitute for very expensive pruning.

Our plantations began to be of significant acreage in the 1970s and became larger in size as our overall tree farm acreage grew. We planted over thirty-five hundred acres in the 1970s, and forty-five hundred acres in the 1980s. Total today is 11,360 acres. Some thinnings have been economical at twenty-one years. An eight-acre clear-cut in a thirty-six-year-old stand surprised all of us with its volume in 1999. This operation has made us rethink our ideas about harvesting at eighty years to probably fifty years. Again, our determination to acquire only high-site lands at our very beginning was a good start.

Harvesting methods have interested Duane Weston and Allen Staringer for the last twenty years. Oxen and horses pulling one huge log over a well-greased "skid road" were gone before I was born, but giant steam skidders and loaders were still in use in the 1940s, although diesel fuel had replaced coal and wood. Today rubber tires have replaced steel tracks. Harvesting machines with the flexibility to reach trees behind trees for thinning and then to pile logs for a forwarder to pick up and take to truck-loading areas have not only created efficiencies in harvest, but also reduced soil compaction and soil disturbance (a siltation factor). Such equipment moves rapidly through a plantation. None of it could be used to harvest an old-growth stand where a "small tree" might be larger than any tree we plan to grow!

Our tree farm area is intermingled with many small ownerships, with owners working in nearby towns or commuting to Everett, even to Seattle, through daily traffic jams. These families like this arrangement. They have horses to ride, small gardens, and relative peace and quiet. On weekends on all four blocks, we may have two hundred or more horseback riders, and quite a few mountain bikers, as well as hikers and joggers. Duane has kept the peace, and our plantations and roads are in good health. The riders have joined clubs, and the clubs have worked to make trails that minimize damage to tree roots.

We are painfully aware of legislation that forces us to obey rules and regulations whose aims are to create the healthy habitat that we *already have* created by our own stewardship of the land. We probably will suffer the loss of 20 percent of our productive land to such rules.

Pilchuck Tree Farm has been and is the host for many meetings of forestry groups. In 1999 Pilchuck Tree Farm was named as the best managed tree farm in our state. We were certified as a "Green Tag" forest, also in 1999.

My family has been honored by Duane Weston's membership on the board of the Washington Forest Protection Association, an ancient organization founded in 1905 to prevent forest fires. Today it is "protecting" tree farmers, both family and industrial, from rules and regulations proposed by environmentalists. At the same time, Pilchuck Tree Farm is a model for forest management.

Allen Staringer has found favorable markets for our trees, both old and young. He doesn't harvest when prices are down. After all, the trees just get bigger. Growing trees for timber in the United States is a very competitive business. The U.S.A.

The Vogelsang Forest—forerunner of Pilchuck Tree Farm. My great grandfather was a farmer and blacksmith who worked also in this forest near Kiel, Germany, named Vogelsang, "bird song." His field lay between the forest and his house and barns. He left his farm to his younger brother in 1848 to escape the militarism that was rampant over all of Europe and brought his immediate family to America. Photo by John H. Hauberg, Jr., in 1988, 140 years later.

Left: The Vogelsang Forest in 1988: A hardwood, leafy, angiosperm forest, requiring a totally different management from softwood, needle producing, gymnosperm forests. Few people are aware of the difference. Seeds and acorns from these trees germinate in the forest "duff" and grow in the shade. Right: Picture taken in 2001: First road built on Pilchuck Tree Farm in 1949. Photo shows three different age stands of Douglas fir. Below: State land: A panorama of Cascade foothills covered with third growth forests of Douglas fir, western hemlock, and western red cedar, with a recent clear-cut greening up with a similar mix of planted seedlings. These gymnosperms, especially Douglas fir, grow well only in full sunlight and germinate rapidly only on mineral soils.

Top: One of Pilchuck Tree Farm's early roads;
Center: A clear-cut with growing plantations all
around; Bottom: Ted Snook, Allen Staringer,
and Duane Weston in the eight-and-a-half-acre
clear-cut of year 2000.

imports logs and wood products from many countries, and Pilchuck Tree Farm has exported logs to the Far East. Our geography, topography, and good soil are advantages we need to stay in business.

The 1960s and 1970s plantations were just reaching the profitable harvesting age, about twenty years later than I dreamed about in Bavaria in 1948. It is a business for the long pull. One must have hope and faith.

Today we never plant just one species because a disease could wipe us out. So we plant fir and hemlock and cedar. That also increases the number of markets. We have over one hundred forty miles of private roads on fifteen thousand acres and can reach any corner of these woods very quickly in case of fire. There are currently few mills out here that can take on eighty-year trees because of the large diameters this age of tree produces and the diameter limitations designed into updated sawmilling equipment. We thin once at twenty-five years and clear-cut at fifty.

Log markets have changed dramatically since the tree farm was established in 1948. The "big is better" concept in log size is a rare operative in this new century. As supplies of large virgin old growth were replaced by smaller second- and third-growth timber, mills have re-tooled in anticipation of more "petite" raw material. Formerly a labor-intensive industry from the woods to the two-by-four, great efficiencies in high tech logging and sawmill equipment have made the harvest and use of small diameter, limby trees profitable. New products such as glue-laminated beams, finger-jointed studs, wafer board, and wood I-beams have also aided in the crossover to smaller raw material sizes and improved resource utilization. Never expected in 1948, these engineered products are often better building components than the massive lumber pieces they have replaced.

Alder and cottonwood

Douglas fir is still king in the Pacific Northwest, but hemlock and second-growth western red cedar have become valuable stocks in the tree farm's timber portfolio. Red alder has experienced unexpected gains to rival Douglas fir values as its light tan wood has increased in acceptance as a replacement for cherry in Europe. Bigleaf maple, once unsaleable except as firewood, is now sold extensively to the Orient. Cottonwood has become an agricultural crop with a seven-year cycle to provide chips for the paper industry.

Although delivered-log values have increased over twenty times from those attained in 1948, and product types have increased manyfold, tree farming will always be a challenging enterprise. One of the keys to survival in the twenty-first century will doubtless be to sustain a variety of species and products to tap all corners of a diverse market.

Kay at graduation from the University of Illinois, Urbana

CHAPTER 20

My Sister Kay

Interchangeably called "SIS" AND "KAY" BY ME, SHE WAS BORN APRIL 11, 1914, TWO years and two months before me, in the Great House in Rock Island. I'm sure Dr. George Hauberg presided over the occasion as he did for my birth. Miss Barbara Ross was probably there too.

Grandmother Hauberg with Kay

Mother with Kay

Kay and I were to see more of each other in our middle years than we did growing up. Those were years when we needed each other and supported each other. But, of course, we didn't see anyone else but each other when we were babies and before going through Audubon School.

Those were years of eating in the kitchen with Miss Ross and the rest of the help.

Dad's albums of the years 1916 to 1924 or so show that we were trotted out for photographs when the families, Haubergs and Denkmanns, got together. At early ages we went on the hikes, went to the big Denkmann houses, and to the Hauberg and Lyford farms—and to Broadway Presbyterian Church.

Left: Kay and John Henry;
Right: Helen Lyford (Simpson), Ada Mary
Lyford (Burke), and Catherine Hauberg
(Sweeney), circa 1917

We both contracted the measles, mumps, chicken pox, and perhaps others that were of little lasting effect, but Kay also had scarlet fever and diphtheria which affected her coordination and her complexion. Both of us had pimples, but hers were worse.

Our big yard brought Kay's school friends as well as mine for sledding, playing in the house, and later for tennis. Kay had a group of friends who called themselves the

"So-Sew Social Club." Our chicken coop was available for them after the chickens were banished and the place cleaned up. In the winter both boys and girls played in different parts of the Great House with the girls taking over the attic. We boys used the front hall for basketball, using a tennis ball and a small hoop. We boys also played in the basement. We all used the elevator. None of this seemed to bother Mother, Dad, Miss Ross or the rest of the help. I think they enjoyed the activity and the laughter.

Kay was Dad's favorite, as I was Mother's. So Kay wore play clothes that were pants and high-laced hiking boots, with a jacket to top it off. Mother smiled at this and turned toward me with advice on improving my table manners. The Black Hawk hikers, mostly women, doted on both of us, but Kay dressed like them and won their hearts. She loved the hikers and being in the outdoors.

Kay inherited Dad's curiosity about the world. I'm sure by the time she was eight she knew the names of all the wildflowers and trees, the birds and little animals that lived in the woods. We competed with each other to come up first with the names of the capitals of states and foreign countries. We did jigsaw puzzles of maps.

When Kay was nineteen, Cousin Hazel Schmoll, a Ph.D. botanist with the Field Museum in Chicago, took her to Guatemala to collect orchid plants. It was the beginning of Kay's lifelong interest in tropical botany. Hazel saw to it that at least a couple dozen orchid plants were installed

Sally Shinn, Dad, and Kay

in our greenhouse along 24th Street. Andrew Reitz, our chauffeur and gardener, was given instructions, and the plants lasted into the late '30s when I began to pick them for corsages for my dates.

Mother wanted Kay to go to Dana Hall and Wellesley as she had done in the 1890s. I'm not sure of dates, but I think Kay went East in 1929. She did not like it. She felt that our German name was held against her and that the Eastern girls

Kay and Prince

ganged up against the very few girls from the west. She was at Dana Hall for a second year when I arrived at Fessenden in the fall of 1930. Mother and Dad came east to Boston for Thanksgiving at Cousin Bessie Lee Howard's Beacon Street house. And we attended a performance of *Porgy and Bess* with Paul Robeson singing the title role. At any rate, Kay enrolled as a freshman at the University of Illinois in Urbana. She joined the Alpha Phi Sorority and was very happy to be back in the Middle West. She was able to keep her precious orchids alive. I know nothing of the courses she took, the friends she made, or her graduation.

In 1938 she married an almost neighbor, Ed Sweeney, seven years older than she. I assisted as an usher at their wedding and promptly lost contact with them until 1945 when I visited them in Washington, D.C., en route to Boston for embarkation to the European front.

Her marriage was a happy one. She loved being married to Ed, and now I'll write a few paragraphs about him.

Ed Sweeney, when I first learned of him, was a professor of aviation law at the University of Kentucky. He was also publisher of *The Journal of Air Law and Commerce*, put out under the banner of Northwestern University. He was very energetic as well as learned. We were all very pleased about the marriage although our father had reservations about his mother who was a D.A.R. (Daughters of the American Revolution), a very snobbish group in Dad's eyes.

Ed asked me to be an usher and I was very honored. I flew east from Seattle to Chicago, then down to Rock Island in time to put on my dinner jacket for the wedding dinner at the Fort Armstrong Hotel that was going on as I rushed in. Mother was putting

The Wedding Party, 22 October 1938

on the dinner and there were no alcoholic beverages, let alone smoking—altogether a very dull affair. I made the rounds of the younger (under fifty!) people there and quietly invited them to join me in the Fort Armstrong Hotel's lounge after the dinner. Some of us carried on for quite a time. The next morning, at breakfast at the Great House, my Mother put her hand on my arm and said, "Thank you for what you did last night." That was all. I was stunned. And I realized that she knew what she had given up for so many years of no social life among her peers because of her beliefs. Did Dad ever think about it?

Kay and Ed moved to Winnetka for a short period of time. He was soon invited to join the international division of the new Civil Aeronautics Board. He was to continue to put out the *Journal of Air Law*, but his new assignment took him to Washington, D.C.

Within months he was given a very difficult task of analyzing the government's subsidies to the airlines for carrying air mail. It was a political hot potato. Ed shrewdly hired the top business auditing firm in the nation to do the work. They discovered, to no one's surprise, that the big airlines with the longest runs got almost all the public's money, and the smallest connecting airlines with the short runs needed the subsidy the most. Congress made the necessary adjustment, but Ed's political goose was cooked.

Congress discovered that every federal agency from the military to the postal department built its own buildings, wrote its own contracts with builders, and hoped for the best results. Thousands of lawsuits resulted with many more in sight. The General Services Administration was created by Congress to take title to all federal buildings, to standardize contracts, to supervise activities, and to liquidate the lawsuits. And Ed was put in charge of the latter. He hired almost every lawyer on the loose in Washington and within four or five years cleared the decks of all the lawsuits. A truly fabulous achievement!

It was time for some sort of reward. Perhaps a seat on the Civil Aeronautics Board? The big airline companies were against it. Perhaps an appointment as Ambassador to Ethiopia? Kay and Ed had traveled extensively in Africa, had met and visited with Haile Selassie, Emperor of Ethiopia. Unhappily, the Sweeneys had befriended the embassies of Lebanon, Jordan, and perhaps Egypt, and were now considered to be anti-Semitic. I was told by the Eisenhower administration that Ed was not going to get any positions and to stop pushing.

So much for the reward for public service.

There were lots of happy times, however. Kay and Ed had many interesting friends. They had moved to 3300 Nebraska Avenue N.W. and Ed had talked Kay into building a swimming pool. It was full of people almost all the time. Among their earliest friends were Finn and Jackie Ronne. Finn was a rugged Norwegian explorer type employed by the U.S. Navy. Jackie became Kay's best friend. My father was entranced with polar exploration and explorers. He had taken me in 1926 to the Paramount Theater in Davenport, Iowa to hear Roald Amundsen talk about reaching the South Pole and we had gone backstage to shake his hand. Now Dad asked the Weyerhaeusers to furnish Finn Ronne with $100,000 worth of lumber to build an American base in the Antarctic! Finn named an Antarctic Range mountain for him and a mountain range for the Sweeneys—a real thrill for all of us.

Kay had another great friend in Marian Stirling through the Women Geographers Club. Her husband, Matthew, had long been subsidized by the National Geographic Society to uncover the great football player-like heads of the ancient Olmec civilization in the Veracruz area of Mexico. Matt was later to get me involved with other scholars of ancient Mexican cultures.

Kay and Ed bought an airplane and soon were members of the Sportsman Pilots Club. And they began to plan flying adventures with friends such as George and Isabel Blodgett. Not to mention inspiring eldest son, Edward, Jr., to devote his whole life to designing and flying anything that could become airborne.

Because of Kay's interest in African plant life, the Sweeneys made several trips into the jungle heartland. On one trip to the Sahara, they meandered into the camp of the Leakey family, famed for discovering the origins of the human race. This led to

The Sweeneys, 1962:
Edward, Jr., Philip,
Ed, Harriet, Kay,
Susie, Johnny

several summers with the Leakeys for the Sweeney children. George Blodgett and Ed planned a Cairo-to-Cape Town trip with two small planes. Ed and Kay's flight ended in a baobab tree in Nairobi where the heat of the day robbed the air of its lifting capacity over the runway. I believe Ed and Kay got off lightly with a broken collarbone and a broken arm. Blodgett later disappeared on a solo flight over South America. His widow, Isabel Blodgett of Cambridge, Massachusetts, was only the first Blodgett to be a friend to the Hauberg family. My daughter Fay married Nat Page whose mother was a Blodgett, and I had become friends with her two brothers, both doctors, one of whom, Dr. E. Donald Blodgett, was involved with programs for retarded children. Isabel Blodgett was their cousin!

All these ventures brought Kay and Ed into membership in the Explorers Club of New York. Ed later became its president.

It was time for our Dad to face the tribulations of the righteous. He was invited to Washington, D.C., to a party given by the Sweeneys to honor him. Much transpired at that party, but all of a sudden I noticed Dad standing with his heroes Admiral Richard Byrd, Sir Hubert Wilkins, Lowell Thomas, and Finn Ronne. Jesse, the Sweeney's butler, came with a silver tray loaded with martinis. I held my breath. Yes, Dad took one, responded to the toast to him by raising the glass to his lips. Did he sip? He put the martini up on the mantelpiece and no one would ever know.

Kay was making annual trips around the world. She was fascinated by the tropical food crops that kept hundreds of millions of people alive. She, and Ed, when he was with her, took very good slides and movies of places and people. One of her annual stops was Ceylon or Sri Lanka, where Edward Sweeney, Jr.'s, mother-in-law lived. Kay began to invite bright, young ladies there to come to the United States and attend Wilson College, of which Kay was a trustee. I believe she put over twenty young women from Sri Lanka through Wilson College.

Although The Kampong in Florida was to become the principal focus of Kay's last thirty years, she could not resist some side-glances. She bought a house in Aspen for Ed and the children to enjoy the skiing and she became involved in the Aspen Music Festivals. She also bought a house in France near the Pont du Gard and spent quite a lot of time there. She joined an old Rock Island friend, Elin Brekke Vanderlip, in support of renovating old French castles. The Friends of French Art was the name of the group. Kay took one of her children with her on most of these annual junkets among French aristocrats with titles greater than their financial resources! Almost all the Sweeneys enjoyed living in France at Castillon du Gard, not far from Avignon.

But The Kampong was very special. Dr. David Fairchild was America's first and major tropical botanist working at the U.S. Food and Agriculture Experiment Station at Bethesda, Maryland. He introduced such fruits as limes and grapefruit to the American

Four of Kay's children at Castillon du Gard. Photograph by daughter Fay Hauberg Page, summer, 1994

table. He also married Alexander Graham Bell's "other daughter." Her sister had married Gilbert Grosvenor of National Geographic Magazine fame and fortune. The Grosvenors and the Fairchilds were very close to one another. Dr. Fairchild had a family compound on the waterfront of Biscayne Bay at Coconut Grove known as The Kampong, and the Grosvenors had a larger one next to it. But when Dr. Fairchild died, his family could not maintain the gardens and they offered The Kampong to Kay!

Kay was thrilled and determined to continue Dr. Fairchild's work. She continued publishing his "Kampong Notes," and persuaded a long list of well-known tropical botanists to write articles for it. Kay was fortunate enough to obtain the services of Larry Schokman as the superintendent of her garden. Our cousin Jim Burke, who, with Ada Mary, visited The Kampong frequently, relates, "Catherine [Kay] had been a guest of Larry and his wife Colleen at his tea plantation in Sri Lanka. Susie and Edward and Sandra Sweeney had also visited Sri Lanka and the Schokmans. With the Sri Lankan nationalization of all tea plantations, Larry decided it was time to move on. He planned to sell tea and spices. This is where Catherine came in. She met Larry, by chance, in London. Larry was invited to come to Florida and employment was agreed on. Catherine sold Larry his residence later, which is across from The Kampong entrance. That was the start of a long and devoted stay." With The Kampong, Kay was in seventh heaven, lecturing widely on tropical plants, putting up scientists from all over the world and traveling around the world almost every year to visit *them*. The *Miami Herald* called her "The Savior of the Kampong."

In 1992, Mr. Schokman was put to the test when Hurricane Andrew blew into Biscayne Bay with wind gusts up to 200 mph and flattened hundreds of shallow-rooted tropical trees. With help from equipment from Disneyworld, almost every tree was stood back up and stayed alive! The Kampong has a fascinating collection of tropical fruit, flowering trees and ethnobotanic plants. Harvard University and the University of Florida conduct month-long summer classes in tropical botany there.

Kay became a very active member of the National Tropical Botanical Garden, with headquarters in New York for fund raising and garden operations on the island of Kauai. It was inevitable that she gave The Kampong to this important organization, which had been chartered by an act of Congress in 1964.

She and Ed shuttled between Washington, D.C., and Coconut Grove until his death in 1967 when Kay made The Kampong her permanent home until her own death.

Anne Gould Hauberg and I had very nice visits with the Sweeneys wherever they lived. Kay always gave a party for us as she had done for me whenever I came to Washington for Republican National Committee meetings. It was at The Kampong that I became friends with Mel Grosvenor and his family. But the Sweeneys and the Mel Grosvenors were also close friends in Washington where the two families made major contributions to the National Presbyterian Church and The Reverend Elson, its pastor. Soon Kay and Ed were persuaded by the Elsons and the Grosvenors to join them in a sunny home in Nova Scotia, adding one more house/home to Kay's already numerous dwellings.

Kay's travels were frequent and extensive and interesting. She could tour the jungles of South America with son Johnny, travel among the homes of French aristocrats with Susie or Harriet, entertain in Aspen, visit son Edward's mother-in-law in Ceylon, take her youngest son Johnny to Japan, Korea and France. She ate every native dish with a seeming cast-iron stomach and could talk about what plants produced the ingredients, and where and how they were grown from seed to harvest and on to what markets sold them and how they were cooked.

Kay was a marvelous sister, energetic, curious, and ready to go anywhere anytime, gregarious, true to her family and friends, warmhearted, generous and caring.

She died January 25, 1995. The *New York Times* ran the obituary included here.

*Ann, left, and I, visit my famous sister, Kay, at
her place in France near the Pont du Gard, 1980s*

Catherine Hauberg Sweeney '32, a lady of few words but many good deeds, was one of seven at her Dana Hall 50th Reunion. She missed her 55th while in France at a meeting of the Friends of French Art, an American organization pledged to restore and maintain art in France, for which she is both a participant in the selection and contributor in the purchase of major works for restoration.

As a botanist, horticulturist and philanthropist, motivated and inspired by her father in her early years, Kay has served as Trustee of Fairchild Tropical Garden and the Pacific Tropical Botanical Garden, Member-at-Large of The Garden Club of America, and member of the International Dendrology Society. Recipients of her efforts and generosity are American Horticultural Society, Coolidge Center for Environmental Leadership, National Council of YWCA, World Wildlife Fund — U.S., National Council of the Metropolitan Opera Association, and Wilson College in Chambersburg, Pennsylvania.

While retaining a life interest, she has given to the Pacific Tropical Botanical Garden her residential estate, **The Kampong**, in Coconut Grove, Florida. This was the former home of Alexander Graham Bell's son-in-law, Dr. David Fairchild, who was instrumental in establishing the U.S. Department of Agriculture Introduction Garden at Chapman Field, Miami. The Catherine Hauberg Sweeney Garden Center at Chapman Field was dedicated in 1978. A report in the **Kampong Notes** of January 31, 1987 describes the Copaifera, an Amazonian tree, that produces up to forty liters of a diesel-like heavy oil that reportedly can be poured directly into a diesel engine. A Brazilian research institute has been running a fleet of Toyota trucks on this fuel since 1978.

Mrs. Sweeney's time, talent and generosity have been recognized through an Honorary Doctorate from Wilson College and a Silver Medal from the Massachusetts Horticultural Society. Upon moving to Florida, she gave to American University her Washington, D.C. house that is now the residence of the University President.

Daughter of Susanne Denkmann, Dana Hall 1883, Catherine Sweeney (Mrs. Edward C.) has kept in touch with her five children and six grandchildren in addition to traveling extensively for meetings, projects, and giving lectures to garden clubs throughout the country.

Researched and written by Ellen Barker Pettit '28 ∎

Catherine Hauberg Sweeney '32

Dana Hall Bulletin.
Summer 1987

Catherine Sweeney, 80, Patron
Of Arts, Education and Sciences

NY Times Feb 3 '95

By LAWRENCE VAN GELDER

Catherine H. Sweeney, a patron of the sciences and arts for whom the Sweeney Mountains of Antarctica were named, died on Jan. 25 at the Miami Heart Institute. She was 80 and lived in Coconut Grove, Fla.

The cause was heart failure, said her son-in-law, Eric Fraunfelter.

Mrs. Sweeney called herself "just a lady gardener," but her efforts on behalf of botany, exploration, education and the arts earned her such honors as a silver medal from the Massachusetts Horticultural Society and an honorary doctorate from Wilson College in Chambersburg, Pa., where she sent eight women from Sri Lanka to be educated at her expense.

She was also a trustee of the Congressionally chartered National Tropical Botanical Garden, the Fairchild Tropical Garden in Miami, the American Horticultural Society, the World Wildlife Fund and the Conservation Foundation. She was a member-at-large of the Garden Club of America and a founder of the Florida chapter of the Society of Women Geographers.

Among other enterprises, Mrs. Sweeney rescued and restored the eight-acre estate called The Kampong in Coconut Grove in 1963. She donated the property, the former residence of the plant explorer David Fairchild, to the National Tropical Botanical Garden as a refuge and retreat for horticulturalists.

After she helped finance the Norwegian explorers Finn and Jackie Ronne in an expedition to Antarctica in the late 1940's, the Ronnes named the Sweeney Mountains in her honor.

She was a patron of the Metropolitan Opera and of the Aspen Institute for Humanistic Studies in Rye, N.Y., and a life trustee and national board member of the Aspen Music Festival and School in Aspen, Colo.

Born Catherine Denkmann Hauberg, she was a granddaughter and grandniece of the two brothers who established the company that became the Weyerhauser lumber empire.

She was a graduate of Dana Hall in Wellesley, Mass., and of the University of Illinois. Her husband, Edward C. Sweeney, a former president of the Explorers Club, died in 1967.

Mrs. Sweeney is survived by her children, Edward Jr., of Black Forest, Colo.; Philip, of Amherst, Mass.; John, of Aspen, Colo.; Susie Kayyali of Coral Gables, Fla., and Harriet Fraunfelter of Washington; her brother, John Hauberg Jr. of Seattle; five grandchildren, and two great-grandchildren.

CHAPTER 21

The Seattle Symphony & Its Revival

1950–1953

a S A BACKGROUND TO MY WORK WITH THE SEATTLE SYMPHONY, I SHOULD DESCRIBE the important role that music had played in my life prior to that association. My father was very interested in music, and that was a tremendous influence on me. Dad sang in the choir of every church he belonged to. When he was in law school at the University of Michigan at Ann Arbor for two years, the Chautauqua circuit not only had speakers such as William Jennings Bryan, but also had drama groups and musical groups visiting the university. These groups fascinated my father. When he took a European tour after graduation from Ann Arbor in 1900, he lived in Berlin for six months. While there he made his operatic debut, as a spear-carrier in the Berlin Opera!

Mother attended many concerts of the Boston Symphony Orchestra while she was in school at Dana Hall and in college at Wellesley in the 1890s.

After Mother and Dad were married, they installed in their new house an Aeolian organ that played from paper rolls. We had a tremendous spread of organ pipes in our house, just terrific. We could put on a roll after dinner and sit and listen to Elgar's "Pomp and Circumstance", or perhaps the "Grand March" from *Aida*. The music would echo through the hallways and rooms. Some pipes were even in the attic to provide an echo. Most pipes were behind screens in the living room.

We also had a Steinway piano that had been linked up to this Aeolian system, so we could "play" piano concertos by Beethoven and Mozart. That was quite a valuable piano. (Many years later when Anne Gould Hauberg and I lived on McGilvra Boule-vard, we sent the piano (which I had inherited) to be refinished. Unfortunately the refinishing company in Seattle had a fire, and the piano was destroyed. Their insurance company bought us another Steinway, but nothing could replace the one we lost.

My parents were not social. We had very few friends over to hear the music, but the Ladies Musical Club met in our big living room for concerts of all kinds. So my sister and I were thoroughly grounded in music because of our parents' interest.

Then there was the Black Hawk Hiking Club, which my father founded in Rock Island in 1920. On these hikes everyone sang. A lot of the songs had come out of World War I, such as "Tipperary" and "Give My Regards to Broadway." We sang songs like "Sweet Adeline," "Someone's in the Kitchen with Dinah," and western songs like "Let the Rest of the World Go By." I still remember the words:

> *With someone like you,*
>
> *a pal good and true*
>
> *I'd like to leave it all behind,*
>
> *and go and find*
>
> *Some place that's known to God alone*
>
> *Just a spot to call our own.*
>
> *We'll find perfect peace,*
>
> *where joys never cease*
>
> *Out there beneath the kindly sky*
>
> *We'll build a sweet little nest,*
>
> *somewhere out in the west*
>
> *And let the rest of the world go by.*

We sang lots of "rounds" as the trucks took us out to the hiking area. One side of the truck would start the song, and then the other side would come in, "Row, row, row your boat." You could get three groups going on that one.

When I got to Hotchkiss at age fifteen, I sang in the glee club and the choir for three years. I was in three Gilbert and Sullivan operettas as a chorus member. We put on *Trial By Jury*, *Pirates of Penzance*, and *HMS Pinafore*. I can still remember a lot of the words to those songs. We sang sea chanties—great glee club music. We gave concerts with girls' schools. In the choir we sang the music of Bach and the great masses by Verdi, Haydn, and Mozart. I sang solos for the glee club and choir. I didn't have a good voice, but I could stay on key. The school brought string quartets to Hotchkiss, and soloists who sang with our groups.

At Princeton I minored in music and got my best marks in that subject. I had the opportunity to learn how symphonic music is put together, and to study the history of music. I just ate it up. I went to many New York Philharmonic Orchestra concerts with Toscanini conducting, and a number of operas as well.

When I came out to the Northwest during the spring and summer of 1938, I attended Seattle Symphony concerts. The orchestra wasn't the greatest, but they did have Sir Thomas Beecham as conductor, and I thought it was just fine. It was a small orchestra of about sixty musicians. They couldn't take on any big works such as symphonies by Berlioz because they couldn't afford to hire that many special players to fill out the orchestra.

In the spring of 1941, my mother had a stroke. Annie and I were married in June of that year when I was working in the big western pine mill in Klamath Falls. We had then been transferred to the Coeur d' Alene, Idaho, white pine mill of the Potlatch Company in September. Annie was obviously unhappy in "milltowns" and my father was lonely in the Great House with Mother upstairs, unable to talk or walk. I decided to leave the Weyerhaeuser Sales Company as a trainee, knowing it wouldn't be long before I would be inducted into the army as a different sort of trainee. In October 1941 I had the company send me back to a Weyerhaeuser and Denkmann retail lumberyard in Rock Island, Illinois. Annie and I lived in Dad's house to keep him company, and we played the Aeolian organ a lot. Mother was upstairs in bed and she enjoyed it. We took Dad to the symphony, and went with him to the *Messiah* at Augustana College. They put on the *Messiah* every year with visiting professional singers, always a wonderful performance.

Davenport, Iowa, is right across the river from Rock Island. A Davenport woman, Elsie Von Maur, who ran the musical scene there, put me to work. In 1995 I received notice that the Quad City Symphony Orchestra was honoring Elsie Von Maur. She must have been ninety-five years old or more. Elsie's husband ran the major department store in Davenport. They were very prominent citizens. They loved the young people in town, particularly those interested in music and art, so Annie and I got along swimmingly with them.

Under Elsie's direction the Ladies Musical Club imported soloists, but they had a budget of only two thousand dollars a year. Elsie very quickly discovered that I was fascinated by music, so she got me the job of helping the ladies sign up their soloists. They were all too timid to deal with impresarios like Sol Hurok and Arthur Judson. NBC and CBS had impresarios as well. I would call them and say, "Well now, the Ladies Musical Club needs a program for next year." You had to work at least a year in advance. They would say, "What's the budget?" I said, "Two thousand dollars, and of course we want Rubinstein and Lily Pons." We got a good chuckle out of that. But because they loved Elsie and got to be rather good friends with me, we wound up with better musicians than our budget called for.

This interlude, November 1941 to May 1943 in Rock Island, was happy even though Annie hated the ugliness of this Midwestern industrial area. In the late spring of 1943 the Army drafted me, and I spent two years in the U.S.A. as both trainee and trainer in both field artillery and infantry, followed by a year and a half in the occupation army in Germany and Austria. I rejoined Annie and baby Fay in the early fall of 1946 in Seattle.

During these three and a half years, I had attended only two musical events, one in Temple, Texas by the Dallas orchestra when I was an infantry-training officer at Camp Hood. The other was in the half-restored palace above the town of Dachau, where a young lady violinist brought the local citizens to tears of relief from the horrors the Nazis had inflicted on them.

Now it was back to Seattle for three years at the University of Washington's College of Forestry and the turbulent cultural scene of a city wanting to shed its reputed dependence on timber, fish, and Boeing.

Since I was the youngest person in the group of people in the early 1950s to bring the Seattle Symphony up to good health and a much better reputation and standing in the community and, we hoped, a national ranking, I am now, fifty years later, unable to find a single soul still alive besides myself who shared in the struggle. What I can't remember is recalled to some extent by Esther Campbell, long gone herself, who wrote a history of the Seattle Symphony Orchestra based on the minutes of the trustees' meetings. Not much fun there. But, at least, she has the names and dates and therefore jogs my memory sufficiently so that I don't have to try to recall "old what's-his-name."

In December of 1949, when I should have been concentrating on buying more land for my tree farm, I became distracted by and attracted to an opportunity to help the Seattle Symphony Orchestra out of its historic troubles. But once again, these months working with the Symphony influenced my future tremendously and proved to be a bit of the serendipity that has blessed my entire life.

In 1946 while waiting to be "retired" from the army, I wrote Annie from Germany to buy season tickets to the Seattle Symphony's 1946-1947 season. The "season" consisted of eight Monday-night concerts in the Metropolitan Theater located in the space which is now in the Four Seasons Olympic's drive-in entrance. It was a cozy space, seating twelve hundred people with a small stage, but at least with a proscenium loft for theater flats, just right for a small orchestra of sixty or so musicians playing Mozart's symphonies and concerti.

Sir Thomas Beecham had conducted the orchestra in Seattle as well as the Vancouver, B.C., orchestra for the three seasons from 1941-1943, the time that it took him to get a divorce from his wife. Now he was back in England and the Seattle Symphony Board of Trustees had hired a Yale music professor named Carl Bricken.

During the intermission of the first concert we attended, I said to Annie, "Mr. Bricken is a very poor conductor. He doesn't seem to be leading, but following the orchestra." We met the Brickens socially over the next few months. Mrs. Bricken was teaching music appreciation at Lakeside School. Their children were bright and attractive. Carl Bricken could tell whether my tweed jackets came from Brooks Brothers or from J. Press. The symphony board, made up principally of socialites, was very pleased. The musicians were not. By 1946 or 1947, they demanded Bricken's departure and went "on strike" against the board which in turn fired them all.

The board of the symphony then got about hiring other musicians but failed in that effort. Seattle simply was too small a city at that time to have an abundance of oboists, violinists, horn players, etc., to make up a second orchestra. So, the socially oriented board members who were not really dedicated to quality music resigned, leaving board members who were without the clout to give or get adequate financial support for the orchestra. It had been a chronic problem of the symphony ever since its 1905 founding. And not only the symphony's problem.

Like all the cultural institutions in Seattle in those days, the symphony's board was made up of prominent citizens who gave money from their own pockets, not expecting professional quality, nor striving to rise above the levels that their personal contributions could afford. The Seattle Art Museum was almost completely financed by Dr. Richard E. Fuller, grand opera was imported from San Francisco, Mr. and Mrs. Bush owned the Helen Bush School, local artists received little attention and sold their work for only hundreds of dollars, and the University of Washington's president was the amiable brother of Seattle's leading banker.

Seattle was, as Sir Thomas Beecham dubbed it, " A cultural dustbin." For an amusing account of Sir Thomas Beecham's "residence" in Seattle, see Hans Lehmann's autobiography *Out of the Cultural Dustbin*. This highly quotable judgment went all over the United States like a new dirty joke. But it went to the hearts of the new post-World War II leadership of Seattle. Bill Allen, CEO of Boeing, and Paul Pigott, the heavy truck manufacturer, determined to make the annual "Community Chest" drives a success after years of embarrassing failures blamed on the Depression and then WWII. They tapped their employees for one day's wages, perhaps high handedly, but the new name United Way of King County suddenly meant sound funding for many civic, health, and youth organizations. Better funding for cultural organizations had to await another creative idea that was about to produce a business base for funding the arts.

Men such as Bill Street of Frederick & Nelson, Eddie Carlson of the Western International Hotels, Paul Ashley, a lawyer with a great sense of what Seattle could become, "Si" Arnold of the Seattle First National Bank, and quite a few others, determined that Seattle would become a great city—the "Venice of the West."

I was swept into this whirlpool in December 1949, when asked to join the Board of Trustees of the Seattle Symphony Orchestra. The Symphony had been a plaything of the socialite descendants of Easterners who brought "culture" to Seattle from Yale and Harvard in the 1890s and the early 1900s. They were serious about history, art, poetry, music, gardens, good schools, literature, good government, etc., and brought their knowledge from their colleges, from travel abroad, and from their own experience to bear on their civic activities. Yet there had never been a commitment to get all these activities coordinated and managed by executives who were as good as the leadership of Seattle's top businesses. "Culture" was a necessity but not worth giving enough money to.

The new generation of Seattle's "downtown leaders" wanted this to change. I was to be their "errand boy."

Annie and I had gone to impresario Cecilia Schultz's recitals of leading artists such as Jascha Heifetz and Lily Pons. We had made the acquaintance of Mrs. Schultz. And we were getting to know the serious music lovers on the symphony board.

One day, Mrs. Schultz, who knew we had a big, although old, four-door Buick sedan, asked me to take her to the Seattle airport to pick up Gregor Piatigorsky, a huge man who made his cello look like a ukulele when he held it in his hands. He was known never to part with it and therefore could not use taxis that had only room for him inside with his cello in the trunk. He would *not* take taxis.

I was glad to oblige just to meet the great cellist. But it turned out to be more than just that. I also had to pick him up at the Olympic Hotel to get him to the Moore Theater, and then take him and the Schultzes to a post-concert private supper and finally back to his hotel. All with the cello guarded beside him at every move. It was a jolly supper. Not a word spoken about music. Gus Schultz never talked about music anyway, so he and the artist talked about the stock market, we all listened and laughed. Great fun and it took place in the same way on a second visit to Seattle by Piatigorsky. I also did taxi service for Lily Pons.

The College of Puget Sound had brought to Tacoma as "composer in residence" a symphony conductor of the French National Radio Orchestra, a well-qualified, experienced man named Manuel Rosenthal. To the satisfaction of the orchestra, the symphony board hired him. The concerts again were good, attendance rose, the music critics were happy. But money quickly became the usual problem.

At the depth of frustration over the Seattle Symphony's failure to raise enough money to put on concerts, let alone pay the musicians, Rosenthal walked from the Madison Avenue bus stop though a driving downpour to our 1031 McGilvra house to ask me to join the symphony board. A week or two later in December 1949, Paul Jarvis, my neighbor across the street and member of the board, came over to ask me to join. I agreed.

In 1950 I was just acquiring acreage for a research tree farm. I was spending a couple nights a week in a boarding house in Arlington. I knew only a few of Seattle's downtown leaders, those I knew being bankers who had summer homes at the Country Club on Bainbridge Island. No other "downtowners" had ever heard of me. But this sort of challenge was identical to almost everything my Mother and Dad believed in, and I was sure they would want me to do it. I knew nothing of the battle that had taken place among board members over the choice of Manuel Rosenthal favored by the orchestra, and Eugene Linden, favored by the board's music committee.

Joe Gandy, the major Ford dealer in Seattle, had become president of the symphony. He and I went around to local businesses to ask for $25 for the orchestra. We were thrown out of the Friedlander jewelry store. It was the most memorable event of our "drive" for funds, but not the only turn down. There was no publicity, no organization. Joe had to run his business at the same time and asked me to take over the Seattle Symphony presidency. I could not do that because I knew no one and vice versa. But I said that I would be executive vice president and general manager for $1 per year. My first salaried position!

I had met a wonderful public relations person named Bill Speidel and I poured out my troubles to Bill. In short order he persuaded the talented public relations people of the Seattle Advertising and Sales Club to make the symphony their cause. A gala Christmas *Messiah* concert was scheduled and with lots of hype all the tickets were sold out. The concert was a great success. The papers were full of the news planted by the advertising club. What next? I could see that unless the business community became involved through membership on the Board of Trustees, we could not reach the new level of funding required.

Bill Street, head of Frederick & Nelson, assigned his top assistant, Hector Escabosa, to the symphony board. It was the first breakthrough. Hector suggested a fashion show with a dance party at, I believe, a hundred dollars per person. It was to be called "Symphoneve" and Hector had persuaded Elizabeth Arden to be the guest of honor. Wow! It was a sell out success!! And the first of the Symphoneves that continue to this year of 2001. I took Miss Elizabeth Arden out on the dance floor, her first dance, she confided, in many years. Annie and I were photographed with the Escabosas, the Gandys, and Miss Arden for Vanity Fair!

With money in the bank, the 1950-1951 season with Manuel Rosenthal conducting was a great success. Everyone looked forward to a second season of untroubled concerts and favorable critics. Also, Ruth McCreery came back as the truly professional manager of the Seattle Symphony, a position she had held with the symphony during its Beecham years. During those days she had built up a $60,000 surplus and all of it was blown away when the trustees, over her objections, rented Husky Stadium in 1945 for a WWII "victory concert," a resounding flop. So, I was relieved of that assignment and joined the music committee.

Before Mrs. McCreery returned, our symphony management offices were on the second-floor storage space of a Sixth Avenue music store next to the Salvation Army, very appropriate. There were three of us there for a year and a half. Vera White handled the complex business of producing and selling tickets. Don Bushell, the first chair orchestra cellist, represented the orchestra, and I had to find theaters for the concert performances. I also made arrangements for rehearsal halls in school buildings all over the north end of Seattle. The symphony librarian, Louis Rotter, had no shelves for the music scores for the musicians so I bought him cabinets with locked doors. Rotter said we had almost no conductors' scores because the British conductor, Basil Cameron had taken them all to England to study them during the summer for the next season (sometime in the 1930s). He was fired during that summer by the righteous Seattle Symphony trustees when an attractive young orchestra player brought a paternity suit against Cameron in absentia. He kept the conductors' scores.

The surprise demise of Manuel Rosenthal as conductor of the Seattle Symphony Orchestra, just as the 1951-1952 season was beginning, was equally dramatic. The music critics liked him. The Seattle audience was very pleased with his music. The orchestra members were glad to have a strong conductor but were growing skeptical of his autocratic personality. I was the chief of staff (at thirty-four?), hearing complaints from varying sides, and the trustees who were watching all this held their tongues and their breath. Rosenthal's wife sang solos in the Epiphany Episcopal Church choir and was well liked. An interesting cast of characters.

The U.S. Immigration Service never said a word to me about Rosenthal's numerous trips outside the country. He guest-conducted the Vancouver, B.C., orchestra several times a year and I believe he visited France, his own country, two or three times. These many trips were in violation of his Green Card permit to work in the U.S.A. that limited his travel.

His last trip to Paris was his undoing. Arriving with his wife, he was confronted with a Paris newspaper headline that announced that his real wife wanted him back and that his so-called wife was just his mistress! Seattle newspapers were not slow to put all this into headlines. On his attempted return to America, the U.S. Immigration Service detained him. All this was a great surprise to all of us with the symphony, not to mention the Seattle music world.

Mr. Wallace Campbell, a wholesale hardware dealer, had become the Seattle Symphony Orchestra president and was wise enough to hire one of Seattle's leading attorneys, Ernest Skeel, who was given complete authority to handle this hot potato. Calling Wally and me to his office, he called the immigration officials. They had only one question of us, "Do you want Rosenthal back or don't you?" Mr. Skeel put his hand over the telephone and asked Wally and me the same question, did we want him back or didn't we? All of the months of incredibly difficult work to strengthen the symphony–its orchestra members, its critics, its audiences, and the trustees' hard work went through my mind. I don't know what went through Wally's mind, but he had shared the same events. We looked at each other and said to Mr. Skeel, "No, we don't want him back." And that was that. A month of scathing press passed as quickly as a summer shower.

The trustees' music committee and I made arrangements with the New York impresario Arthur Judson for guest conductors for the 1951-1952 season. Mr. Gordon Scott became president, a man respected by the business community. If I recall correctly we had two seasons of guest conductors. The most popular was Arthur Fiedler of the Boston Pops. There were also Maestro Gaetano Merola of the San Francisco Opera, Wallace Harrison of the Los Angeles Philharmonic, Maurice Abravenel of the Salt Lake City Symphony, and others.

With the 1951-1952 season planned, scheduled, and sold, the symphony trustees had to act quickly to engage guest conductors well enough known to favorably attract our concertgoers. The music committee labored furiously, meeting in Hans and Thelma Lehmann's house to decide on conductors and what music was to be played. My two favorites were Gaetano Merola, maestro of the San Francisco Opera, and Arthur Fiedler, of the Boston Pops.

Ruth McCreery had replaced me as symphony manager, but I still had the duties of meeting the conductors at the airport and taking them to the Camlin Hotel, chosen mainly for its great chef in the top floor Cloud Room. Knowing Fiedler's and Merola's tastes, I would buy a pint of Olympia oysters in the Pike Place Market, take it to the chef with instructions to come into the dining room wearing his tall chef's hat to greet my guests and inform them of the availability of Olympia oysters. Both men loved this personal attention.

Arthur Fiedler came out for one concert in November of 1952 and stayed to conduct a second concert a week or two later. He was eager to see the Pacific Northwest. Ruth McCreery called me to see if I could arrange for him to visit the Weyerhaeuser operation at Snoqualmie Falls. I quickly called Eddie McIntyre in Tacoma, a public relations man taking Weyerhaeuser's biggest customers around woods and mills as well as feeding them well and talking about the company. We picked Fiedler up on a very snowy day. Ruth was concerned about his catching cold and told me to keep him in the car. Our trip through the well-covered mill went well and Eddie headed us to the woods.

We drove through a grove of huge trees, preserved for McIntyre's trips and a mile or two further came across two loggers felling hemlock trees of thirty to thirty-six inches in diameter. Before I could stop him, Fiedler was out of the car in knee-deep snow to go up to these amiable Swedes to ask them in what direction the tree they had already begun to work on would fall. When they indicated the direction, Arthur bet them five dollars they couldn't drop it in a very different direction. The Swedes spit on their gloves, moved the chain saw cut around, and won the bet. Fiedler came back into the car in high spirits and it was time to go back to the Camlin Hotel in Seattle.

The next morning I got a call from Cy Mott of Blythe and Company saying a strange man named Fiedler wanted to buy a thousand shares of Weyerhaeuser stock and had given my name as a reference! I told Cy that Mr. Fiedler was good for a lot more than a thousand shares! Several years later, I met Arthur Fiedler again and asked him if he still had the Weyerhaeuser stock. He had added even more, he said.

The public liked these concerts, even though they were played in various rented auditoriums such as the University of Washington's old Meany Hall, the balcony of which was already condemned, the Moore Theatre on Second Avenue at Virginia, the Metropolitan Theater "inside" the Olympic Hotel, the Music Hall, and the Orpheum movie theater, and lastly, the old Civic Auditorium, which was a cavernous, flat-floored structure designed for boxing events and for marching by veterans' organizations. There were six thousand folding chairs that let out protesting squeaks whenever any occupant moved.

Under these circumstances we were not building a good orchestra with a good musical director and conductor, an audience of committed attendees and financial supporters. Also the critics were becoming very vocal about the quality of the music.

The Seattle Times had hired a serious music critic from Cincinnati to replace Maxine Cushing Grey who for years covered all of Seattle's cultural events. The Times wanted a specialist in music. His name was Lou Guzzo. He took his job seriously, sizing up the orchestra playing as bad, the concert halls worse, and the symphony leadership as inept.

Symphony president, Gordon Scott and I went to the Seattle Times editor-in-chief and begged him to get Mr. Guzzo to tone down. We said we knew the orchestra was not the greatest, but asked for his critic to consider our efforts to rebuild. Some favorable comments about our concerts would help, while the bad press was only hurting our efforts. Lou agreed and became our friend and ally and can be credited with an important role in the ultimate development of a successful Seattle Symphony Orchestra.

Just as the "guest conductors" strategy was working through its second year, the impresario representing one of them called before the concert to say his man was very sick and unable to conduct. But "would we accept the services of a young protégé of Arturo Toscanini named Milton Katims?" It turned out that Hans Lehmann had met Katims and urged the music committee to accept. The subsequent rehearsals and the concert began a love affair between Milton and the orchestra and their audience that went on for twenty years. Two seasons after Katims' first concert, he was named musical director and conductor.

The Seattle World's Fair brought about the complete remodeling of the Civic Auditorium as the new Seattle Opera House. The symphony finally had a "home" but had to share it with the Seattle Opera, the Pacific Northwest Ballet, Billy Graham, and rock 'n' roll bands. And now financial support began to come from many sources.

PONCHO, Patrons of Northwest Cultural Organizations, was organized by Kayla Skinner and Paul Friedlander. The annual auction raises hundreds of thousands of dollars. The Corporate Council for the Arts brings more annual funding from the business community. And symphony trustees now give annual support in dollar amounts not even imagined in the old days. Individual contributors give thousands and corporate support is in the hundreds of thousands of dollars.

My last fling with the Seattle Symphony came with the concept of the Corporate Council for the Arts. I don't know for sure, but Ned Skinner must have had a hand in creating it. He was on Boeing's board of directors and William Allen, Boeing's president, had been "in on" Seattle's rebirth in corporate support for the United Way, whose agencies did not include arts organizations.

Also Dr. Richard Fuller had started the Seattle Foundation, which would receive estates as well as gifts in support of needy groups, including the arts.

The first two years of the CCA found Ned, Sheffield Phelps and me doing all the soliciting. Corporate executives were still of the opinion that their money was going only to Sheffield and Patty's dance group and John H. Hauberg's symphony. So we were "fired" as solicitors and Peter Donnelly became the professional manager after resigning the directorship of the Seattle Repertory Theater. Today the major arts organizations and many small theater and music groups are well supported from these professionally managed fund-raising organizations.

Whew!

CHAPTER 22

Republican Politics, 1956–1964

W HEN ANNE GOULD HAUBERG AND I WERE IN HAWAII ON THE ISLAND OF MAUI for the Christmas holidays of 1955, I got a phone call from Norton Clapp. He told me George Kinnear, who had been the Washington State Republican finance chairman, wanted to retire. Norton had been talking to my cousin, Fritz Jewett in Spokane, about getting me into that position and Fritz was enthusiastic about it. I told Norton I would think about it and call him when I got home.

I called Fritz and said "I don't know a lot of people in Eastern Washington, but you are probably the most prominent citizen in Spokane. Everybody in Eastern Washington knows who you are because of your position with the Weyerhaeuser interests. If I get into this thing I would want to have your complete support and the ability to talk to you whenever I need to do so. The next problem would be that I've probably got to get a good contribution from you to start with, so I can tell people that you felt this was a good cause." He said, "All of that is perfectly possible." I made the same talk to Mr. Clapp and he agreed to give me his complete support.

I knew nothing about the task, except that one was to raise money for the politicians who sought office as Republicans. Nineteen fifty-six was a presidential election year, when Eisenhower was up for reelection. I looked forward to going to the convention, but Mort Frayn, who was the state party chairman, said the position had been promised to D.K. MacDonald, a great fund-raiser for the party. D.K. had said there was one thing he had really wanted to do when he retired, which was to attend a national convention. So even though theoretically I was an automatic delegate as one of the top three administrators (Mort Frayn, and a state vice chairman from Eastern Washington), D.K. attended the convention in my place.

Otherwise, 1956 was a banner year for Republicans in the state of Washington. I organized the financing and election of the entire Dan Evans team to the state legislature.

It was very easy to raise money for Eisenhower's re-election. He was one of the most popular men in the world at that point. The Democrats put up a sacrificial lamb who got nowhere. I can't even remember who it was.

Money came flowing in and was passed out to both the state and national committees. I began to attend meetings of the national finance committee in Washington

D.C., meeting people who were household names—Firestones, DuPonts, etc. It was quite a heady experience to attend meetings with all of these powerful persons. The meetings were always well staged and very stimulating. Everyone got acknowledged and applauded, including me, although I was the newest person on the committee. Eisenhower, of course, won the election hands down. Then there was a hiatus until his inauguration in January 1957.

Annie and I were invited to all the parties attending the inauguration. We stayed with my sister in her house in D.C. Kay had volunteered to entertain all of the entertainers for the various balls. There were at least six dance halls signed up, with entertainment provided by such stars as Ella Fitzgerald, the Kingston Trio, the Brothers Four—all the great entertainers of the day. The balls lasted until about 3:00 a.m. Then because we were staying at Kay's house, lo and behold here were all the entertainers at her house. I found myself talking to Ray Bolger, the famous scarecrow of *The Wizard of Oz*. It turned out that he had collected several paintings by Mark Tobey and he wanted to learn more about Mark. One thing led to another and I suppose I probably talked to him until about 5:00 a.m., when everybody went home to bed.

From then on it was a much harder fight. Eisenhower was in, but Democrat Senators Jackson and Magnuson were absolutely entrenched in the state of Washington. We always had to find some victim for them to beat. The idea was that if we didn't put up someone to oppose them, all the money they would have used would support some other Democrats for public office. My recollection of one of these problems was typical. Magnuson was running for re-election. I don't know how many terms he had already had. No Republican of any stature wanted to take him on. We finally heard about a young man who was born and raised in Chehalis and was now in Spokane, named Bill Bantz. He agreed, and said he would need at least fifty thousand dollars. Not very many people wanted to contribute to a losing cause.

I called a meeting of major givers in Seattle and said "We have to come up with at least enough money to get him on the road and make an appearance." So with many groans and moans, about a hundred guys came up with fifty thousand dollars. Then it was my job to flank big Bill Bantz with the knowledge of promoters and other people. He went down to defeat, gathering one of the most overwhelmingly small percentages anyone ever got.

Somehow or other we wound up with six or seven Republican congressmen, although both senators were Democrats. We had a Republican governor. I think it was Langley. All of the big industrialists in town wanted to put a right-to-work initiative on the ballot. The industrialists didn't want power to be in the hands of the unions. They wanted to hire the people that they wanted to, whether they were union people or not. So a right-to-work initiative would bring out a tremendous union Democratic vote. Normally union people don't vote, because they don't feel they have any control over our system at all. But when their positions are attacked, they respond to labor leaders. They feel their jobs and right to strike are on the line.

People behind this initiative were Paul Pigott of Paccar, Bill Allen of Boeing and Bill Street of Frederick & Nelson. I felt I had been placed in this job to produce winners, because all of us had so much at stake, and asked Norton Clapp to help. He said, "You are absolutely right." He called a luncheon meeting at the Rainier Club. It was a very small group. I explained what was at stake, that we could possibly lose all of our congressional seats, we were certain to lose the governorship, and we probably would lose our then majority in the house of representatives in Olympia. I urged them not to put this right-to-work initiative on the ballot, because it would bring out a strong union vote, and the Democrats would gain and we would lose.

It was just like trying to stop a strong wind by standing up and blowing into it. Bill Allen got up and said he had a meeting in Renton at Plant 2. Mr. Pigott had a meeting to go to, and one after another they left. Bill Street, head of Frederick & Nelson, was the only one that stayed. He said, "This is a matter of principle, and I firmly believe in it." I said, "I don't quarrel with you at all, but I'm here to advise you how to win elections, and you are doing everything to defeat yourself." He said, "I can't help it. I have to stand on principle." He then sent me about six books on the virtues of right-to-work. But of course it was not in the real world.

My predictions came true. We lost the governor, we lost the house. In Washington, D.C. we lost five out of six of our Republican congressmen. And the initiative was badly beaten, too. That Christmas at the Debutante's Ball, Bill Allen came up to me and very brusquely said, "Well, John, you were right." He shook my hand and very quickly turned and left. I thought it was very big of him to do that. I had worked hard for what I knew had to be done, and I had lost because of him.

Then we had another ballot issue, similar to right-to-work, and that again did great damage. It was going on the ballot in May. This was about 1960. I called a 7:30 a.m. breakfast meeting at the Washington Athletic Club the morning after Christmas for about forty of the state's top givers. I said, "You guys are shooting yourself in the foot again. I'm just your servant and I'm not going to tell you what to do, but I am going to tell you what I think you ought to do, which is to kill this initiative."

D. K. MacDonald got up and said, "John, I have three checks in my pocket for two thousand dollars each in support of this initiative, and I'm going to give these checks back to the men who wrote them."

Charlie Clise said, "I think we're barking up the wrong tree. We have to get people elected first, and then work on right-to-work, instead of bringing it up as a ballot issue."

In Tacoma, Reno Odlin, a wonderful Republican fund-raiser, stood up in the meeting and said, "I'm going to give back the checks that are in my pocket." So I was flush with success. But I scheduled a meeting in Spokane and ran into a buzz saw. They were very conservative and weren't in the real world at all. So the initiative went on the ballot, and, of course, it lost and cost us some more seats. It was altogether a sad story.

In 1960 Eisenhower could not run again, and Nixon had captured the public fancy at that point. He was traveling everywhere and making speeches. He was a very difficult man, but otherwise quite popular. At the Chicago nominating convention, I was by this time on Nixon's committee representing the Northwestern states. I was sitting with the national Republican chairman, Leonard Hall. Everyone was wondering where Nixon was. It was an evening meeting, and we were all having a drink and relaxing, but where was Nixon?

Suddenly Hall got a phone call from Nixon. He said, "I'm in New York City in Nelson Rockefeller's apartment." Nixon was making a deal with Rockefeller to get his support and the support of the New England states. At issue were education, housing and jobs for minorities, mainly black people, that the New Englanders were insisting upon for the platform. I was on the platform committee. The southerners, who were Taft-type people, had spurned all of these suggestions and Nixon said he would not run unless he could get this platform changed. So each one of us on the platform committee, who happened to be also members of the national finance committee, was assigned three people from the south or middle states, with the missions to change their minds and change the platform to reflect Nixon's demands.

I was completely unsuccessful with two of my three. The third one I managed to swing toward some of Mr. Rockefeller's ideas. It was a bitter battle, but the platform was re-opened and changed. Nixon came on and was nominated. President Eisenhower would not support him. He didn't say anything bad about him, but he would not say anything good for him. We were told not to say anything about this. It was certainly some convention.

In the fall of that year, Annie and I were invited to dinner at the White House with the Eisenhowers. Their guests were President and Mrs. Marcos from the Philippines. We left Seattle with our dinner clothes and flew to Washington, D.C. Again we stayed with my sister. Annie said she had only brought a short dinner dress and she was a bit worried about it. My dinner date was to be Mrs. Arthur Summerfield, the postmaster general's wife. She volunteered to call Pat Nixon and find out what Pat was going to wear. Pat said she was going to wear a short dinner dress.

Kay's butler-chauffeur-head gardener, Jesse, put on his chauffeur's hat and drove us through the White House gates. At the dinner, Mrs. Summerfield was on my right. On my left was a very distinguished lady who was the dinner partner of Secretary of

State, John Foster Dulles. When I had an opportunity to ask him a question. I said, "What are the basic ingredients of democracy, which we are trying to spread around the world?" He said, "The first one is Christianity. They should be Christians, and then they should be educated." Well, of course, these were two things that all kinds of people weren't.

I found my experience in politics sometimes exhilarating and challenging, but quite often frustrating, and in later years I have left the grassroots work largely to others.

Bellingham Public Schools

ADMINISTRATIVE OFFICES: ROEDER SCHOOL BUILDING
DUPONT AND I STREETS
P. O. BOX 878
BELLINGHAM, WASHINGTON 98225

GORDON L. CARTER
SUPERINTENDENT
HARLAN W. JACKSON
ASSISTANT SUPERINTENDENT
DR RICHARD L. GREEN
ASSISTANT SUPERINTENDENT
VANCE H. CLARK
BUSINESS MANAGER AND
SCHOOL BOARD SECRETARY

LESTER F. FELDMANN
COORDINATOR SPECIAL SERVICES
EDGAR A. DOLL, Ph. D.
GERALDINE L. DOLL, Ph. D.
CONSULTING PSYCHOLOGISTS
BRUCE HOWELL
THOMAS R. FUNK
SCHOOL PSYCHOLOGISTS

April 24, 1968

Mr. John Hauberg
1828 Washington Building
Seattle, Washington

Dear Mr. Hauberg:

Following is a resume of our discussion, as I recall it, regarding Sue which took place at the time of your visit here on April 18.

1. We reviewed the desirability of working out a systematic transition for Sue from her graduation at Devereux School to a life situation. This transition should afford her as much satisfaction and as large a future as possible. It should not be a pocket placement but rather an opportunity for the fullest possible expression and enjoyment of her capabilities.

2. Such a placement might very well include a job analysis of what lies ahead, namely, a systematic programming of occupational possibilities. I am thinking of this as involving a horse ranch with many different avenues for operation, such as breeding, training, perhaps wrangling, dude ranching, rodeo riding, breaking and training of new stock and all the opportunities that a horse ranch could offer.

3. One thought here is that perhaps we could obtain the services of Joe and Jane Smith as managers of such a ranch. You may remember him as the business manager at Devereux School. He is an outdoor man of many talents, she is an unusual person from the standpoint of companionship and chapøaronage. If their services could be available, I think this would be highly satisfactory. A place itself might be found in such a general neighborhoos as Tucson, the Tetons, Albuquerque, or Phoenix, so that Sue would not be fenced in but would have ample opportunity to enjoy life and earn an independent living. This plan would set her up as relatively independent of home without actually separating her from home.

The above ideas can be expanded in detail. At first it would be desirable to have as much time as possible on such a ranch with a routine tie-in with Devereux School. It would be important to be continuously on the alert for a stable program. As periods of poor adjustment develop she could be returned to Devereux for re-adjustment, the presumption being that the periods of independence would gradually be increased while the returns to Devereux would gradually be decreased. Companionship might be provided for her through individual friendships or through dude guests.

It is a little difficult to set this forth in precise detail but the general plan seems feasible. It would be of the utmost importance to have the right people in charge. Both Mr. and Mrs. Smith satisfy these requirements. Beyond that, a working relationship with Devereux could be continuously maintained.

I think we should move as soon as feasible on such a program so that when Sue graduates a month from now, we are prepared to move into the next phase of her development. It would be desirable to collaborate with the people at Devereux as soon as feasible with a view to having everything set at the time Sue graduates. After that we would make accomodations to circumstances from time to time as they develop.

A copy of this letter is being sent to Dr. Ferguson and the people at Devereux for their consideration as to specifics. I think it would be desirable to confer with Devereux as soon as some definite plan is developed. Of course, the actual location of a ranch for Sue would be a major undertaking. We would also need to determine the character of the facilities, the nature of the animals to be bred, and the extent of services to be offered, and so on.

Cordially,

Edgar A. Doll

Edgar A. Doll, Ph.D.
Consulting Psychologist

EAD/ef
cc: Dr. Ferguson

CHAPTER 23

Work for the Handicapped

WHEN OUR DAUGHTER SUE WAS BORN IN 1948, THE OBSTETRICIAN WAS IN DOUBT about her future. He called in a pediatrician right away, who announced that Sue would never walk or talk. I was crushed by this news, but my wife, Anne Gould Hauberg, said he was wrong, and she refused to accept it. Sue came home with us and was a wonderful baby.

In 1950, two years after Sue was born, we had a little boy, Mark, whose gray matter never developed. At the end of a very painful year, we found a foster home for him with Mr. and Mrs. Hart Ritz over in West Seattle. Hart was a janitor in the public schools and they had no children of their own. Hart and Ann Ritz were delighted to take care of Mark, which was very difficult. I think he really was in pain all of his short life. He died at the age of four and a half at Providence Hospital.

In 1953 Sue entered Helen Bush Pre-School for two years. Meanwhile at the University of Washington a very interesting educator, Eleanor Evans, had set up an experimental preschool in which the new concept of structuring was developed and employed. The school was marvelous. One of the teachers was a young woman named Myrene, who later married Walt McAninch. She was a most unusual person. She had three majors, one in psychology, one in child development, and another in education. She suggested that Sue come to live with her and her mother, Violet Kennedy, and her grandmother, Grandma Marsh.

Their house was near Roosevelt High School in the University District. Grandma Marsh was an old school, pioneer spirit, where everything was possible, nothing was impossible. She was going to see to it that Sue could speak and do arithmetic and all that sort of thing. Vi Kennedy provided the income for the family. I think she worked for an insurance company. Myrene was all fired up with her new charge, and of course we were supremely happy to have such intelligent, energetic people surrounding Sue. This was in the summer of 1955, I believe, and Sue lived with them for several years.

The Pilot School

By 1960 we became very involved in special education for children who had problems far worse than Sue's. That was the beginning of my work in developing organizations that would involve handicapped people throughout their lives. The first organization was called the Pilot School. Sue had attended Bush Pre-School for two or three years and did very well, but we wanted to explore further the concept of structuring. Many children with IQs of 85 to 100 had lots of potential, but they had a hard time developing the thought processes leading to intelligent conclusions. Structuring began with such concepts as hot and cold, day and night, various types of weather—rain, sleet, snow. Myrene was a top person in this field. After Sue's experience at Bush, I thought it would be a good idea to start a school with Myrene as the head of it. I bought a house at the corner of 10th Avenue North and Aloha. Myrene was to be the headmistress. She recruited a faculty and student body.

At that point my accountants said, "John, you need a board of trustees so you can get the school set up as a 501(C)(3) organization and make tax-deductible contributions to it." I knew only one person I thought was strong enough in the field of children's health and education for children to advise me, and that was Dr. Jack Docter, who was the chief of staff at Children's Orthopedic Hospital (COH) and a friend from Bainbridge Island. I asked him if he could come up with the names of some people who might serve on the board. I thought it would be good to call it the Pilot School so the kids would think of it in terms of piloting airplanes or ferryboats. It didn't occur to me that it was a pilot project, but of course that's what it was.

Jack Docter suggested Dr. Tim Chapman from his own staff at COH, and several people from the UW. I invited them all to lunch at the Harbor Club to discuss the school's board and structure, and to invite them to be on the board. Those people became associates of mine for a long time. Dr. Charles Strother was eventually to be the head of the new school and Dr. Alice Hayden his right hand. There was Dr. Bob Aldrich, an opera lover, who went on to become head of the National Institute of Health's child education division, Dr. Robert Deisher, Dr. Sidney Bijou, a speech and hearing person, and Dr. Norris Haring, in special education. During lunch I told them I had chosen the house at 10th Avenue North and Aloha because it was so easy to get to from the UW. I wanted a very close connection between the school and the various departments at the UW that pertained to such a school—for example, the education department, department of pediatrics, and the school of nursing.

They all thought it was a great idea, but suggested that the location wasn't as convenient as I had thought, because many students on campus would need a car to get there. The next morning I received a call from one of them. He said they had talked this over with Dr. George Aagaard, new head of the medical school at the UW, and he would like to discuss it with me. I had one of the most delightful conversations with him, because of his enthusiasm for the concept of the school. He had done a lot of thinking about it since he had been approached and said the UW had just acquired two little residences, each with a yard, on Brooklyn Avenue, south of 42nd Street and on the southwest fringe of the campus. They would like me to sell the house on Aloha and contribute the proceeds to setting up the new Pilot School in those two houses.

Annie and I were thrilled. We were living at 1101 McGilvra Boulevard, and it was very easy for us to get to the campus. Myrene then became a member of the faculty, which was headed up by Dr. Charles Strother. All the ideas I had for getting something started in this direction came true with a bang. The Pilot School carried Sue through to about sixth grade, so this would have been about 1959 or 1960.

Sue thrived in this school. I was interested in getting children started in their early years. The Pilot School by 1962 ran out of program for her. Later it was folded into the Child Development and Mental Retardation Center (CDMRC), another project that came to a successful conclusion at the UW, which I will discuss later in this chapter.

I had heard about the quality of the Devereux Foundation, which had a unit near Santa Barbara. In 1962 when Annie was undergoing treatment at the Pennsylvania Institute in Philadelphia, it was time to get Sue into a new school. Sue and I went down to Devereux and found it very attractive. They liked Sue and Sue and I liked them so she was enrolled. They had horses, which was a big plus as far as Sue was concerned. She was there through her high school years, and received, in 1968, a State of California high school diploma upon graduation from Devereux.

Sue was clearly above any of the students at Devereux in her abilities, and the staff realized that she was just a slow normal child. They put her to work in a very interesting way. There were several children from the state of Washington there. There were the Huffine twins from Olympia, the sons

Above: Pilot School house, another house next door;
Below: Sue, Myrene McAninch, and another student

of wonderful parents, Sherman and Noochie Huffine. Noochie was a Schmidt of the Olympia beer company, and Sherman was its attorney. He was a very outgoing person. Even though his sons were handicapped, one of them played the piano by ear and could play anything if you hummed the tune to him. The other was a little more involved, but neither one of them could live independently. The Huffines became lifetime friends of ours. The two boys always telephone Sue when they come up here for Christmas vacation.

Devereux had Sue shepherd these four or five young people from Santa Barbara airport to Seattle via either Los Angeles or San Francisco airports, taking them through whichever airport for the final flight to Seattle. She never missed a flight. Sue has always been a good traveler and knows exactly how to order tickets, make necessary reservations, etc.

Annie and I were very encouraged by her experiences and schooling at Devereux. We were thrilled when she received a California High School diploma. We went to the ceremony taking Granny Gould and Myrene with us. Now it was time for Sue to come home and learn more about working and the world. (See Chapter 30 for photos.)

Since she had fallen in love with Arab horses already, we looked for an Arab farm and found a Mrs. Wayne Moore on an eighty-acre place near Arlington, Washington, with more than a dozen friendly young Arab horses which ran up to greet us when we came up to their pasture fences. Sue spent two years there, during which her own Arab horse farm east of Stanwood was being built and finished in 1971.

Meanwhile, I had had a concept of a vocational training center for handicapped young men and women in their early twenties to teach them how to live and work in a community. Back in 1958, Dr. Temple Fay (Uncle Bunty to all Fays) had told me about a man and wife, both Ph.D.s, who left Philadelphia because so many people wanted their counsel for their handicapped children that they could not carry on research. The Doctors Doll lived on a little ranch just south of Bellingham. They enrolled Bellingham School District children physically, mentally, and emotionally handicapped, in their program—more simply defined, perhaps, as learning by working, both alone and in groups. Bellingham had acquired two Ph.D.s for very little salary.

Dr. Doll's letter of April 1968 also mentioned "a systematic programming of occupational possibilities." His students, both boys and girls, built small structures, learning to use tools and materials. If mistakes were made, the structure falling down, or material unraveling, well, the kids just did it over again.

I thought of young people from all over, even out of state, coming to a residential vocational program, living and working together, learning to use the bus, the laundromats, the civic facilities such as swimming pools, etc. Also to show up at work on time and get along with people.

Mrs. Moore's ranch near Arlington 1969–70   *Annie, Sue, Dr. Edgar Doll*

The tree farm owned a sixty-acre tract, which had an old house, an orchard, a dairy barn, and plenty of room for dormitories, a mess hall and offices, pastures, strawberry beds, etc. This all seemed just right for my vision. I created a board of trustees for Victoria Ranch and we set off into the never-never land of leadership, funding, tuition, recruiting. And pleasing parents.

A brochure announced our intentions. We struggled for ten years, more or less, before throwing in the towel. But many wonderful people worked hard together. I realized that Devereux succeeds because of a big endowment, a national reputation, and wealthy parents living all over the U.S.A. The following is how we began Victoria Ranch.

The new board heard about a young man named Chuck Wrobel, a public school special education teacher. He and his wife moved into the old house. We enrolled five boys who lived downstairs with the Wrobels, and four girls who lived upstairs. It was kind of a primitive operation, but they got the old dairy barn dunged out and made it a place where they could be indoors when it rained. There was an open loafing shed for the cattle. For a while the program of growing things and making things was very successful. We graduated quite a few kids to Mount Vernon and Everett, who lived mostly in boarding houses operated for handicapped persons and worked in those cities in modest jobs, but arriving on time, doing the work, getting along with the boss and fellow workers. The theory was sound.

We had the benefit of the interest of Dorothy Bennett, who was the Snohomish County School Superintendent. The city of Edmonds in this county already had a good school program for the handicapped. Dorothy had learned much from that. She and our board thought our residential program might serve the rest of the county. Hazel Verables was a stalwart board member who took charge of a one-room school-

Sue Hauberg and friends

house for the retarded east of Mt. Vernon in Skagit County and Sue worked for her. So there was a ferment of ideas and activities. Sue had learned to drive, a terrific accomplishment that enabled her to do all sorts of things. Her interest in horses grew to become greater than working in Hazel's school.

Chuck Wrobel very quickly moved on to Minneapolis to accept responsibility for vocational rehabilitation in its schools. He later became head of special education for all Minnesota schools. We outgrew the house. It became obvious that we had to build some buildings, and had to have a larger student body to justify the expense. The board had trouble raising the money. Hardly anybody in that area knew anything about giving or getting. Somehow you have to learn these things in big cities where giving and getting was customary and accepted. We hired an architect, and pretty soon we had two dormitories suitable for twelve boys in one and twelve girls in the other.

Each member had an individual bedroom, with bathrooms down the hall. We began to reach out to get a more powerful administrator. We went through several of them. It was always a financial struggle to balance tuition and subsidy. At one point Victoria Village had graduates working as baggage handlers at Sea-Tac Airport, and also working in the restaurant there. The school had a turnover as people learned and then left. There was no dearth of young men and women who needed our program. But, again, few could pay full tuition.

Long after I had stopped being the president of the board or even a board member, Victoria Ranch developed greenhouses, berry patches, an orchard, and they had a dining room and kitchen attached to the administration building. All of these young people had something to do. But the program was simply too expensive for the funds available.

We tried to interest the Department of Institutions, now known as Department of Social and Health Services (DSHS) which gave us a pitiful amount of money because we were an addition to its already strained budget. And the Snohomish County Schools were similarly strapped. Perhaps it was the residential feature that brought the program down. But we had to give it up. The buildings were purchased by an organization called Chrysalis. They tried for five or six years to make a go of it, funded by as much in contributions as they could get and the DSHS, and they just couldn't do it. They fell into financial problems. We started it around 1970, so seventeen years later they were still looking at the impossibility of raising enough money from public sources. It has been closed now for several years, and the property sold.

Origins of the Child Development and Mental Retardation Center: Victoria Village

Between the Pilot School and Victoria Ranch came the establishment of the Child Development and Mental Retardation Center at the University of Washington. Washington governor, Arthur Langley, had appointed a Governor's Advisory Committee on Mental Retardation in the 1950's. Jack Docter, chief of staff of Children's Orthopedic Hospital was on it. A man named Van Hinkle, the Director of Child Development for the State of Washington, staffed the committee. On the committee were Drs. Deisher, Aldrich, and Dr. Bob Hunter from Sedro-Woolley, who was at that moment head of the state medical society. They had looked at the whole problem of mental retardation in the state and concluded that there had to be a training center for all kinds of disciplines involving research into brain damage and including a special education training department. The advisory

Victoria Village

committee had published a pamphlet titled "Everybody's Child," in which the principal recommendation was that such a center be established at the University of Washington.

About that time Jack Kennedy was elected president. His oldest sister was retarded and his family was very interested in the whole problem. In late 1962, the Kennedys got Congress to pass a "Mental Retardation Research Facilities" act, which called for six centers, two in the East, two in the Midwest, and two on the West Coast, funded from a total $50 million federal grant. Each institution would presumably get one sixth of that and would set up research programs in a university medical school. Our state was ready for this, but it caught the other states unprepared. We decided to go for it. The facilities cost $10 or $11 million. The federal government was going to put up all but about $3 million of that. That $3 million had to come from the state as part of the state's support of the University of Washington's building funds.

The University had a problem, however. In November 1962, the state legislative committees that had oversight over budgets had already put a limit on the amount of new construction funds the legislature would give to the University of Washington for the 1963–1965 period. In other words, the building fund had been "put to bed" and the UW lobbyists were very reluctant to try for more through their own lobbying. They felt it would be much more suitable for an outsider to do the lobbying for the $2.5 million, completely separate from the building fund which had been settled in November 1962.

I was still the Republican state finance chairman in 1962 and I knew people of both parties all over the state so I volunteered to lobby for the special extra $2.5 million from the state of Washington's 1963-1964 budget toward the facilities to be at the UW. To start with, I donated $250,000 to the UW on behalf of this new center for mental retardation. I lived in Olympia for all of January, February and March 1963. I moved in with UW lobbyists Fred Thieme and Bob Waldo at the Olympia Hotel in Olympia and began to buttonhole all the legislators. I could sense the reluctance of the legislators, and particularly the ones from Eastern Washington, a region that traditionally has a deep resentment of the UW, its size, its importance, and the amount of money it had to have every biennium to stay alive and improve.

Part of the lobbying for the CDMRC involved getting the support of all of the daily newspapers in the state of Washington. I organized a three-man committee to head up this lobbying effort. It consisted of Fred Haley, of Brown & Haley Candy Company in Tacoma, a leading Democrat and intellectual in the state of Washington, Lou Thrailkill of Spokane, who was vice-president of Washington Water Power, and myself. Fred and I toured all nineteen Washington cities that boasted local daily newspapers. I wrote an editorial just as a guide to what I presumed the editors would rewrite. All nineteen papers were impressed with Mr. Haley and Mr. Thrailkill being on the committee. None of them had ever heard of me, but they all ran my editorial verbatim. Even though I thought it was pretty well written, I was a trifle disappointed in the editors; prior to that I had always believed they wrote their own editorials.

I learned the names of every single legislator and senator and their wives. I took them to dinner, bought them martinis, and shared the exhaustion of the legislators as they fought each other day after day in the capitol building and recreated at night in such places as the Oregon Trail, a nightclub south of Olympia. Many evenings were spent at the Oregon Trail dancing away our blues. I always was out there buying my new friends a drink and dancing with their wives so I got to be one of them. I loved it. Gradually the sentiment toward the University's bid for this unusual facility began to get through to them. The center was to get its operating budget from the National Institute of Health. Finally the legislature agreed to a joint session of the senate and house to discuss the bill and pass it. I knew by this time that it would succeed, but we didn't take anything for granted.

Dr. Charles Strother of the UW, who was the director of the Pilot School and was well known to people with handicapped children all over the state, got something like three thousand people headed for Olympia for this joint session, to sit in the galleries and cheer for the passage of this bill. I had to get to the governor, and, of course, he was a Democrat—Albert Rosellini, a very nice guy. I had never met him and couldn't quite figure how I would get in because of my official Republican position.

One night we all were gathered at the Oregon Trail and it was getting toward the end of the session. People were tired, we were dancing, and the music was playing. It was about one in the morning. One of the wives said to me, "I bet you can't dance that lady over there off her feet." I said, "I can only try." Nobody told me who she was. I asked her to dance, and said, "I noticed that you are such a good dancer." She said her name was Marge Gunderson. We danced, and we danced, and we danced until finally she said, "I think I'd like to sit down." So I came back rather triumphantly to my table, and we all laughed and went home.

I felt that I just had to see the governor the next morning. About 11:00 a.m. I went to his office. The outer office was absolutely full of people, maybe forty or fifty, waiting to see Governor Rosellini. I went up to the reception desk, and lo and behold, the commander of the reception desk was Marge Gunderson. I said, "I want to get in to see the governor." She said, "John, you're next." So I went in and began to talk to about this thing. He quickly said, "I've watched the progress of the bill and I know about you and your contribution to the University. The bill is going to pass and I'm going to sign it." I thought that was just wonderful.

Governor Albert Rosellini signing the bill authorizing $2.5 million for the University of Washington toward construction of the Child Development and Mental Retardation Center. March 21, 1963. Back row: Lou Thrailkill, left, and the two tall men in the row, John H. Hauberg, and Fred Haley, with legislators. Front: Marjorie Lynch, legislator, with Governor Rosellini. Missing but so important: Dr. Charles Strother.

I said, "Well, Governor, we're going to have a dinner in April celebrating the victory of the bill, and you've got to be there." He said he was looking forward to a vacation away from all this. I said "I've already talked to President Kennedy's sister, Eunice Shriver, and she's coming out to make the major address at our victory dinner. As governor you are the top person to greet such distinguished company." "Okay," he said, "I'll be there." The bill passed unanimously in both house and senate, the governor signed it in the presence of Democrats and Republicans, and so the UW had its $2.5 to $3 million toward building the facility as well as annual federal funding for operations. It was one of the greatest experiences of my life.

It bothered Annie that I had to be away from home for so long, but she knew it was necessary and for a good cause.

The bill passed in March 1963. The victory dinner with Eunice Schriver was in April at the Edmond Meany Hotel. The governor was there and by this time we had become good friends. Today whenever I run into Al Rosellini, we talk about the CDMRC, and he says, "It was the crowning achievement of my administration."

The new University of Washington's Child Development and Mental Retardation Center was planning on two buildings, including one for medical research into the causes of mental retardation. The other was to be a school for researching the education problems, an actual school for children called the Experimental Education Unit (EEU). It took a couple of years before the architects and the UW could get all this together. Annie was particularly interested in having good architecture for the EEU. She made a donation so that artists could design something in brick for the outside of the building, and that was a wonderful contribution.

There was a double groundbreaking ceremony. Doctor Strother and I were photographed, each of us with a foot on the spade as we dug up the first shovelful of earth for the building. That picture never saw the light of day because Senator Magnuson showed up and took full responsibility for getting the national congress to pass this bill, which he probably had. He and Dr. Odegaard, president of the UW, also were photographed each with a foot on a shovel, so that was the picture that got printed.

The bill for CDMRC called for a citizens' advisory committee, and I was, of course, named its chairman. The committee never met. The UW is a monolithic organization that doesn't brook much advice from outside the academic ranks. After the buildings had been completed, I went out there twice to see about calling a meeting of the advisory committee and got brushed off. Nevertheless I was very close to the EEU. It was headed up by Dr. Norris Haring, with whom I have been friends ever since. Dr. Alice Hayden and Drs. Strother, Aldrich, Deisher and Bijou all taught there. I lunched with them all at the University of Washington Faculty Club many times in the ensuing years.

Very shortly I began to hear from parents whose children had been at the EEU. They wrote me letters of appreciation for what I had helped to create.

The Foundation for Handicapped Children later called Lifetime Advocacy Plus

Van Hinkle, the State Director of Child Development, and I became great friends, and that led to many subsequent activities, such as the beginning of the Foundation for Handicapped Children (FHC), in about 1963. Its purpose was to provide guardianship care for handicapped children after their parents had died. This was an obvious extension of programs for early schooling and the work of Victoria Ranch in teaching the handicapped to live independently. Ralph Munro, the secretary of state (of Washington) and an old friend, was of great help in getting the FHC started.

So we started on a statewide basis. We had marvelous people from Spokane, Ellensburg, Yakima, Walla Walla, and up and down the west side of the state. I was elected president. We had a board and we set about raising some money. We did not own a building, but rented space.

This again became a terrible struggle to raise money to provide active guardianship personnel. We did not propose to get any money out of DSHS, since we knew how little the state legislature gave them to do what they were already supposed to do. So how do you get parents to write into their wills leaving funds to the foundation to take care of their children? The idea was that if the child was living independently or with a relative, using funds which had been donated by the family, a supervisory person would call on them regularly to find out what their needs were—if they'd been to the dentist recently, were they getting good food, did the apartment manager provide enough heat, were they being harassed by anybody, did they have friends? Our people were to make these calls about once every six weeks. A caseworker for the foundation saw about thirty people on a regular basis. We started out with two or three caseworkers, and today it has thirty or forty caseworkers all over the state. I am honorary chairman of the board, which is statewide. Today the organization is called Lifetime Advocacy Plus (LA Plus). It is struggling, but I think it's here to stay. Around six hundred people are being cared for by the Foundation and it is doing very good work.

There are good and bad things to say about divorce, and also about abortion. When you work with retarded people as much as I have, you find that when a retarded child is born, particularly if it is a boy, a divorce takes place in more than half the families. If the child is a girl, then it's up to the mother, and the dad often feels that if the mother wants to keep the child, that's her responsibility. I became an advocate of mandatory fetal inspection. If a fetus were defective, a doctor could recommend an abortion.

Once the family of a handicapped child can no longer provide the services he or she needs, it falls on the community. It costs the public at least $100,000 a year to maintain a retarded child.

When I see how well my daughter Sue is doing with her life today, I feel a great sense of gratitude to those who helped to guide her through her early years, including her mother and Myrene McAninch and her family, members of the medical profession who offered guidance, and all the gifted educators who were able to teach to her strengths. I am also grateful to the legislators and to Governor Rosellini, who listened to our campaign to obtain a proper education for handicapped children.

The key word in all these programs is "funding." Without such support none of them succeeds and lasts beyond initial years of enthusiasm and optimism. I am enthusiastic and optimistic and now know what I should have done to begin with, researched the funding basis for each program. Needs are obvious. The ability to pay for services is limited. Public funding is at best shaky because it must come from state, county, or city institutions where every dollar in their budget requests is fought over by the legislature, county and city councils, etc. Adequate funding from tuition never reaches its goal. And annual drives for charitable contributions are almost impossible for small groups. The Devereux School depends on the big Devereux Foundation; the CDMRC required and received support from the National Institutes of Health.

But it seemed to me that I had to do something. And the parents and teachers I worked with were wonderful, many of them friends for all my life.

*The "Box of Daylight" hat is quite old, depicting Raven holding
the box in his flight back to "the people on the beach in darkness."
Now in the Seattle Art Museum.*
© *The Seattle Art Museum, Gift of John H. Hauberg*

CHAPTER 24

Collections

LIKE LOTS OF BOYS I COLLECTED STAMPS FROM AN EARLY AGE. MISS ROSS, GOVERNESS TO sister Catherine and me and nurse to Mother, bought me a simple stamp album for worldwide stamps and I began to learn about where all those countries were. Since Great Britain dominated a huge chunk of the world, it seemed that most stamps were red or pink and had King George V's portrait on them. Mother and Dad brought home stamps from their trips to Egypt and the Holy Land in 1924 for my benefit. Then came the whole family's visit to Europe including England, Finland, Germany and France. The album was getting full. Little stickers held the stamps in place so that one could remove them for trading or to replace with a better sample. At Hotchkiss in 1931 and 1932 I was buying stamps for a special British West Indies album. *Lots* of King George V! By age eighteen I realized that I could spend a fortune on stamps and never come close to collecting them all. So I quit.

But my knowledge of geography had increased dramatically. I knew where Swaziland was, and Kuwait and the Cameroons. All very useful, no doubt. One of my best friends at Hotchkiss was Harry Whitin of Whitinsville, Massachusetts. I don't remember him as a stamp collector, but when he died in 1997 his obituary in the New York Times proclaimed him one of America's greatest philatelists! I visualized him immersed in stamps and albums and was sorry for him. I had long ago sold all my albums to a Seattle dealer for quite a tidy sum which probably was spent on the beginnings of a new collection of something or other.

Annie and I drove to Tucson in 1946 to visit Granny Fay to see about bringing her to Seattle. There, and en route, we began an interest in contemporary Navajo rugs and pottery, and Hopi and Zuni jewelry. They were the roots that branched into Pre-Columbian art and Northwest Coast Indian objects.

But first, I had to go back to college for a degree in forestry, and we had to buy and furnish our house at 1031 McGilvra Boulevard. Annie took care of the interiors, including a new dining room bay window with a sculpture by Everett Du Pen in the garden outside to look at. I believe this was the first work we ever commissioned.

We were ready to acquire some craftwork to go beyond the polar-bear rug we had brought west with us from the House-in-the-Woods in Rock Island County. We couldn't do much because I was busy in school, Annie was busy taking care of Granny Fay who had come to live with us and was bedridden. But we did buy some driftwood sculptures by Guy Anderson. We had made a start and in 1949, following my University of Washington graduation, we, along with sister Kay and Dad, drove east to Ward, Colorado, and Annie and I wound up in Arizona's Canyon de Chelly in the trading post there. The trader's vault was filled with beautiful Navajo objects, collateral for the loans he made to the Indians to buy breeding stock for their herds of sheep. We bought some lovely things that had been forfeited by the Indians unable to pay back the loans in dollars. So another "start" had been made.

I will make no effort to apply specific years in the 1950s, 1960s, and 1970s when we began trips to Mexico and to abandoned Haida, Tlingit, Tsimshian, and Kwakiutl (Kwakwaka'wakw) villages. In themselves, the trips did not result in purchased objects. But they stimulated a great interest on my part in the dramatic objects used by both Mexican and Northwest Coast cultures in their ceremonials and their burials.

One day we were in New York and went into Andre Emmerich's gallery to look at contemporary art. I had heard of his affiliation with several anthropologists in Mexico and asked him if he sold any pre-Columbian Art. A couple of hours later I found that I had bought $100,000 of his finest objects! I was "hooked!" I developed an important collection over the next years to about 1972. There were lovely Maya vases, bowls, and figurines. Many gold pieces from Panama and Costa Rica, and a very early, important Olmec (800-1200 BC) figure of a priest shaman turning himself into a jaguar to be able to converse with his jaguar gods. The priest's ears and nostrils had become feline, his hands were paws. All this meticulous "carving" had been done with abrasive sand on wet thumbs to create the modeling of shoulders, arms, legs, and back. A truly fabulous work acquired from a German collector by Andre Emmerich.

After a great trip in 1969 with Gillett Griffin of the Art Museum of Princeton University to the greatest of the then-known Mayan sites (abandoned villages!), I began to trade with another dealer, Ed Merrin, also in New York. He had a greater variety of objects, perhaps not quite as elegant as Andre's pieces. But Ed took

Maya vase, 600–900 A.D.

274

Top left: Ceramic burial figures, Jaina Island, Mexico, man & wife, 600–900 A.D.; top right: Maya vase, 600–900 A.D.; right: The Olmec were-jaguar

chances in purchasing from "the pirates" who bought from the Indian peasants looting tombs in the jungle not yet known to archeologists. I came to New York with Annie almost every year in November to shop, see plays, visit galleries and see friends. One of these trips produced a visit to Ed Merrin's gallery. He had a small Maya stela, the like of which no scholars had seen at the time. Ed was very nervous about the authenticity of the work. But Gillett had taken his Friends of the Princeton Art Museum to a remote site in southern Guatemala near the Pacific Ocean. There we saw huge stones carved with twining tree branches and leaves. Chiefs looked more human than classic Maya,

Toltec, or Aztec kings. I thought that Ed Merrin's little stela was authentic and early. I bought it for $30,000. In 1999 Sotheby appraised it at $2 million!

In 1969 the New York Metropolitan Art Museum celebrated its 100th birthday with six major exhibitions. One of them was "Before Cortes." And I was asked to loan the little "were-jaguar" figure of the priest (or shaman) transforming himself into a jaguar and the Maya stela. I attended the conference of scholars, archeologists, and collectors a few days before the show opened to the public. The Met put me up with the great Maya scholar, Sir Eric S. Thompson, in a hotel room across Fifth Avenue from the museum. He was certain the stela was authentic. The conferees said my two works were the hits of the show.

Linda Schele, a University of Texas scholar, and one of three chosen by the National Science Foundation to "crack" the Maya hieroglyphic writing, chose my stela for her Ph.D. thesis. It was a brilliant analysis of subject matter. The date of 197 A.D. caused scholars to push back the period of "Classic" Maya to a "Proto-Classic" period of 100–500 A.D. maintaining "Classic" for 500–900 A.D. Linda later included the Hauberg stela in the "Blood of Kings" exhibition at the Kimbell Art Museum in Fort Worth in 1986.

I later sold the were-jaguar figure to the Dumbarton Oaks collection in Washington, D.C., feeling that it belonged among the greatest, most elegant pre-Columbian pieces in the U.S.A. The Maya stela will go to the Princeton University Museum by bequest to be among its peers brought together by Gillett Griffin.

Maya (Hauberg) stela, 197 A.D. Now at the Princeton University Museum

The stone in the jungle at El Baul, uncovered by Professor Ed Shook of Harvard. Memories of this carving convinced JHH that Ed Merrin's Maya stela was authentic.

In 1972 the U.S. Congress passed an act making it very difficult to import "national treasures" of other countries. That meant that the finest ancient treasures would remain in the countries of their origin, a good act, I felt, but the end of collecting pre-Columbian art for me. That act later led to "repatriation" legislation, but I don't believe any other countries went that far. This new act, passed in the 1990s, was to affect my next interest in Pacific Northwest Coast Indian art.

I have never been interested in the numbers of items in any of my collections. The excitement of owning rare, beautiful objects is enough. It is exciting to discover that what you already may have owned for many years has a history of its own. And when this happens, then you suspect that many of your other treasures might tell fascinating stories if only they could speak. The greater the beauty of an object, the greater the chance of this being true. For the same reasons, the rareness of a beautiful work bespeaks the probability of a previous high-ranking ownership.

While the great pre-Columbian kings of fifteen hundred to a thousand years ago had sarcophagi of heavy stone at the base of tall pyramids and many objects of gold and jade buried with them, the aristocracy kept hundreds of artists busy too. They had their own burial areas as well. Thus there was a great variety of objects for household worship, personal adornment, and burials. Such made up the bulk of my pre-Columbian collection. They are handsome, made of all sorts of material, such as clay, flint, obsidian, stone, gold, silver. Even a few wooden things and cloth weavings have survived. Each culture had its own shapes and patterns of adornment. It was just great fun to follow the dates and the areas of origins as the collection grew. Although I tried to specialize in Maya and Olmec cultures, I had objects from Peru, Ecuador, Bolivia, Colombia, and Panama as well.

This collecting excitement was enhanced for me, in both my major collections, by visiting the places where these mysterious, beautiful objects were made and used. My wife and I made a half dozen or more trips to Mexico, Guatemala, Colombia, Bolivia, Ecuador, and Peru. We met scholars and collectors, and went to see the museums. Once we met the president of Peru and once the president of Guatemala. These trips were arranged by the American Federation of Art to which we belonged and of which I was a trustee for twelve years, again a group of collectors of all kinds of art.

A few pictures of some of my favorite pre-Columbian figures will suffice to define the scope of the collection.

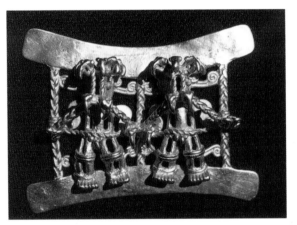

Gold brooches, Panama, 600–900 A.D.

Pacific Northwest Coast Indian Art

I have always believed that the greatest art of any culture is produced for its most important royal, imperial, priestly, and tribal ceremonies. The greater the scope and power of an empire, a region, or a faith, the greater the need for fabulous trappings that elevate the rulers or priests above the ordinary. While bishops and cardinals can afford silver and gold, and later fine paintings, only a pope can create a Sistine Chapel, a St. Peter's Basilica. The same with the kings and emperors of France and Spain. The same with Maya kings and Inca rulers. The same for the chiefs of the Haida, Tlingit, and Kwakiutl (Kwakwaka'wakw) villages.

The Pacific Northwest Coast was not as isolated as self-centered Europeans believed. The Europeans had big ships driven by the wind. The Indians of the Pacific Northwest Coast had big canoes powered by the muscles of men, and that limited the scope of their travel. But long before Captain Cook arrived offshore in 1778 at Nootka Sound, there had been trade with tribes as far south as California. The Haidas canoed to trading centers such as the Dalles on the Columbia River. The Fraser River was a trade route for Coast Indians to trade with the Plains Indians.

Our "Indians," now more sensibly called "Native Americans," call themselves, with pride, "the People." They were "here" long before the first European traders arrived

Chief Scow Potlatch House, poles by Arthur Shaughnessy. Now in the Seattle Art Museum. © The Seattle Art Museum, Gift of John H. Hauberg

in the late eighteenth century. How long before is currently (1999) a hugely debated question. The Bering Sea bridge theory puts the "people" as coming from Asia during two ice ages, the first eighteen thousand years ago, the second about seven to eight thousand years ago. The Indians themselves believe that their ancestors were created right where they are today—on the beach. Their creation beliefs parallel our creation beliefs written in Genesis, but in a different place. Just as white man's creation belief has for most people given way to a scientific evolution belief, so Native Americans are divided in belief today. Their legends survive in the stories of Raven who discovered "the people on the beach" and who soon "brought Daylight in a Box to them." And so they had light—sun, moon, and stars.

When Pat Baillargeon and John Robinson and I visited many of those beaches in the 1960s and 1970s, we could well believe that "the people" had been there a long time—at least for centuries. Those beaches were chosen with great care for many reasons. For food supply, shelter from the storms and possible enemies, for building materials, fresh water, and room for their houses. They were so beautiful it was hard to believe that the Indians had not been there forever.

I could go on about how white man's diseases decimated this population. Many villages had so few people left that a church and a school could no longer be supported. As Pat and John and

Top: The village (still very much alive and well) of Gwayasdums on Guilford Island not far from Alert Bay. It is the village of which Bill Scow is chief and from which the Seattle Art Museum's totem poles come. The village site is ancient with all the vital ingredients of a great beach, running fresh water, level ground for its houses, and protection from storms by the offshore islands. Bottom: Gwayasdums Village, circa 1900.

I float-planed to shore, only a totem pole or two peeked out from the spruce forest that had invaded from the rear. Moss covered the floors and the fire pits of great houses. Only a few big timbers remained to suggest the power of the architecture of the village. We found the paths that were behind the houses ringing the beach. The paths connected the people at one end of the beach to those at the other end. There were obviously sunny fields where, perhaps, the wash could be hung up to dry. But on to collecting their art.

Although my father had enough local Indian art to fill up a small museum in Rock Island, Illinois, I had not even bothered to go out to find arrowheads. *His* collection was good enough for me. I think my curiosity began in 1949 when Annie and I and my sister Kay visited Canyon de Chelly, putting up at Cosy McSparron's Thunderbird Inn which had four guest bedrooms attached to his trading post. Mrs. McSparron was encouraging the local Navajo weavers to return to the old native dyes and designs and get away from the popular garish Navajo blankets (rugs) of the time (the same for jewelry design and pottery). We were entranced with the results and made sizable purchases.

I was also getting acquainted with Professor Erna Gunther at the University of Washington, a good scholar and author and lecturer. She worked in a pavilion left over from the Alaska-Yukon-Pacific World's Fair of 1908 held on the University of Washington campus.

The collection had been encouraged by Judge Thomas Burke's family. There were hundreds of baskets, canoe paddles, some masks, and some fine totem poles. It was an anthropologist's collection with little deliberate attention to "art." One found stone axes and mortars and pestles, baskets to carry clams and oysters and berries and fish, fishing equipment, split cedar bark capes and room dividers, building tools, etc.

Professor Gunther told me one day that she had been offered the "Waters Collection" for ten thousand dollars, a very reasonable price. Phil Padelford and I went out to the campus to look at it and found it was a truly fine gathering of many objects not included in the University of Washington museum. Erna was appalled at the price and was about to turn it down with a letter of indignation. Phil and I raised the ten thousand dollars in a few days.

In gratitude, Erna let Phil and me each buy a small item for twenty-five dollars. I was offered a raven rattle, because Erna already had three or four of them. It was the first object in my Pacific Northwest Coast Indian collection.

I thought I could help the University buy other similar collections or just individual pieces. Erna told me she had turned down the great Rasmussen collection of five hundred terrific objects for twenty-five thousand dollars. I was again amazed that the University of Washington could not find the money. She replied that she hadn't dared to ask anyone there because it was "too much money." Soon I found out that Dr. Fuller had been offered this collection at the same time and price. Dr. Fuller said he did not have storage space for it. The Portland Art Museum was more *professional* about it and raised the money from a few friends. They later sold two or three of the five hundred objects and got their twenty-five thousand dollars back. It is a larger collection by more than twice the number of objects I gave to the Seattle Art Museum forty years later. I could hardly believe the Rasmussen collection could have slipped away from Seattle.

But this story illustrates the attitude of the white European-oriented people of the Pacific Northwest toward the perfectly acculturated native inhabitants. Although

The future collector of Pacific Northwest Coast Indian art invaded his father's collection of Sauk and Fox Indian artifacts at an early age.

Erna Gunther knew and appreciated their culture, she didn't think it was worth anything. Dr. Fuller would not even consider their art among his treasures, taking up valuable shelf space. He did have a few Pacific Northwest Coast Indian things, but I doubt if he ever looked at them. (It was not until the 1960s that there was a first showing of Pacific Northwest Coast Indian art curated by Bill Holm, whose knowledge and appreciation of this art vastly exceeded Dr. Gunther's).

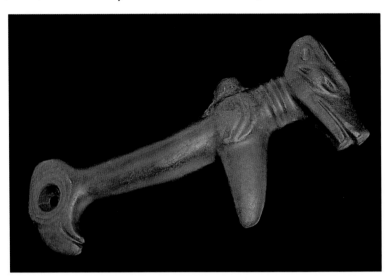

Left: The "Captain Cook" stone club. © The Seattle Art Museum, Gift of John H. Hauberg Facing page: Sarah Stone's sketch in 1778

After helping Dr. Gunther with the Waters Collection, I was in Victoria wandering up Government Street and saw eight great masks of the Hamatsa Society's initiation ceremony. They were offered at one hundred dollars apiece. I told Erna Gunther about them and this price. She did not hesitate to say that the price was ridiculous. I bought her a round trip ticket to Victoria, and she went to look at this treasure. She returned and reported that they were very good and that she would like to have them. So I bought them and gave them to the Burke Museum. I had nary a letter of thanks from her or any person at the University of Washington. A few more objects given with the same lack of response convinced me to buy for myself, and so my own collection began.

Annie and I were in New York one autumn day and wandering past the Sotheby auction house on Madison Avenue. I looked in the window of a gallery in that building and spotted some very small but elegant Northwest Indian artifacts. I went in and bought them and made the acquaintance of Mr. and Mrs. J. J. Klejman, dealers mostly in the classic works of Egypt, Assyria, Greece, and Rome. They visited England and France every year and bought treasures from old families in need of money to pay estate taxes. Many objects had been in these families for more than two hundred years. Wealthy aristocrats had supported the scientific voyages of Darwin and David Douglas of Douglas fir fame, and other explorers. J.

J. Klejman was the answer to their needs. And some of them had objects from North America's Pacific Northwest Coast. The Klejmans knew nothing about them, but did put a few in their gallery's window.

One time I went to New York and Mr. Klejman showed me a check from Nelson Rockefeller who had been in a week before my arrival and cleaned out all the Pacific Northwest Coast Indian things. This happened several times and was discouraging. Some years later, Rockefeller told me that Klejman had showed him my checks. In the long run, I won this little race as Rockefeller's interest changed.

Klejman had brought back an unusual looking stone club which he accurately ascribed to the Pacific Northwest Coast. Its style and appearance proclaimed its age, at least well before 1800. The Englishman who sold it said it had been in his family for more than two hundred years and called it a "slave killer club." This was plausible since even in the 1850s Indian chiefs were supposed to have killed a slave during a potlatch to impress guest chiefs of their host's wealth. There was also the "cannibal society" among the Kwakiutl (Kwakwaka'wakw) to back up the belief. The stone club was inexpensive and I was glad to have it.

Eight objects were loaned to the "Sacred Circles" exhibition put together by Ted Coe of the William Rockhill Nelson Gallery of Kansas City. Coe had gathered five hundred objects of native tribes all over the U.S. from dozens of collectors. The catalog was excellent. It was a great honor to be a lender to the show, which opened in London in 1976 and in Kansas City in 1977. I went along to the Kansas City opening banquets and was delighted to find myself assigned as escort to the rather flamboyant Duchess of Argyll, herself a lender to the show. Oh, the joys of collecting!

More on the Stone Club

Several years went by. One day Mr. Klejman phoned me in an audible state of excitement. In a rare bookshop in London a "Sketch Book of Sarah Stone" dated 178_ had been found. Miss Stone worshipped Captain James Cook who, like Charles Lindbergh in my generation, had been a hero in his own time. She had asked Mrs. Cook if she could sketch all the objects Captain Cook's crew had brought back from the captain's last voyage from 1776-1779 and delivered to her. Permission granted. And among the objects sketched was my club! So Captain Cook had collected my stone club in Nootka Sound in 1778! Perhaps it was a gift to him from one of the two major chiefs in the area, Wickaninish or Maquinna.

Of course, the club was old when it came on board the "Discovery," so its origin could easily date before 1700.

I acquired, through dealer Mike Johnson, an almost complete set of masks, rattles, and cedar bark withes for the Hamatsa (cannibal) Society's initiation ceremony, about thirty-five pieces in all. The major masks were the work of Willie Seaweed and Mungo Martin, both still alive, and recognized, with Arthur Shaughnessy, as the outstanding carvers of this century among the Kwakiutl (Kwakwaka'wakw) nation. It was a real coup. Without really knowing anything about the actual individual native artists, I had acquired great works by them. I also acquired Chief Bill Scow's potlatch house totem poles on Guilford Island only after he found no market for them in Canada. Again this showed the lack of interest by American and Canadian "whites." The de Menils and a woman in Florida buying for the Denver Museum, and I had the field to ourselves. Not that there were no others collecting fine pieces, but we were buying a lot of them.

So the collection grew piece by piece. A steel sword more than two hundred years old, a "Box of Daylight" headdress, a superb Chilkat blanket, a strong Kumugwe' mask, pipes with tightly organized animal forms, an eagle helmet that had been in the 1804 battle between the Tlingits at Sitka and Baranoff's soldiers and Aleuts, a "soul catcher," two flannel jackets covered with ermine and beaded flower designs.

And then it was over. By 1985 many Indian youths had finally become interested in their traditions and their languages. No more would "grandmother," the usual custodian of the family treasures, be able to sell them. Collectors bought and sold among themselves, but they knew the prices to be asked and paid. I had had my fun and it was time to contemplate what to do with them.

Annie and I could show only some sixty pieces in our house on McGilvra. Yet there were more than two hundred objects. Later in the 1980s, some thirty-five were crammed into the house in North Seattle bought and remodeled for Ann Homer Hauberg and me. When my grandson, Ben Page, was three, he refused to go down the staircase lined with the masks, which scared him so. They were powerful!

The Seattle Art Museum's long struggle for a downtown location was resolved and money raised for a new museum. I gave a million dollars for three galleries, and turned the collection over to the museum staff, especially Steve Brown, curator, Paul Macapia, photographer, and Mike McCafferty, Seattle Art Museum's brilliant designer. We set out to plan a book about the objects that would be not only an art book but also a textbook on

Top left: Eagle war helmet, worn in the Battle of Sitka, Tlingits vs Baranoff's Russians and Aleuts in 1803. Now in the Seattle Art Museum; Center: Bent box; Bottom: Killer whale pipe; Right: Ancient steel dagger, indicating that the Tlingits had learned the metalworking techniques of welding and riveting before 1700 A.D. All © The Seattle Art Museum, Gift of John H. Hauberg

Left: Ermine robe with beaded felt trim, Tlingit; Right: Grizzly bear frontlet on a dancing hat with ermine trim, a basket of walrus whiskers & flicker feathers, Haida. A great treasure.
© The Seattle Art Museum, Gift of John H. Hauberg

Indian ethnology. Steve, and Bill Holm, the great expert but working for the Burke Museum almost full time, knew the old time principal speakers and leaders of each of the seven major nations—Tlingit, Haida, Tsimshian, Kwakiutl (Kwakwaka'wakw), Nootka, Bella Coola, and Coast Salish.

I invited each group to come in turn to Seattle at my expense, to look at the objects from their nation, to wear them, dance them, and talk about them in both English and in their own language.

A Native American photographer videotaped the proceedings. Much of all this found its way into the book, to be called *The Spirit Within.* I want to express right now my great appreciation of all those activities to Steve Brown. With counsel from Bill Holm, Steve guided each phase from inventory to the illustrations and the text of this wonderful book.

The book was designed by Katie Sims. Paul Macapia's photos are superb. The tribal scholars wrote excellent essays, objects were given their names in both English and native languages, Steve wrote object descriptions that were revealing of the meaning each one had to its tribal members. And Gail Joyce of Seattle Art Museum's staff shepherded the book to its publication when it seemed several times to have bogged down.

The quality of both the exhibition in the three galleries and the book are beyond my wildest dreams. When I first saw Mike McCafferty's mounting of about one hundred

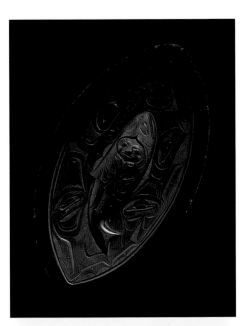

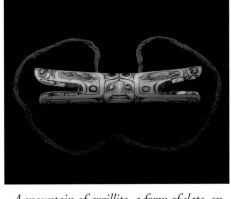

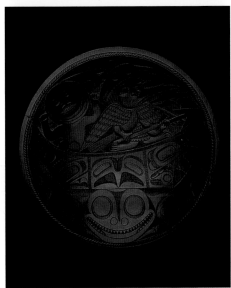

A mountain of argillite, a form of slate, on Graham Island in the Queen Charlotte Islands, gave the Haida exclusive rights to work this material. Lower left: The plate is the work of the famous Charles Edenshaw. Upper right: The box, carved by John Robson, was purchased in Juneau the day before its owner died. It depicts the legend of the crow who taunted the crab for his awkward shuffle, but let the crab come close enough to catch its wing and begin the crawl back into the water. The crab apparently relented in time. Lower right: soul catcher. All © The Seattle Art Museum, Gift of John H. Hauberg

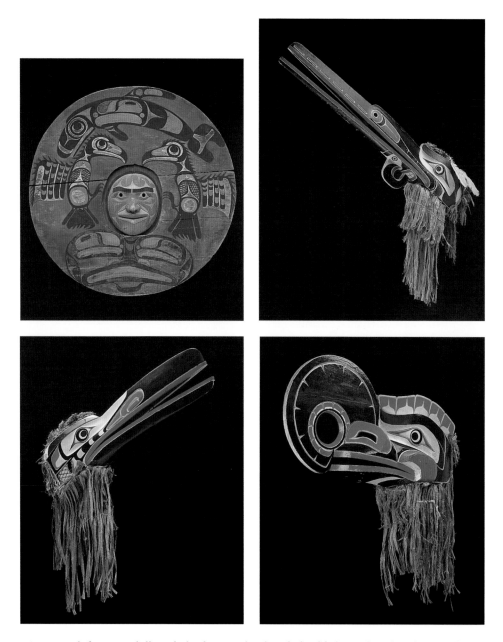

A sun mask features a killer whale above and a thunderbird below. The other three masks are worn and danced during a Hamatsa society "taming" potlatch with the "Crooked Beak of Heaven" at lower right. They are the work of Willie Seaweed and Mungo Martin.
All © The Seattle Art Museum, Gift of John H. Hauberg

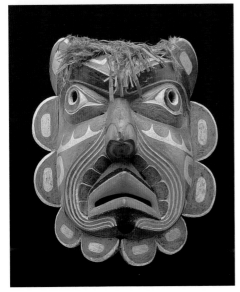

eighty objects, I could not believe they were mine. Where did they all come from?

What had happened to the pre-Columbian collection? After 1972 there was no more collecting of that and so I sold it for almost all the money I needed to buy, over the years, the Pacific Northwest Coast Indian collection! The Maya stela remains in my personal collection. I gave about forty "leftover" small pre-Columbian works to the Seattle Art Museum. There appears to be little interest in these objects in Seattle, while everybody seems to resonate with the Pacific Northwest Coast Indian collection.

I have given several lectures about the Indian collection to the Museum's docents, and have also given slide talks to the Diet and to a full house at the Sunset Club.

While I have not bought any "old" works for years, I do have a small collection in my office in Pioneer Square of works by contemporary Pacific Northwest Coast carvers who have become very fine artists.

Glass Collection

I served as a trustee of the American Crafts Council for twelve years from the mid-1960s. Most craftsmen were weavers, potters, jewelers, and woodworkers. Annie and I became good friends with Mrs. Vanderbilt Webb who founded and funded both the World Crafts Council as well as the American Crafts Council. We became very close friends with Jack Lenor Larsen, born and raised in Bremerton, and now a world-renowned textile designer. We also met and hired Jim Plaut of Boston to be a consultant to us in all of our projects. At Plaut's suggestion, we went to a World Craft Congress in Lima, Peru. Those were heady days of frantic comings and goings to New York, Washington, France, England, and Spain. When the froth had blown away, or settled down, we found that we had not succeeded in getting Mark Tobey's approval of a museum to be named for him, we had not created a Pacific Northwest Council of interested people from Portland to Vancouver and Boise, but we had created the now-famous Pilchuck Glass School with Dale Chihuly's idea and our funding and guidance.

The detailed story of Pilchuck Glass School is told in another fine book with that title, written by Tina Oldknow. So I won't tell it here. But of course Annie and I began to acquire glass objects. At first they were gifts from the artists. In a couple of years our Pilchuck artists/teachers were also instructing at Haystack Mountain and Penland summer craft schools. And slowly a market developed with Pilchuck alumni in the lead.

We bought small objects to begin with, the early work of Harvey Littleton, Dale Chihuly, Ben Moore, Flora Mace and Joey Kirkpatrick, Billy Morris, Fritz Dreisbach, Howard Ben Tre, the Libenskys, and others.

Glass works today tend to be large. But masterpieces of glass blowing, Murano style, still can be quite small, and, of course, very, very elegant, such as works by Lino Tagliapietro and Richard Marquis. The subtle etching on black glass done by Paul Marioni and Walt Liebermann have not caught on with the public at large, though they are prized by others, including me.

Meanwhile, Dale Chihuly has become a "National Treasure," decreed by President Clinton, and is represented in almost every billionaire's new house all over the world!

Today we, Ann Homer Hauberg and I, have a modest collection of perhaps thirty glass works, both early work as well as their latest. Properly mounted and lighted, these works are very beautiful and very satisfying to own and show to others.

All these give life to our houses and joy to our families. It has been a great pleasure to live with all these treasures.

Paintings and Sculptures

Like Dr. Fuller, I was more attuned to objects for many years. I did buy works by Guy Anderson, Paul Horiuchi, and Alden Mason in the 1960s. With my marriage to Ann Homer in 1979, I "discovered" that I had a wife with a keen eye for collecting paintings. We have bought them whenever we have traveled—Italy, Spain, Germany, New York, San Francisco! In a New York gallery she found a painting that was done, to our amazement, by an Eastern Washington painter, Robert Helm. Our house is a happy mix of exciting pictures from all over.

However, most of our art is from regional artists, such as Helm. My first interest in art was the result of my marriage to Annie Gould, and she was devoted to Mark Tobey, Morris Graves, James Washington, Guy Anderson, and Philip McCracken as well as many craftsmen and jewelers in the Pacific Northwest, such as Ramona Solberg and Ruth Pennington. The Seattle Art Museum held an annual exhibit of Northwest artists. So I gradually, and somewhat tentatively, became an art collector, buying works by Tobey and Graves, Anderson and William Ivey, a screen by Paul Horiuchi, the Eastern Washington painters, Helm and Hansen, a sumi by George Tsutakawa, then large canvases by Fay Jones and Alden Mason.

From Italy came two paintings by Mimo Palladino. Ann Homer Hauberg has added two paintings by Francesco Clemente. And we have small iron sculptures from Germany.

Our present kitchen/family room holds works by San Francisco Bay Area artists. A very big picture by Roy DeForest was bought by Ann Homer Hauberg. We also purchased works by Paul Wonner, Saul Steinberg, Mike McCormick and Joseph Raphael.

Then there are many photographs and prints from all over, plus glass work by Chihuly, Bill Morris and many others.

We also commissioned art for our current house in Seattle. There is a crystal column by the Libenskys, a stairwell sun-and-shadow display by Ed Carpenter, and stained glass panels by Cappy Thompson.

Red Tie *by Gaylen Hansen*

Boneyard *by Robert Helm*

Self Portrait *by Francesco Clemente*

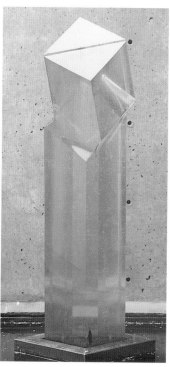

Stanislav and Jaroslova Libensky: a crystal column in a pool lit at night

"Abstract" *Six fold screen collage by Paul Horiuchi*

Saint George in Squareland
by Roy DeForest

Cassandra's Sister
by Ann Wolff Warff

Vase, 1985
by Ulrica Hydman-Vallien

Angel on a Tightrope
by Catherine Thompson

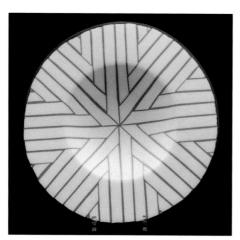

Slumped Plate *by Klaus Moje*

Etruscan Vessels *by Dante Marioni*

Left: Soft Cylinder;
Below: Macchiapair; *both by*
Dale Chihuly

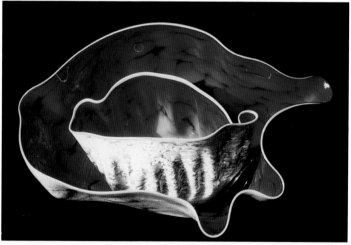

Spiral Wrap *by Benjamin Moore*

"Serie Fratelli Toso-Split"
by Marvin Lipofsky

Red Soldier
by Charles Parriott

Standing Column Number 12
by Howard Ben Tre

Don Johnson Has a Vision of a Corn
Muffin and Decides to Hide His Cocaine
in a Potato Patch *by Ginny Ruffner*

Shard Pot *by Richard Marquis*

The Whole Soul Summed Up
by Christopher Wilmarth

Balanced Parabolic Arc *by Harvey Littleton*

CHAPTER 25

Seattle Art Museum & King Tut

aFTER ANNIE GOULD AND I BEGAN TO DATE IN 1939, I LEARNED THAT THE GOULDS were great friends of Dr. Richard Fuller, his mother and his sister, Eugenia Atwood. Dr. Fuller was very fond of Annie, and had been devoted to her father. In the early years of our marriage, my work and then my army service took us away from Seattle, but when I returned from the army in 1946, Dr. Fuller began to invite us to the openings at the Seattle Art Museum. These were all black-tie affairs. Before long we were also being invited to his house for cocktails and dinner prior to the openings. At that time he was unmarried and lived with his mother. He seemed to like us very much. We were happy and we were young, and interested in art and architecture as well as music.

We began to see more and more of the Fullers and the Art Museum, and also were getting acquainted with local artists. Annie was very interested in the arts and crafts. We became acquainted with a widening circle of regional artists, such as Mark Tobey, Morris Graves, Guy Anderson, Carl and Hilda Morris of Portland, University of Washington jewelers Ramona Solberg and Ruth Pennington. This was a new experience for me. I knew practically nothing about visual art, coming from the Protestant ethic of the Midwest. While my family had a rich musical background, they considered paintings and sculpture to be "Catholic stuff."

Annie's family had close ties to the University of Washington, both of her parents having taught there, and we became closely involved with several members of the faculty. Her cousin, "Cully" Moore, who designed the Aurora Bridge, was a professor of engineering at the University. The family was close to Milnor Roberts, who was dean of the school of mining. He and his twin sister, Milnora, lived together and they were involved in everything cultural in Seattle—symphony, theater, etc. We all went to opening nights of plays at the University of Washington's Show Boat floating theater, then under the direction of Professor Glenn Hughes. Almost every occasion in those days was "black-tie," and we went out several nights a week. The Roberts were always there.

I believe that Dr. Fuller wanted a member of the Gould family on his board of trustees to maintain contact with the family. This was quite appropriate, since Carl Gould had designed the Seattle Art Museum. Dr. Fuller also may have felt that my appointment would bring a touch of youth to the board, so I became a member in 1949.

I was thirty-three, quite a bit younger than the other board members of the Seattle Art Museum, and I remained as an active board member until October 1995, when I became an honorary board member.

The Seattle Art Museum board was a rubber-stamp board for Dr. Fuller, just what he wanted. His connection with the museum was all-encompassing. He was the founder, the president, the curator, director, paid all of the bills and salaries, did all the collecting—and he wanted it that way. He didn't really think he needed a board, but his lawyer, Raymond Wright, convinced him that for tax purposes he had to have one. There were eighteen or twenty members, and they all were close friends of the Fullers.

The required annual meeting was perfunctory, and there were few other meetings. Raymond Wright served as board secretary, and he would write the minutes in advance as if the meeting had already taken place. Dr. Fuller would then read the minutes straight through without discussion—"it was moved, seconded and passed that so and so would be reimbursed in the amount of..." No vote was ever called for, of course. Dr. Fuller would then report on his collecting for the past year, there would be a youth education report by Mrs. A.M. Young, a docent report by Dorothy Lahr, the treasurer's report by Mr. Henry Judson, who always concluded with "The Museum finished the year in the black." Everybody chuckled. Then came the election of the board. No new business ever came up. It was entirely a social affair.

Dr. Richard Fuller had a tremendous fortune as far as Seattle was concerned at that time. He was the son of a physician and an heiress. His father, Dr. Eugene Fuller, had made very shrewd investments for his family and this was the foundation for his son's fortune, but Dick was also a skilled investor. He invested in local firms, such as Northwest Glass Company and Heath Tecna Corporation, and made a great deal of money on those investments. He was a very bright man. His undergraduate degree was at Yale, and he had a Ph.D. in geology.

In 1931 Dr. Fuller and his mother, Margaret E. MacTavish Fuller, became interested in providing an art museum for Seattle. Dick Fuller had gone around the world in the 1920s with his mother, sister, and brother, and they purchased art at every stop. Because of his interest in geology and stone, he was drawn to jade carvings and the pieces he acquired make up the backbone of the new Asian Museum's collection today. Originally the Fullers gave the city $325,000 for a museum. That was an immense gift, more like $10 million now. The city agreed that the proposed museum would take the place of the pergola in Volunteer Park, which had been designed by the Olmsteds. In making their gift, I think the Fullers required that Carl Gould would be the architect. An art deco masterpiece was the result.

Dr. Fuller initially brought things to his house, for family enjoyment, and for many years larger sculptures weren't of interest to him. Even after the museum was built in 1933, he had many treasures in his house. When we went there for dinners we were permitted to pick them up and examine them. Soon they became too expensive for us to touch. Eventually, they found their way into the museum.

Dr. Fuller attended the openings of all local art galleries, of which there were only three or four at that time. He usually bought, because he wanted to show his interest in the local art scene, and knew that his presence meant a lot to the galleries and their artists. But basically he was an "object" collector and not very interested in pictures. All during the Depression, he was able to acquire great pieces of Asian art, and the Seattle Art Museum became an important Asian Art Museum. He was known to every dealer in Asian and Near Eastern art and to the directors and curators of the outstanding museums all over the world from Japan, India, Egypt, and Europe to the U.S.A. It was a bit of a fraternity.

There were few collectors of art of any sort in Seattle in those years. Charles and Emma Frye had a fairly extensive collection of nineteenth-century painters of the German academic school. They offered it to the art museum, and Dr. Fuller sent Sherman Lee (who had come to the Seattle Art Museum as a professional curator of Asian art) down to inspect it. Lee came back and sneered that the collection was "nothing but sheep." Dr. Fuller was happy with that assessment because he didn't want to give any space to the Frye collection anyway. He already had twice as many items in storage as he could display. Later on that became a ratio of maybe twenty to one. Mrs. Charles "Emma" Stimson collected Mark Tobey, Morris Graves, and other leading local artists. Mrs. D.E. Frederick collected important church art from the Renaissance. Dr. Fuller welcomed their art into the Museum. But he remained aloof to the world of European and American painting and sculpture. He was "object-oriented."

At the time I joined the board, the Seattle Art Museum was very much Dr. Fuller's own province. He had never built much of a staff because he didn't want one. He didn't go after funds because he wanted to meet all the museum's needs with his own considerable resources. It was terribly nice of him, but it also made him the only collector of note in Seattle, and because he wasn't in the habit of showing other people's work, there was a very narrow focus to the collection. Meanwhile, museums which didn't have a great patron or patroness turned to professionals to help them buy. They bought the great American works of the '20s and '30s and they bought French Impressionists, etc., all of which escaped Dick Fuller, who was interested entirely in oriental art, made all the acquisition selections, and was embarrassed by offers to help.

He did have a Northwest Annual, which was his commitment to the local arts scene. All kinds of people exhibited in the early years: Tobey, Graves, Callahan, Anderson, and a great many artists from Eastern Washington, Western Montana, and the Boise area submitted paintings in the early days. But most of the pictures were single works of amateur "Sunday painters." He also had a photography section in the Northwest Annual and the local printmakers had their own annual exhibit. After the Northwest Annual had gone on for several years with Tobey, Graves, Callahan, and Anderson collecting the main prizes, these artists rarely entered a picture. That left the prizes to a wide number of local artists who were usually never heard from again. Each artist, or "Sunday painter" produced a "Northwest Annual" picture. At the opening night, each artist stood beside his or her picture, waiting for Dr. Fuller to come past and make a comment. It was always, "Very interesting."

Not only did Dr. Fuller fail to actively seek outside funding, he even discouraged people giving anything more than about twenty-five dollars. Mrs. Cebert Baillargeon, a board member, offered to see if she could get corporations to become fifty-dollar members, and he asked her not to do it.

There were people who would have been more than willing to give to the art museum, but they had never been asked. It seemed likely that Dr. Fuller didn't want any fund-raising programs because he would lose some sense of power if contributors became influential in museum decisions. Walter Wyckoff said to him one day in my hearing that he wanted to give the museum five thousand dollars. Dr. Fuller replied, "Walter, I wish you wouldn't do that. It's terribly embarrassing to me."

When the museum was offered the permanent loan of paintings and sculpture from the fabulous Kress collection of paintings, it was necessary to build three new galleries. Surprisingly, Dr. Fuller, with difficulty, agreed to accept these as a gift from Norman Davis, a board member. Davis was an Englishman who had come to the Puget Sound country and founded a brewery in Tacoma. He was a collector of classic art and coins. He and Dr. Fuller had become great friends.

About 1944 Sherman Lee had been hired by Dr. Fuller as a professional oriental curator, and greatly raised the museum's stature. (He later went directly from the Seattle Art Museum to become director of the Cleveland Museum because of his great knowledge). Dr. Fuller appointed Lee and Davis to select from the Kress collection the paintings to be on permanent loan. This was recognition of his own lack of knowledge in the area of pictures; however, he trusted both of these men and valued their expertise. The new galleries, one of which had a special cove ceiling to hold the Tiepolo ceiling mural, were a tremendous addition to the museum.

Dorothy Lahr ran a two-year docent training program. The docents needed an activities room where they could meet, store their hats and coats, eat lunch, and so on. The room was to be a one-story structure added to the east side of the existing museum walls. I suggested that we build a gallery on top of it, and gave fifty thousand dollars to establish the Carl F. Gould gallery. The offer was grudgingly accepted and my name as donor was never mentioned.

By the early '60s, Dr. Fuller realized his Asian collection had grown so much that it had to be curated by a professional. He hired Henry Trubner, who came from the Royal Ontario Museum in Toronto. He was an autocratic Austrian scholar who knew Asian art, but Dr. Fuller was not about to give his curator the right to buy anything without his approval. However, Trubner brought much additional prestige to our fine Asian collections. He and his father before him were widely known to the scholars and directors of museums with Asian works all over the world. When he and his wife, Ruth, led a group of us to Japan and Korea, we were impressed with the great respect for him shown by these directors of major Japanese museums, private collectors, and the artist families who had been producing ceramics for centuries. Later Dr. Fuller hired a very shy but immensely knowledgeable curator, William Rathbun, who added many art works of Japan and Korea to our collections, becoming curator of Asian art after Trubner's retirement. Bill was made director of the newly designated Seattle Asian Art Museum in Volunteer Park, after the new Seattle Art Museum was built in downtown Seattle. He did an incredible job of displaying the Fuller collections of Asian art with help from Seattle Art Museum's display genius, Mike McCafferty. Dr. Fuller would be immensely happy with the results.

The aftermath of the Seattle World's Fair in 1962 presented an opportunity of which Dr. Fuller took full advantage. At the close of the World's Fair he asked the City to give one of the buildings to the Seattle Art Museum. The building was remodeled and air-conditioned. Although it was only a Band-Aid solution to the museum's need for expansion, it did present new possibilities for exhibits. Virginia Wright and I funded the first-year salary of Charles Cowles, the first curator of contemporary art, and he began to show the huge canvases of the New York abstract expressionists, and the work of pop artists such as Roy Lichtenstein in the new building. The Northwest Annual was also moved to it. Finally, Seattle was being exposed to "New York art" in its own art museum. Jinny Wright and Bob Dootson were to open galleries selling "contemporary art," but both failed to gain the necessary support to stay in business.

Dick Fuller's health began to fail in the late '60s, which caused him to spend less and less time at the museum. It reached a sad state of affairs when he had to be carried up the steps. Dr. Fuller had begun to lean on me a bit as a vice president of the board. I suggested to Albert Kerry, who was the first vice president, that he and I and Bob Arnold, who was the treasurer, form a trustee triumvirate to meet with the staff and find out what the problems of the art museum were. Then Albert would have lunch with Dr. Fuller at his house and pass our recommendations along. I felt these would be more acceptable to him coming from Albert Kerry, who was Dr. Fuller's most trusted friend. Dick agreed to this arrangement. As we passed our ideas along to him he concurred with all of them except a recommendation to replace the museum auditor with a younger and more vigorous accounting firm, which could provide us with needed information more quickly and accurately. The accountant also did the Fuller family's work, and Dick did not want to hurt his feelings.

There were some interesting incidents involving our work as trustees. His accountant advised that an outside annual inspection of the securities in Dr. Fuller's safe deposit box was required by law. It contained stocks which funded the Margaret E. Fuller purchase fund for the museum, as well as all the stocks which were providing Dr. Fuller with the money he gave the art museum, at the rate of several hundred thousand dollars a year. Albert Kerry and I were asked to make this inspection and then verify in a notarized document that indeed the certificates were there which were supposed to be. I was terrifically impressed with Dick Fuller's ability as an investor. There were U.S. Steel, Standard Oil of California, mining and oil stocks primarily from his father. He believed in real values, and they paid very good dividends. Then he had local stocks, in which he had invested and made his own fortune.

By 1970 Dr. Fuller must have recognized that he would not be able to get back to running the museum on a daily basis. Albert and I persuaded him to appoint a long-range planning committee, consisting of three of his best friends. Part of their report recommended that Dr. Fuller would retire and the board would select a new president.

So we held the famous November 1972 board meeting. As usual, Dick Fuller read the minutes which had been prepared for him before the meeting. When it came to the part which read: "It was moved, seconded and passed that the report of the long-range planning committee be accepted..." Dr. Fuller paused after "seconded" and didn't say "and passed." He was aware of what was in the report, and at that point we knew he was not going to accept it willingly.

A board member then moved the passage of the long-range planning committee's report. Someone else murmured a second. Then there was dead silence. Dr. Fuller would not call for the motion. The ladies on the board broke into tears. Dr. Fuller's friends stood and someone said, "Dick, we just have to have a replacement. If you should die before we could find somebody else, it could be that your lifetime work might be lost. You surely don't want that to happen." Everybody pledged their friendship and their lasting devotion to Dr. Fuller. And he still wouldn't put the motion. Finally Betty Fuller, who served on the board and was sitting next to her husband, put her hand on his arm and very sweetly said, "Dick, it's time." He called for the vote and adjourned the meeting.

About a week later, Dick called me and said, "John, I'd like you to succeed me as president of the board." I said, "When would you like me to begin? I think I'm ready to do that." I took office in February 1973.

One of the most challenging events that took place while I was president was the King Tut exhibit in 1978. When we first learned of the show in 1976, it was already on its way from Egypt. It was to have two eastern venues, Washington, D.C., and New York, two in the Midwest in New Orleans and Chicago, and then two on the West Coast. Los Angeles would be one, and the sponsors were undecided on what city would be the second western venue. The Egyptians who put together the King Tut exhibit were well acquainted with Dr. Fuller and the Seattle Art Museum. When they decided on the second venue on the West Coast their friend Dr. Fuller came immediately to mind, and thus the Seattle Art Museum was confirmed. This was wonderful news to all of us, but I wondered why there was nothing in our files about its coming to Seattle until it opened in Chicago.

Annie and I visited the King Tut show in Chicago in July 1977. A man named Woods, who had been head of Sears Roebuck, was the president of the Field Museum, the place for the "Treasures of Tutankhamun." I called him and said I'd like to talk to him about the King Tut show. I wanted to find out what problems he thought they had and how they were solving their problems, such as parking, selling tickets, and the interior design of the show, who would manage it, and so on. It was obvious that he had given the matter a great deal of study.

"First of all," he said, "we're not letting the staff of the Field Museum run the show, because they would then be off their regular jobs not only for the four months it was here, but a month before and month afterward. I hired a professional manager, who in turn hired the staff to run the show. For parking we have Soldier's Field, an immense football stadium in Chicago." They did have very long lines for admission. People stood in lines for hours to get into that show. But the Museum had made memberships available that would let the member in with a much shorter wait. So Annie and I learned a lot from that visit.

Later we went down to New Orleans for their exhibit. In contrast to Chicago, they had turned their entire museum and its staff over to the King Tut. It was a small museum, and to make room for King Tut, their greatest treasures went into storage (in fact, almost everything they had), and their staff was retired from their regular jobs to handle the King Tut show. Also the New Orleans Art Museum was in a park, which was to take all the parking. It rained for practically the entire duration of the exhibit and the park became a sea of mud. We learned some more.

Based on all that, I decided the King Tut show would not be held in the Seattle Art Museum. We would have swamped the neighborhood with parked cars, and people up there would never have forgiven us. A Seattle Art Museum board member, Malcolm Stamper, president of Boeing, provided two men to make an intensive survey of possible sites for the exhibition and recommended we petition the City of Seattle to pre-

305

pare the 1962 World's Fair building known as the Flag Plaza Pavilion with air conditioning for our use and future uses. The city agreed, spending almost a million dollars in expectation of thousands of people coming to Seattle for the show.

I asked the board of the Seattle Art Museum for permission to hire a professional to direct the King Tut exhibit. I prevailed upon Ewen Dingwall, who had managed the Seattle World's Fair so successfully, to accept the position and he did an outstanding job. The King Tut show in Seattle attracted one million, three hundred thousand people in attendance. The ticket problem was solved by having advance tickets sold in box offices already existing in the city such as the Seattle Center building and the Opera House, keeping those offices open from 7:30 a.m. to 11 p.m. People purchased their tickets stating a day and an hour. They would be admitted to the exhibit within five minutes. The museum sold over twenty-five thousand new memberships by promising favored status for admission. As it was in all the other cities, the exhibit was a great success. But the attendance in Seattle was the largest, even besting New York and Chicago. Even better, we made a net profit of over a million dollars!

I was president for five years, and determined not to stay in that role for forty years as Dr. Fuller had. And the board would never have permitted it. It was someone else's turn and that person would have to make many changes.

The old guard was still very much around at that point, but the art world was changing rapidly. Following my term as president, Bagley Wright became president and I became chairman, a newly created title. Bagley was much closer to the business community than I and soon brought onto the board many younger, and smarter, people. We needed them badly for the next event.

By far, the most controversial event to take place during my years as an active board member was the decision to move the museum downtown. The move was a long time coming and encountered many roadblocks along the way, but there is a great deal of satisfaction when a difficult mission is finally accomplished. I thank Dr. Richard E. Fuller for his tremendous gift to Seattle, and for his confidence in my ability to provide leadership to the Seattle Art Museum as it embarked upon a new era.

A Moving Experience

The board of the Seattle Art Museum, made up of Dr. Fuller's close friends, became aware that we could display only about five percent of the artifacts Dr. Fuller had collected from the time he took his round-the-world trip with his family in the 1920s, until he retired as head of the museum in 1973. It had reached a point where the art in storage was of equal value to the art on display, and almost all of it would be of interest to the public. The board and Dr. Fuller always had assumed that we would simply expand into space between the existing art museum and 15th Avenue East. We needed about an acre of space. That part of Volunteer Park wasn't used very much, although there was a great deal of lovemaking under a certain Atlas cedar tree with very low-hanging branches.

We finally arranged a meeting with the Capitol Hill Community Club, chaired by Ibsen Nelson, a very fine architect and a solid citizen. Dr. Fuller, Mr. Kerry and I presented our case, and I was not at all surprised that the Capitol Hill Community Club people were very much opposed to any expansion of the museum in Volunteer Park. The density of population around the park had increased dramatically. Most of the original houses had by now been turned into apartments. The number of cars over the years had increased greatly. Every time there was a museum opening, the park and the neighborhood were jammed with cars.

We were firmly put down by the community representatives. We checked with members of the City Council to see whether the Community Club's decision was compelling against our aspirations. The council assured us they would not vote against the Community Club and would respect the wishes of the neighborhood.

Over the heartfelt and strenuous objections of many old friends of the Fullers and the Seattle Art Museum, the board commissioned The Richardsen Associates to make a study of downtown sites. The "center" of downtown was discovered to be an area where Westlake Boulevard began at Pike Street. This thought was to be our beacon for a long, unhappy time.

However, J.C. Penney decided to close its downtown store. They gave the J.C. Penney half-block downtown to the Seattle Art Museum as a charitable deduction worth $8 million to them. So all of a sudden we were presented with half a block of downtown space and a building we could either tear down or use or sell. And it was close to Westlake.

At about that time, the downtown office-building bubble burst. A Canadian firm that had overextended itself by buying the buildings between University Street and Union and Pike, between First and Second Avenues, went bankrupt and we were able to negotiate the purchase of that site with them. We formed a committee with Bagley Wright as chairman and began to try to put together something that made sense from the standpoint of our own abilities to raise money and take advantage of this opportunity.

For a short time we worked with Mayor Charles Royer who wanted the Seattle Art Museum as part of his plan to develop Westlake. Royer asked Bagley Wright and me to go with him to Montreal, where a developing firm, Mondev, that had made the best presentation for Westlake Park to the Seattle City Council, was headquartered. The firm wanted us to take the top three floors of a major building in the Westlake complex. For a time we thought that was a fine idea, but then we realized we would not be our own master. We would just be tenants on the top floors of a building, with very little ability to expand or deal with the public. We paid an architect named Giurgola several hundred thousand dollars to see what he could do with the Art Museum in the Westlake site. He was a charming man who had done huge enterprises in Australia and some interesting work in Boston, all of which recommended him to us. This did not work to our benefit, however. In paying him and some other advisors we lost a great deal of the money which we had made from the King Tut show. When we withdrew from the Westlake area, we incurred the wrath of the mayor. However, we were free then to proceed with the purchase of the University-Union block. I will spare the reader the story of the fund-raising, but the voters of Seattle approved many millions, while individuals and foundations gave more.

My entire collection of Pacific Northwest Coast Indian art was given to the museum. Long before the new museum came about, I had decided that I was not going to be the owner of these things. I was going to give them to the public for education and enjoyment. Prior to their going to the museum, I had most of the collection in my home. Until the objects were beautifully displayed in the museum, I had no idea that I had so many items. I was as astounded as the Seattle public. It is a spectacular display, and even to this day (2001) it is what the public remembers from their visits to the Seattle Art Museum.

The new museum has received promises of many works from collectors in town. We now have some splendid collections of New York abstract expressionists and the art periods that followed it. Some local collectors have told the museum they would donate what the museum needed from their collection, either by bequest or perhaps some of them are already giving parts of their collections. There is no doubt that the beautiful new museum will give great impetus to collectors to make valuable additions.

A French city in the land of Monet

CHAPTER 26

Travels

I'VE DONE A LOT OF TRAVELING IN MY LIFE, ALTHOUGH MANY OF THE TRIPS WERE repeats of the same kind. Anne Gould Hauberg and I made five or six river trips with Hal and Elizabeth Hirsch, of Portland, Oregon. Hal was a trustee of Reed College, where I met him. Elizabeth was absolutely charming. They invited us to go on these outings down rivers, all in Oregon. The Illinois, the Rogue, and the Salmon Rivers were all different. We used the same boatmen on all the trips, but the rivers were each very different. Ann Homer Hauberg was my companion on the last trip on the Rogue. Fay and Sue went with us to the local National Parks, Mt. Rainier, and the Olympics. And there was one trip to the Southwest, the Grand Canyon, and Carlsbad Caverns in Texas with Sue and Fay and Fay's friend, Jayme Clise.

I particularly cherish our family winter breaks at Castle Hot Springs, Arizona, which was a ten-acre oasis some twenty-five miles across a desert wasteland from the nearest highway. It was here that Sue found her big interest in life. The resort featured rides out into the desert, usually with a well-organized picnic in a dry wash where cottonwood trees shaded our noontime stops. A small number of cowboys with good horses organized all these junkets. We never missed a single one of them during the five winter vacations we were there. The cowboys put Sue on a small horse named Fox at the stables and let her sit there. Sue rode with me on my horse a couple of times, and then rode Fox on her own from there on. Fay, of course, was already an accomplished rider and needed no help. The resort doctor was a bird watcher and could imitate each bird's song. He joined almost every ride/picnic. A tiny nine-hole golf course was fun; a tennis court and the hotel pool rounded out the options. We loved it.

The next five years found us at Hana Maui where we learned the Hawaiian songs and to play, a little, the ukulele and do the hula dances.

We always felt we should take our children on other trips as much as possible. After children are fifteen or so they don't want to go just with their parents. So we took Fay when she was ten on a Patriotic Tour. It included, in sequence, one or two days in Williamsburg, then to Washington's home at Mt. Vernon, the Lincoln Memorial, the White House, the Capitol building, various museums, picnics with my sister and a swim in her pool. On to Philadelphia and its Liberty Bell, Independence Hall, then to New

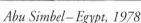
Abu Simbel – Egypt, 1978   *Anne Gould Hauberg – Camel Ride*

York to the United Nations, Empire State Building and more museums. Thence to Boston and Concord, Bunker Hill, the old North Church, and the bridge where was fired "the shot heard 'round the world." Sue had her turn when she was eleven or twelve.

In 1977 we began to prepare for our Seattle Art Museum sponsorship of the King Tut show in 1978. Although I can find no mention of its coming to Seattle in my 1976 journal, I am sure that our director Bill Woods must have received such information. Maybe so. But the museum's buildings and grounds committee met on January 5, 1977 to discuss the logistics of the 1978 King Tut show, and where to put all the people, the cars, etc. From then on there was a steady build-up of discussions and decisions. These all led to a fine trip for Annie and me to Egypt in February 1978.

I felt we should know something about Egypt that might enable us to talk more intelligently with the various curators who were sure to come with the show. The Friends of Princeton Art Museum, a group of museum supporters, scheduled a trip up the Nile and we joined that trip. It was a sternwheeler which had been built in Memphis, Tennessee, and somehow shipped on the deck of a very broad vessel all the way to the Nile. The cabins were absolutely miserable. The toilets were between the window and your bed, so that you got the stench of the toilets before you got the fresh air, if there were any such thing.

Karnak

The food was catered to the boat at various stops, and the caterers were not competent to coordinate anything so we had a very difficult time with the food. Then the two three-hundred-horsepower Universal engines broke down twice, although one of the occasions led to a beautiful evening. We had to tie up to the left bank of the Nile. The crew lowered the gangplank and we went from the deck of the boat onto the sands of the desert. There was a full moon, and someone from Princeton had brought along a battery radio. By the light of the moon we danced under the palm trees to music from the radio. It was probably the most glamorous evening I'd had for a long time.

The monuments of Egypt are superb. One thing that impressed me was that granite comes in so many colors. The Egyptians used these color combinations, and carved immense statues of various pharaohs in varying colors. One pharaoh would be immortalized in red granite, and the next in green or black. Our tour leader, a man from Wilson College who had been on many trips in that area, could read Greek, Sanskrit and Egyptian hieroglyphics. He took us around the huge compounds of Karnak, Luxor, etc. We saw only the most interesting things there, so that our interest never flagged. We could count on him to walk past thousands of things that other guides might have talked about, but with unerring knowledge and taste he took us to the most fascinating places on this tour.

The group concluded its Nile River trip at Abu Simbel, a new location for the huge royal statues, because the Aswan Dam had put the old location under water. Then back to Cairo, the Sphinx, the pyramids, a ride on a camel, and (for me) a visit to its great museum.

My First Trip to China

In the fall of 1978, I parted company with Anne Gould Hauberg. I agreed not to bring the divorce to a conclusion for a year, honoring her desire to observe a tenet of her Baha'i faith, a "think it over" period.

So the invitation to join the Washington Council on International Trade (WCIT), mission to China was more than welcome. I was to represent Weyerhaeuser Company since I was on its board, and also the "cultural interests" of Seattle.

It was a very interesting group. Our leader was Dr. George Taylor, head of the Far Eastern Institute at the University of Washington, a man of vast knowledge of China, fluent in its language (he had taught at the University of Beijing for several years in the 1930s), charming and witty. The group included bankers, engineers, port commissioners, architects, foundation people, educators, and those of us representing specific companies such as Boeing, Weyerhaeuser, and Western International Hotels.

We all hoped to make contacts that would be useful to us in some way or other. But the Chinese travel people who took over the management of our group and its itinerary had other ideas. We were to be impressed by China's progress from the days of the building of the Great Wall and the Ming Tombs. So we saw what they wanted us to see in Beijing, Shanghai, Canton, and cities in between.

It wasn't much of a trade mission. We didn't really have time for the businessmen to sit down and talk with people, since the sightseeing took up all the time. We were under the eyes of three young Chinese-communist travel guides, two men and a woman in their late twenties, all speaking excellent English. They were with us for the entire trip. We had lots of fun with them. By the time the trip was over the three of them wanted to come back to the States with us, although I suspect they felt that way even before we arrived and had visited all the Chinese mandatory sites.

The academics on the trip visited the universities in each city. Dr. Taylor was, of course, most interested in the changes in China's higher education since the end of the so-called Cultural Revolution. Then we had the dean of agriculture from Washington State University, and several other professors from the UW. Bill Jenkins, chairman of Seattle First National Bank, and I roomed together. We decided to visit the universities along with the academics. While they were talking academic business, we would go out and talk to the students. Most of them could speak only one or two phrases in English: "What is your name?" and "How old are you?" If you said you were fifty-five I don't know that they could translate that. But some of the students could speak a little English. Taylor and the academics were fascinated by what the universities were teaching, and of course Bill and I were fascinated with the kinds of students who were going there.

During the Cultural Revolution (1966-1976) the wife of Chairman Mao, who had become senile, seized power. Anybody who wore glasses, could speak a foreign language, or was a leader in the villages, would be rusticated to farms all over China or killed outright. Some twenty-five million Chinese were killed during the ten years of the Cultural Revolution. They closed the schools above the sixth grade, so none of these college-age people we met had been to high school. An educated public was not to the liking of Madame Mao.

Following the breakup of the Cultural Revolution, the first thing the universities had to do was bring the students up to speed through junior high and high school levels. Since most books had been destroyed, there were few books in the library and they were tattered and torn. We were told that when the professors dug the textbooks out of the dung heaps, the books weren't in good shape. Each book had to be read by maybe a thousand students. The students were eager to learn about America and they were thrilled to talk particularly to Bill, who had a wonderful way of dealing with these young people, having seven children of his own.

All but one of the universities had returned to a classic education along with teaching communist economics, but in Nanking the university was in the hands of a woman who was a very hard-core communist so the entire curriculum was the communist dogma.

We visited four different universities and found that the Chinese young people were vital and curious about everything. They had the feeling that Chairman Deng Xiaoping was opening up their world and they wanted to participate in it. When they learned that Bill was a banker they hoped he could take their name and address "and if you have a chance to employ us you could give us a call." Bill got quite a kick out of that. One of the students said, "Of course, the trouble with the United States is the spread from rich to poor is so great."

Bill said to him, "Well, what does a peasant get in China?" It was 25 yuan a month. That was about $15 a month. The bottom level in the cities was about 80 yuan a month. Millions of Chinese were getting 25 yuan a month. Bill asked what a teacher got. A really good teacher got about 150 yuan a month. Bill said, "What do you think the university president might get?" Well, he might get 500-1,000 yuan a month. "What about the military. What does a lieutenant get?" He got 125 yuan a month. "What does a general get?" Well, he gets 2,500 yuan a month. Bill said, "Well that's 25 yuan at the bottom, 2,500 yuan at the top. That's a spread of one to a hundred. I get one of the top salaries in the U.S., about $750,000 a year." They thought that sounded like a lot of money, but Bill said, "Our minimum wage is something like $3.75 an hour. You multiply that by two thousand hours, that comes to $7,500, so the bottom level of employment in the U.S. would be one to a hundred as well." These students were just amazed.

The group had a meeting with one of the vice presidents of the politburo, in charge of science. He had been with Deng Xiaoping in Seattle. We were supposed to make a presentation. The audience was to last only an hour, but he obviously didn't have anything to do and when we got close to an hour he said, "Why don't we all just relax and we can be here another hour. I find this very rewarding." Stan Little represented Boeing, and the Chinese official wanted to hear about Boeing, so Stan had five minutes to talk about it.

Each one of us had a chance to speak. I felt it was appropriate to say that the Weyerhaeuser Company had been one of the very first companies in the U.S. to take booths in the famous Canton International Trade Fair that took place every year. He said that yes, Weyerhaeuser was well known to them as a fine company. I said, "By the way, I also represent the cultural interests in Seattle, and we would like to have exchange programs, both musical and fine arts, with your country." He thought that could be arranged, and we are getting exchange programs now from China—opera, dancers, etc., although I don't believe I had anything to do with it.

The trip was spectacular. We visited tea communes, which, of course, were well chosen for us. We bypassed communes which were still deep in the mud, and got to ones that were considered modern. One had a sawmill. It basically had two logs. One was a hardwood log from the Philippines or Indonesia, and the other was a Douglas fir log from the U.S., usually a fairly sizeable log. They cut them up with handsaws so they utilized every sliver of the log somehow or other, but they needed that log to keep four or five or maybe ten men employed. When they used that log they ordered one more, not having the capital to have an inventory of logs, or even an inventory of lumber.

They are working hard at modernizing, both at the newly opened universities as well as some of the communes. They were generating clear water supplies and aqueducts to carry it to villages. We had an abortionist on our trip, who always met in each village with the so-called country doctor. Each commune has a doctor who is trained to deal only with a fairly simple area of medicine. I think the most common task for which the doctor is trained is bringing babies into the world. He can treat common colds, broken bones, etc. He is available to anybody who has even just a sniffle.

From these doctors, our abortionist got contraceptive devices, IUDs, and he came home with about fifty different IUDs. An odd thing to collect, but he has a fine collection from China. Through him we got involved with the concept of the country doctor. Here we are nineteen years later and in this country we are still trying to provide medical services to everybody. But we don't have partially trained doctors who can open infirmaries that anybody can go to for very little money for very small medical problems. If I have a small medical problem I go to a highly trained doctor, and that costs Medicare and my insurance company a lot of money.

We met a man from Seattle, an insurance executive, who had just witnessed a brain operation with acupuncture providing the anesthetic. He said it worked fine. The chap was conscious the whole time and said he had no pain. When it was all over he asked someone for a cigarette.

When I came back, I kidded with several doctors from Virginia Mason Hospital. I said "I'm sure you must have an acupuncturist on the staff," but they were horrified at the very thought.

In Hong Kong, because Bill was chairman of the biggest bank in the state of Washington, we were invited by the president of the biggest bank in Hong Kong to go to the racetrack. Bill took me and the Boeing executive, Stan Little, with him. We went to lunch. The host from the Hong Kong bank was in New York buying a bank for his company, but his wife was there. She was charming and made us feel at home.

Although the races weren't fascinating, the people we met were. I found myself sitting beside a Chinese lady, beautifully dressed in a golden sheath, who wouldn't talk with me at all, at least to start with. On my right was a wizened little man named Mr. Lee, who, I was told, was the richest man in Hong Kong. He and I got along fine. I finally said, "Why is this lady not talking to me?" He said, "Oh, she will, but right now she's figuring the daily double. She usually wins." She went to the window to place her bets and when she had finished she was a great chatterbox.

Haiti

I suppose you could say that our overseas travel began with a surprise trip to Haiti! It was winter of 1958 in Seattle and Annie's Uncle Temple (Bunty) Fay invited us to bring Sue down to his outdoor clinic near Sarasota, Florida for his inspection. We thought a day or two was enough for that and made plans to go on to the Bahamas. We never got there!

The day or so with Dr. Fay turned out to be very rewarding later on. We then drove across the state to Miami's airport for the sun break, as planned. But the hotel people in the Bahamas had all gone on strike! Pan American Airlines refused to fly anybody to the Bahamas because there were no hotels operating and Pan Am would just have to fly them back.

Annie and I had heard about an Episcopalian minister in Haiti who was encouraging local artists. Some very fine work was forthcoming. So Pan Am found space for us to fly there and made hotel reservations in a fine hotel several miles from and perhaps a thousand feet higher in elevation then the city of Port-au-Prince. There were four of us, Annie and I, Sue, and her tutor, Myrene. We spent a week there from January 15 to 23, a very exciting week.

We were met by a taxi driver at the airport who quizzed us about why we came to Haiti! The country was in the turmoil of a new dictator, Duvalier, making deals right and left with those who paid him the most. Were we here to do that? Before the driver went on we assured him that we were interested in art! His tone changed completely. He was half-Mexican and half-Haitian and an intellectual knowing the educated middle class in Port-au-Prince. In fact, he was going to a party the next night and invited us to it.

We settled into our nice rooms at the Hotel Creole and soon went out on the streets, teeming with a pre-Mardi Gras spirit. Our friendly taxi driver took us to artist studios and we began to buy paintings.

The dinner party was amazing. The men were doctors, lawyers, educators, and other professionals. The girls were not their wives, but were probably the mistresses of these handsome, French-educated men. It was a "demimonde" society. When one of the men asked Annie to dance, and another one asked Myrene, I could only ask their "companions" to dance. Soon we were learning Haitian dance steps. We were invited to their next party about a week away!

A roadside market

Nineteenth century French influence on Haitian architecture. Port-au-Prince

Haiti turned out to be a very photogenic place, its people, its architecture, its farms, and its markets. A few photos tell the story.

But Duvalier's people noted our association with the educated middle-class

The Citadel of King Henri Christophe

people and Annie's friendship with an American former military man who was seeking an audience with the dictator, but looked on with suspicion by his "protectors." The hotel manager talked to me about these things and urged me to get out of Port-au-Prince as soon as possible. We did, flying over the mountains to a quiet city, Cap Haitien. Waiting for a plane to Miami, we visited the Citadel of Henri Christophe, a giant fortress built by King Henri to discourage Napoleon from further thoughts of recapturing Haiti.

Our first trip to Europe, 1959

Phil and Fay Padelford went on their first trip to Europe in 1955 and Annie and I were very jealous. In a Princeton alumni weekly issue, I read an article by a Princeton classics professor about an ancient mystery. "Morgantina was once a city but exists no more." So stated the Greek writer Strabo (64 B.C.–19 A.D.) in the chapter of his geography describing the inland towns of Sicily. For nearly two thousand years after Strabo, Morgantina was still as if vanished from the face of the earth, a city as thoroughly lost to history as any Atlantis. Its rediscovery is an archeological detective story. I had to go to Morgantina.

So when Joe and Janey McCarthy said they had plans for an expanded European trip, and Janet MacDonald Paulson said she and Chester would like to go also, Joe found a way to bring us six together in the big, famous cities of Europe about every ten days and leave each couple to explore on its own in between.

Annie and I left Seattle February 27, and after a brief stay in Rome and a week in Florence, we arrived in Sicily and the Classic World. A letter from the chairman of Princeton's Department of Art and Archeology directed me to the town of Piazza Armarina and its Jolly Hotel. And a letter from the director at the dig, Professor Erik Sjoqvist told me that Giuseppe, the dig's guardian, would expect me to knock on his door. So it was all arranged. Giuseppe opened the door of his little house wearing an orange and black Princeton Reunion cap! He carried a broom and a bucket of water as he showed us one wonderful mosaic tile floor after another, brushing away the protecting dirt and then bringing the colors to life with water.

Morgantina had been a big city in the days of the Punic Wars (264-201 B.C) between Rome and Carthage but had made the mistake of espousing the Carthaginians. When Rome ended victorious, it destroyed Morgantina, giving the site to the Spanish mercenaries who had helped Rome win. Professor Sjoqvist's realization that he had discovered the city came from finding ancient coins marked "Hispanorum," or " of the Spaniards." I was thrilled.

An unexpected additional thrill came when the hotel people asked me if I were here also to visit the "Emperor's Hunting Lodge," not far away. I had never heard about it. Built in the waning years of the second century A.D. by one of the many short-lived

A floor tile mural from the Emperor's Hunting Lodge in Sicily near Piazza Armerina. The Paulsons came over to Sicily from Rome. We rented cars and visited many Greek sites on the island.

One of many Greek temples in Sicily

Roman emperors, it has been covered for over a thousand years by a mudslide. The Italian government was spending many lira to develop its murals, rooms, and fountains as a tourist attraction. This work had just begun. Italian archaeologists had rebuilt the villa in lucite to let in the light so that one could see the colorful tiles on walls and floors. Spectacular!

I will leave the rest of the ten-week trip to photos, which will take the reader up the Italian boot through Rome, Venice, Vienna, Paris, Freiburg, Stockholm, and Copenhagen. We didn't have a list; we just wanted to see everything!

And it was not "over." Annie and I made many more journeys based on themes such as Renaissance gardens and villas, museums of all sorts, Etruscan digs, visits to Kay in France, etc.

A picnic with Seattle friends before going on to Chartres

Detail from the Cathedral in Freiburg, Germany

Black Forest Country near Freiburg

*Fontainebleau
Palace*

*A managed
French forest near
Fontainebleau
Palace*

*Sculptures in the
garden of Carl
Milles in Stockholm*

*Wisley Gardens
in England*

*The Etruscan coast
of Italy–a visit
prompted by Guy
Anderson who spoke
to us about Etruscan
civilization before
Romans conquered it
some five hundred
years B.C.*

"First trips" to Mexico, Colombia, Guatemala and Peru and "first trips" to Japan, South Korea, and Cambodia were all ahead. Annie made several trips with Ramona Solberg to Israel, Istanbul, and, I think, to Mexico, and she took Sue to Holland at tulip time.

Fay went to Europe in 1960 with a high-school group led by a Bush English teacher. She and Nat have also traveled to many places.

Ann Homer Hauberg and I have joined Seattle Art Museum and American Federation of Art groups in at least a half dozen ventures from Europe to South Korea.

CHAPTER 27

Life with Ann Homer Hauberg

A Prologue: Monday, August 20, 2001

I HAVE TEN DAYS, MORE OR LESS, BEFORE I HAVE A HEART OPERATION, WHOSE OUTCOME IS in doubt. After all, I am eighty-five, although, as always, an optimist. Still, there are very important things to say, to write about, that I would hate to leave unsaid.

I have brought my autobiography reasonably up to date, but it is almost all about my parents, my childhood, youth and education, marriage, years in the army, getting my tree farm started, successful civic life. Even wrote a bit about my own children, but little about the last twenty-plus years, my happiest years.

Once upon a time, in 1978, I realized that I was going to make a change in my life that would bring great happiness to me. I hoped the change would make another person happy, too.

Both of us had had many years of happy first marriages, had children we loved and were proud of, and many friends in common. We were about to drop a bomb on this situation. Not a happy outlook.

I first met Ann Homer Brinkley at a Seattle Foundation luncheon when we were both honored for civic leadership. She was president of the Children's Orthopedic Hospital and I had founded programs for the retarded. This must have been about 1963. We also met at the annual duck dinners of the Alberta shooting group of Brinkley, Davis, Eddy, Garrett, Padelford and myself. We were soon going to see more of each other.

Ann and Jim bought the Woolsey house next door to ours on Bainbridge Island in 1966. The Brinkleys were charming, liked tennis, had a small powerboat for picnic dinners on the spit on Blake Island. We had a pool and the Brinkley children enjoyed that. It was a very happy time. The summers went by pleasantly.

I became more and more immersed in organization work in the management of my own tree farm, on the Weyerhaeuser Company board, the Republican Party of Washington State, programs for the retarded such as Victoria Village and the Pilot School at the University of Washington. It was a disastrous overload.

My then wife, Anne Gould Hauberg, filled her life with encouraging young artists who adored her and came to many parties at our home on McGilvra Boulevard. We were not on the same train in Seattle, although we traveled very well together to the great centers of the world and to some of the most remote. And we were proud of the art with which we filled our houses. Also I enjoyed Anne's brothers and cousins, and took care of her mother and Aunt Jean Fay later on.

Jim Brinkley was having difficulties with his business. That household was becoming strained as was mine.

Much of this was understood at the time by our friends and families. But none of us expected that Ann and I would fall in love.

Ann had graduated from the University of California at Berkeley. She was widely knowledgeable in international affairs, read a lot of English and American literature and loved music and poetry. So we had a great deal in common and enjoyed each other's company. We began to listen to Puccini's great tragic operas on records, at her house and at mine. We read poetry aloud to each other.

Each of us had found new visions in each other, as our first marriages became less and less happy. But right here is the place and time to say, again, that we both had many happy years with our first spouses.

Marriage

At the end of 1978, we had each notified our spouses and friends that we would seek divorce with intent to marry, and so, on December 1, 1979, Ann Homer Brinkley and John Henry Hauberg were married in Carmel, California at Ann's sister Rosemary's house in the presence of our children, other family, and a few friends. There were tears and laughter. Ann and I had begun a new voyage. We were sure it would be smooth sailing, and so it has been.

Behind me were the 1970s, troublesome days of the Seattle Art Museum's first efforts to find a downtown site for its expansion, preparing for the 1978 June opening of the King Tut show, educating myself about Egypt by visiting it with a Princeton group in early 1978, and then the fun of Tut in Seattle in June.

Nineteen seventy-nine was a very busy year in many other ways. We began by visiting Ann's family and friends in California in February, and went for ten days to Bora-Bora in the South Pacific, one of the world's most beautiful places and about as far from Seattle as possible.

In the spring of 1979, I was invited to go to China with the Washington Council on International Trade to stimulate trade with a seemingly newly rich country. It was a great trip capped by a two-hour visit with a vice-premier of the communist fourteen-man politburo. Lots of fun, but the Chinese suddenly realized they were out of money to buy anything from lumber to engineering services. They had great needs for such infrastructure items as roads, airports, hotels, office buildings, power plants, dams and flood control and more, which is why our group and groups from other states had been invited to come to China. But now, the Chinese realized they had no money.

In 1979, I received a University of Washington Recognition Award, the Denkmann family had a reunion in Big Sky, Montana, and Ann and I bought a house just south of The Highlands from John and Virginia Tytus on July 1, 1979, and persuaded Bob Shields to design its remodeling.

In the fall of 1979, Ann and I went to Bedford, Massachusetts to visit Fay and Nat, and Stan and Sally Page, then on to New York to shop for beautiful things to live with, see a couple of plays, and *Carmen*, go with Bob and Bobbie Wilson to the Carlyle Hotel to listen to Bobby Short, and to Princeton to meet Class of '39 friends at the Yale game.

At last to Carmel, and our marriage, December 1, at Rosemary and George Blackstone's house with our families in attendance.

Two happy people and very much in love, and now, August 21, 2001, looking back on almost 22 years of bliss.

Our First Year

Ann and I were married December 1, 1979, on the "threshold of a new year and a new decade and in the midst of threats to the American economy and its military security. Inflation was in double digits, the auto industry was in a deep slump, and signs of a deep recession persisted."

So ran the *Wall Street Journal's* January 4, 1980, "Monday Outlook." Were we concerned?

A nice letter to the two of us from Governor Dixie Lee Ray got 1980 off to a good start and a heavy January snow kept us from getting to town. We went to New Orleans for a business meeting of the Denkmann family and Ann met my favorite cousin, Marietta Reimers Schneider, and most of the rest of the Denkmann clan.

During 1979, we had bought a lovely house in the Northwood area just south of The Highlands. It was ready for us to occupy upon our return from our short honeymoon in Mexico, and we lived in it while it was being remodeled by Bob Shields in a small way to suit us entirely. The house had great views of Puget Sound and the Olympics beyond. There was a swimming pool on the lower

Fred Reimers, Ann and John, Marietta Schneider

level opening out to a fine deck for parties. Soon our many mutual friends were joining us there. And the Seattle Golf Club was only five or ten minutes away for Sunday golf and get-togethers. Jean Jongeward designed the interiors, finding room for the major part of my Pacific Northwest Coast Indian collection as well as for paintings that we almost immediately began to collect. We lived there for thirteen years, during which the house was featured in *Architectural Digest*.

Top: Win Wright, Ann, John, and Bob Barnes in Maui
Bottom: JHH at Tatoosh House in 1978

But the remodeling of our new house, Northwood, was moving slowly during 1980, so we adjourned to Maui to golf and play tennis with Bob and June Barnes, Win and Kathy Wright, the Kitchells, and Bob and Dorothy O'Brien. A Kona wind had stripped the beach of its sand, but more gentle winds were bringing it back. Under Ann's guidance, I was reading the great French classics of Dumas and Victor Hugo. Ann also recommended the Russian author Gogol.

We returned home to be welcomed, on March 27, by an eruption of Mt. St. Helens, not yet the big one, but a hint from the gods. There would be more and finally a huge one in the weeks ahead.

Back home we discovered our Tatoosh House as a weekend retreat. We walked around the marsh, listened to a lot of Italian opera records. Ann curled up on the bedroom window seat and read. I went forth with a pruning saw to shape the trees.

Then there was the colossal salute to our marriage as Mt. St. Helens blew its top in May 1980. We were treated to a helicopter fly-over in August as the Weyerhaeuser board made one trip, perhaps too close to the crater, as sulfur fumes filled our 'copter. Our wives were then treated to a more conservative visit. But the devastation was enormous. Ann and I were to revisit the site every five years to the year of this chapter, 2001.

Ann and I were at Tatoosh that weekend and felt a series of thuds at 8:32 a.m., exactly the moment of the eruption some seventy-five miles away. At first, I thought our tree farm road builders were working on Sunday, blowing stumps for a right-of-way. But Sheff Phelps called us to turn on our radio and the eruption was the news of the entire day and the days following too.

We began a long series of wonderful trips with various groups of people, beginning with Hal and Elizabeth Hirsch and friends, related to Reed College, of which Hal and I were trustees. A July ride in MacKenzie River boats down the Rogue River in Oregon was almost too exciting as our boatman washed out an oar in a roaring rapids and we missed a big rock by inches. Ann's keen eyesight spotted nests of geese more quickly than anyone else. In another year we had a beautiful trip on the south fork of the Salmon River, again with the Hirsches, and our Reed College friends.

A fine event was another "Woodbrook Hunt" in April at our tree farm's Victoria tract. This "fox-less drag hunt," as the *Everett Herald* called it, was a joint meeting of the Fraser Valley Hunt Club of Vancouver with the Woodbrook Hunt of Tacoma. John

One of the many rapids on the Rogue River. We had just made this passage and were nearly overturned. This group had a rubber-inflated raft, not nearly as much fun.

Davis, one of our closest friends, was Master of the Woodbrook Hunt. When all hunters were mounted, John welcomed one and all riders and friends, called out the safety rules, and off went some twenty or thirty horses and red- and black-coated riders and the pack of hounds. Meanwhile, Franny and Manson Backus had "dragged" a bundle of cloth soaked in some animal's urine over the trail to be followed. When the score or more

With John Handley Davis,
Master of the Woodbrook Hunt

hounds picked up this scent, they took off pell-mell, sounding off as loud as they could. Our convoy of cars of friends went to places along the route to watch this procession roar into view and disappear over the hills. Very exciting. At the end of the "hunt" there was a huge picnic in the big barn in our meadow. One year we roasted a whole ox over an open pit for several hundred guests. Altogether, there were probably four or five of these events.

Another yearlong pleasure was the development of Pilchuck Glass School's tenth year. More housing for students and staff was needed. Architect Tom Bosworth had designed two dormitories for twelve students each with pairs of bedrooms sharing a bathroom. We built both of these dormitories, but the students and staff said they were too luxurious. We later found out that the problem was lack of privacy for sex. The roaring hot furnaces and glory holes, the intimate relationships required in the glass blowing process created urges we had not suspected! The other need was a change to a full-time director.

Pilchuck had grown beyond the ability of part-time director Tom Bosworth and his wife Elaine, who had become the full-time registrar while managing the Bosworth family full time. Both Bob Block and I came simultaneously to Alice Rooney who was director of Allied Arts in Seattle. Dale Chihuly agreed, and we approached Alice who was ready for a job change. We had solved housing and leadership problems and were ready for the summer! Ann and I walked from Instant to the campus almost every weekend during the summer to enjoy a chance to talk to the artists, watch them work, and have lunch with the whole gang. On the first of August, Ann and I walked from Tatoosh up to a "pig roast" staged by Fritz Dreisbach. It became an annual event not to be missed.

Ann, Nat, Fay, Carey, Ben, and the Great House

In late May, we were off to Chicago, St. Paul, and Rock Island to meet Ed and Luche Uihlein, my Hotchkiss classmate and Princeton roommate, Weyerhaeuser cousins in St. Paul and dozens of cousins and old friends in the Tri-Cities. Also to visit the Great House, the House-in-the-Woods, and the Hauberg farms.

Back home the Seattle Art Museum was still in the throes of finding a new location, and the Pilchuck Glass School was having a hard time with leadership. Katherine White's great African collection came to the Seattle Art Museum through efforts by Ann and me, Jane and David Davis, and the Bagley Wrights.

We survived an incredibly busy first year filled with a few isolated activities not to be repeated, but with more of the same for the most part over the following years.

Now began the wonderful summers on Bainbridge with Ann's children, enjoying the pool and tennis court and Sunday-night picnics on the beach. Over the following years, each child was to marry. Each marriage was a joyous occasion. The ensuing grandchildren have been lots of fun for Ann and me.

We have joined Ann's brother and sister in Carmel, San Francisco, and Palm Springs on many occasions. My children, Sue and Fay, and Fay's tribe of Pages have also joined us for many holidays.

Ann and I looked forward to the every-five-year trips with my Princeton Class of '39. We went "Up the Rhine with Thirty-nine," "Pasta and Wine with Thirty-nine," and I found that my classmates were not any more interested in "art" than any other slice of American college graduates might have been and it saddened me. But at least I introduced three or four friends to museums in Holland, in Basel, and in France's smaller cities.

We joined Seattle Art Museum tours to Japan with Henry Trubner and to China with Mimi Neill Gates conducting. After the latter we went on our own to Cambodia and its great ancient city of Angkor Wat. As it turned out, our visit there was during a brief lull in the fratricidal wars in Viet Nam and Cambodia.

Another "vacation" was a great trip to France, in September, most of the time with Sheff and Patty Phelps. We picked up our Audi 5000 diesel in Brussels and drove through Rouen to join them for two days in Normandy. We spent a day at Omaha Beach and its huge cemetery where the bodies of the thousands of American GIs killed in the D-Day assault are buried. All of us were in tears as we walked the rows of crosses. Officers and enlisted men were side by side as were Christians and Jews, whites, blacks, Asian Americans, and Native Americans. The nearby museum filled in all-too-many details of the battle.

Sheff and Patty went on to Brittany, while Ann and I went to visit the Chateau district just south of Tours along the Loire River. We enjoyed the differences in sites, architecture, and gardens at Chenonceaux, Villandry, Chambord, Amboise, and Blois.

We went to the cave country, putting up at the Cro Magnon Hotel in Les Eyzies. Patty and Sheff were in another town nearby. We "did" some very interesting caves and the nearby museum. By this time, Sheff and Patty Phelps and we were "doing" some towns separately and then coming together again. We went to Albi together to visit the Toulouse-Lautrec cathedral and then Ann and I went to Carcassonne to see the old walled town. We were together at Les Baux and a fabulous dinner at Beaumaniere.

Ann and I went to Aix-en-Provence to Hotel de Pigeonnet and the Vaserely Museum, also the main street, the Cours Mirabeau. Both of us now were having tummy trouble from all the rich French meals, with more of them to come. We and the Phelpses went to St. Paul de Vence to visit the Matisse Chapel and the Maeght Museum. We went on to lunch at the hilltop town of Eze and killed a couple bottles of Tattinger 1973 at $75.00 per bottle. Oh well!

A few days later we were back in Seattle. It was raining hard.

Thanksgiving was in our new home in Northwood with Sue, down from her stables, Fay and Nat and Carey and Ben, newly moved from Massachusetts to Mercer Island, happily nearby! Marion and first husband Bernie Hyde, Jim and friend Bettina Collins and her five-year-old daughter made an even dozen for a great turkey dinner. I showed a carousel of slides of the "old days." Fine day.

Christmas found Sue with us opening stockings around the breakfast table, then to the living room to open presents. I took a walk with Winner. Izzy, Jimmy, Marion and Bernie and Alison, and all the Pages came to a fine turkey dinner, starting a long Christmas tradition. Afterwards there was a Jacuzzi hot tub and swim for everyone.

We closed out 1980 at Tatoosh with Sheff and Patty and Winner. Much champagne and bridge until 2 a.m.

The Dow closed the year at 963.99. Gold at $591. Weyerhaeuser stock was at 39 and paying $1.30 per share dividend.

So, marriages, births, holidays, seasonal vacations, schools for our grandchildren and their own accomplishments, travels to fascinating places, a few deaths of senior members of our families, houses, books, art, theater, sports and many parties have established traditions that we all cherish. Even the highlights of our life together fall into a pattern.

Ann is a warm hearted, gregarious lady who brought many friends into my life. I added many friends and relatives to her list.

I like some lines from a song by the Irish Tenors:

"Life is an ocean, Love is a boat.

In troubled water, it keeps us afloat

When we started the voyage there was just me and you,

Now gathered round us, we have our own crew."

Left: Ann Homer Hauberg; Right: JHH and Winner at Northwood

Ann Homer Hauberg

John has asked me to tell you about myself, since I am a part of his life story. I don't have much information about the Homer side of my family. Daddy was a younger brother who was kept out of the Homer family business and had to make his own career. He was a mining engineer for awhile, and then went into the insurance business in Seattle where he met my mother, Marion Wiley.

The Wiley side suffered a terrible tragedy when my grandparents, Charles and Lida Wiley drowned in Princess Louisa Inlet when grandmother fell overboard from a boat and grandfather tried to save her. They were caught in a whirlpool.

My mother was only twelve years old when this happened, and her two brothers Lawrence and John were younger. An aunt and uncle in Illinois raised all of them, but the boys never really recovered from the loss of their parents. A cousin in Illinois was Virginia Wiley who came to Seattle later, "Aunt Virginia" Price Patty.

After my mother married Carl Homer, they lived in Seattle at 1101 36th Avenue East just five blocks from where John and I live now. When I was nine, my sister Rosemary and brother Charles and I moved with Mother and Daddy to Hillsboro, California. So I really grew up in California. Charles now lives in San Francisco and Rosemary Blackstone lives in Carmel.

I went to Hillsboro Grammar School, a public school, and then to Sarah Vicks Hamlin School for Girls, where I graduated from high school. My father had an insurance firm in San Francisco. My parents had a happy marriage. Daddy was difficult, a New England Yankee, but I would say that my mother ruled the roost. She was active in everything, and was particularly interested in the garden club. She loved to play bridge. They joined the Burlingame Country Club in Hillsboro and played a lot of bridge with another couple there. My father died first, and not long after that my mother died.

When I was a youngster, I liked to play tennis. I had a lot of friends. Hillsboro Grammar School was far from our home. Mother drove me there, and I walked home, usually with a string of boys following me. Then I went to the University of California in Berkeley and pledged Kappa Alpha Theta, and was president of the house. I graduated with a degree in international relations, which has been a major interest of mine. I read a lot about it. During World War II, I worked for the Office of War Information in California. I was in the Philippines division, and wrote for them. I loved it, particularly when the UN started in San Francisco.

In 1947, when I was twenty-three, I married James Brinkley, from Seattle. I used to come to Seattle on school vacations to stay with my aunt and uncle on Bainbridge, and that was how I met Jim. I had only known him three days when we got engaged. I think I was awfully hasty. We were married in the garden at home.

When Jim and I were first married we lived in Longview, Washington, where he worked for a paper company. Then we lived in Eugene, Oregon, and finally in Seattle. We had four children—one boy, the eldest, and three girls. We had a summer place on Bainbridge, which the children really enjoyed.

John Hauberg lived next door on Bainbridge, and I had known him for quite a while. Neither of us was getting along very well with our spouses, but divorce was a painful decision. I think my children were sorry about it, particularly Alison, the youngest. They liked John very much. Now they are all married, Izzy (Elizabeth), Marion, Jimmy, and Alison. I feel fortunate that my children have always been very good friends with one another. Alison lives in Washington, D.C., but the others live here in Seattle. Jimmy is an M.D., Ph.D. at the University of Washington, and so is his wife, Sheila.

She is at Harborview, and Jimmy is at the medical school. Alison is studying to be a Montessori teacher. Their father has remarried to a wonderful person. Because of the children, whenever there is a family gathering at their house they invite all of us.

I have six grandchildren. I enjoy them a lot. They absolutely love John. We have nice big family get-togethers on holidays.

I share John's interest in art. We have similar tastes—I wouldn't buy anything if he didn't like it. I enjoy listening to music. John and I used to love to play tennis together, before my hip problem. We belong to the Tennis Club. Also we have enjoyed golf at Seattle Golf Club. John is just wonderful to be married to, very warm. I get along well with his children, Fay and Sue.

We have a lot of friends and enjoy entertaining. We like to give small dinner parties now and then, but we've entertained as many as fifteen or twenty-five. We found good caterers, Allen Sarno and Vida Collery, so it's easier to have a few more. Sometimes Vida cooks the dinner in our kitchen, other times she brings it in already prepared. For holidays she will bring in the turkey, then cook everything else here.

We love to travel. We have become very close members of John's Princeton class, and enjoy traveling with them. I like to go to Europe the best. In other chapters of this book, John has described some of the wonderful trips we have taken with his Princeton classmates.

I was active in the Seattle Garden Club. We don't have a garden at our current house in Seattle, but there is quite a garden at the Bainbridge house. We enjoy a small house on John's tree farm, and have enjoyed decorating it ourselves. It has become more home-like as we have taken some of our paintings there.

I'm so glad that John has taken the time to write his life story. I know family members will treasure it for many years to come.

The Caboose on Bainbridge
"Bought in the first PONCHO auction. The caboose was
set up on about thirty feet of ties and tracks and furnished fun
for the kids for many years."

CHAPTER 28

Homes at Bainbridge Island, 601, and Tatoosh

Bainbridge

I N 1955 ANNIE AND I MOVED INTO 1101 MCGILVRA BOULEVARD, WHICH WAS DESIGNED for us by Roland Terry. He and Annie basically designed it, and I didn't get to say a lot about the plans. But it was a super house and I liked Roland. Like all good architects, he gives you more than you expect, and it's always good.

When Annie and I built the Bainbridge house in 1955–1957 I was a more active participant. Fay was thirteen and Sue, nine. We had enjoyed using the Gould house on Bainbridge, known as Topsfield, just up the hill from our waterfront property. Many of our best friends were on Bainbridge in the Country Club area as well as the flats. Mrs. Gould, Annie's mother, had been living elsewhere, but she felt more comfortable on Bainbridge and wanted to move back into her house, to which she had come as a bride in 1914. It was designed by her husband, and held many happy memories for her.

In 1952 I had been approached by Milnor Roberts, an old friend of the Gould family, professor of mining engineering at the UW, who lived with his twin sister, Milnora. They had taken Annie and me under their wing in the early years of our marriage and were great friends of ours. We went to a lot of UW cultural events, openings of plays at the Showboat Theatre, for example.

Milnor liked me very much. We were both members of the University Club, and were very compatible. He was probably in his eighties in 1952 when he approached me and said that a man he and I both disliked was pestering him to sell the lot that he and his sister owned on Bainbridge Island. Milnor felt certain the people at that end of Bainbridge would not enjoy having that person in the group. I told him I would buy it, but I wanted no one to know that I had bought it, because the minute it was known, everybody in the area would start telling me what I should be doing with it. Then Annie and I could proceed with a house in due course. Annie felt the same way I did. Dean Roberts asked twenty thousand dollars for something like three hundred feet of Bainbridge Island waterfront property. I thought that was pretty high at the time, but in retrospect it was the best deal I ever made.

In 1955 I hired Roland Terry to design a summer home for us on Bainbridge. To our delight, the drop in elevation from the road to the top of the beach was somewhere in the neighborhood of ten to twelve feet. That would give the house a certain prominence. The drop from road to house would be very graceful and we would have room on all sides for a swimming pool, tennis court, vegetable garden, cutting gardens, etc.

Roland and I worked very closely together. I wanted to be on the ground floor. I was weary of walking up so many steps as we had to do at 1101 McGilvra. If you got to your automobile and forgot something, you had to climb something like thirty-four steps to get to it. I don't think we ever considered an elevator in that house. We were young and vigorous, and at the design stage the prospect of all those steps hadn't bothered me, but they became a reality to deal with.

I therefore thought that in the Bainbridge house our bedroom should be on the ground floor. That meant that everyone else would be above it. I wanted the house to be open and cheerful, with great views from all the rooms. We had huge sliding doors everywhere so we could open up the house when that was desired. John Davis literally rode his horse through the living room at one point. He was invited to do that just to show the open aspect of the design when the sliding doors were open.

We didn't have the swimming pool right away, but we did have the tennis court. We left as many of the existing trees as we could, but the soil was very thin, and after we had a couple of very strong windstorms we were down to two major fir trees side by side out on the lawn. Today they aren't there because one was blown down and fell against the house, damaging the roof. We didn't want the other one to do the same thing. That was probably in the '70s. Arthur P. Nute, our next-door neighbor, said that when he built his house in 1912 there really wasn't anything on our lot at all. It had been pastured by the farmer, and Arthur could actually see the Country Club clubhouse up on the point from his house. By 1955 or so the place was covered with Oregon ash and vine maple, and a lot of blackberry bushes. There were many yellow jacket nests. There probably were rats also, but I didn't see any. So it had to be cleared. When the clearing was done, the two fir trees were no longer supported by the surrounding brush, with their resulting loss.

We ended up with a bedroom downstairs with dressing rooms and a bath, and then five bedrooms upstairs, with three baths. Only one of the bedrooms had its own bathroom, and two pairs of bedrooms shared a bath. It seemed to be an ideal combination for a summer house.

We wanted a low maintenance garden, and hired Noble Hoggson to do it. We were very pleased with the results. We built a barn with stalls for two horses. At the outset, Fay was riding a huge horse named Big Red. She had kept it over at Topsfield. She was a beautiful little blonde girl, and perched on top of Big Red she presented a picture that really tugged at your heartstrings.

We finally gave Red to someone because Fay got involved in riding in hunter-jumper classes. She was so good that we bought a better horse, named Rayhak's Rahwan.

She rode him to the finals in Hunt Seat Class state championships in Washington and Oregon. We also had one of my Grandfather Denkmann's carriages, and we made room for that in the barn. We found someone who did a superb job of restoring it. He even sent to France for the rickrack trim that was typical of a Victorian carriage. But we never could find a team of horses to pull it. Finally I gave the carriage to the Seattle Museum of History and Industry, where it is today.

Then I had Grandpa Hauberg's buggy that my Aunt Rosetta used to drive as she made her rounds giving piano lessons to the farmers' children. That was lots of fun. Johnny Davis had a Connemara pony. The first time around, the pony kicked the traces into smithereens. Johnny was embarrassed and bought another pair of traces. We finally did have a ride in the buggy.

The tennis court was a huge success. The only court in the area was the one at the Country Club, and even as summer members of the club we had not had the right to use their tennis court except during the annual tournament. Increasingly, the Country Club members lived there year-round. When Annie and I started to go there in the 1940s, almost no one lived there on a year-round basis. That was true to some extent on the flats. Our tennis court was very popular because it was the only one that everyone who didn't belong to the Country Club could now use, so there was lots of action. The annual tennis tournament on our court went along with that of the Country Club. We were very close to the members of the Country Club. All the men were also members of the University Club, and the women of the Sunset Club.

Our house was immediately written up in magazines. Roland Terry knew that the only way for an architect to advertise was to get magazines like *Architectural Digest* and *House Beautiful* to write up the house. And so he arranged that.

We built the swimming pool in 1960. While the house was being built, we became conscious of the fact that although we didn't have a high bank, we really didn't have much of a beach, due to the interesting configuration of the Nutes' pool next door. The tidal currents swirled around the end of their pool and cut into our lawn tremendously.

We built a bulkhead out to our property line and straightened out the beach, filling the hole behind the bulkhead with dirt that was excavated to build the house. We had Roland Terry design this special raised beach above the bulkhead, with steps down to the beach proper. Our families love that little beach. We have Sunday night grills there almost every weekend in the summertime.

We thought we would use the house from the Fourth of July to Labor Day, but we liked it so much that we wound up going over there usually on Memorial Day weekend. At one time we tried moving over on the first of May, but both of us were much too involved in the city for that.

The summers were great. We had a lot of people our age that we liked and who liked us. At that time I was gathering land for the tree farm I was involved with the symphony and on several boards with programs for handicapped kids. Annie was also involved in countless projects. I went to town a lot from Monday through Friday. But that has blessedly given way now to the point where I come to town maybe twice a week after moving to Bainbridge for the summer.

The Bainbridge house is a splendid house. We had a man named Conrad Jacobson who had been a laborer on the construction crew. He lived on Bainbridge, and he hinted to the contractor that he would like to remain on because he knew where everything was, all the wiring, etc. So we took on Jake and it was a great thing. He not only worked for us but he worked for everybody else. He was a jack-of-all-trades. He's not a caretaker, but he did the gardening and looked after the house. I think Norwegians have quite an artistic sense. In the fall, Jake would bring to town a huge branch of vine maple in great color. He knew exactly what to do with it in our house in town, where we had a stairwell that was twenty-four feet to the ceiling.

He found a wonderful piece of driftwood which he brought to our new beach and set up. We call it Neptune's Throne. It just gives so much character to our beach. Great eagles and cute little kingfishers enjoy this perch.

We wanted more privacy for the yard so we brought in about a thousand cubic yards of dirt and created an artificial orchard that drops off just before you get to the area at the side of our house. We planted some apple trees. It's also a great parking area for the house, and a place where the horses can graze, and people can sit.

When Annie and I parted company, she kept the house on McGilvra Boulevard, which she later sold, and I took the house on Bainbridge. My new Ann and I spend most of our summers there, and still find it a delightful and restful ambience. It is an easy commute to my office on those days when I need to tend to business there.

Sometimes we round up some old chums for a game of golf. Ann and I love to read, and on a good hot sunny day after we've played nine or eighteen holes of golf, we sit out there in the yard, or sit by the pool and read. We both like to swim. We usually swim a few laps every day. Our children and grandchildren enjoy it. We invite them all the time, Sunday nights especially.

My first visit to Bainbridge was another example of the serendipity that has pleasured me all through the years. As a young bachelor recently arrived in Seattle, I was invited to a coming-out party, the debut of a young girl who lived at the north end of Bainbridge. The fleet was in, and they were very much a Navy family, so dozens of plebes and young officers were invited to this party. The question was, where the heck were we all going to sleep? My roommates at Princeton and I had entertained some plebes during a Princeton/Navy game, and one of these chaps attended this party. We remembered each other and were invited to stay at Mrs. Gould's house. We were six-foot four and six-foot five respectively, each weighing probably two hundred pounds. We had to share a twin bed!

My Navy roommate and I got up in the morning and walked out on the old golf course, and up to the Country Club tennis court, which was very primitive. You had to roll it yourself. It reminded me so much of the two summers I spent at Hyannisport on Cape Cod. The facilities were primitive there also, but everybody enjoyed it. The main thing was to have some way of enjoying friendships and have a good time at a summer place at very little cost.

There were two ferry dock options in the '40s and perhaps '50s. The ferry from Seattle stopped at Winslow, and then it backed across Eagle Harbor and made another stop at Eagledale. There were ferry docks all around Bainbridge Island, where the so-called mosquito fleet used to take people to their summer residences. For Mr. Gould, for example, the ferry landed at the Country Club dock. There was no road to Topsfield, so Mrs. Gould would take Annie and Carl and Wyck on foot down to the ferry dock. The closest dock to our new house was South Beach. There was another one at Pleasant Beach. Earlier they went into Rolling Bay, and all the way to Port Madison. They were small ferryboats, passenger only. The road system was really primitive. Everything now depends on automobiles. It's no longer that relaxed atmosphere of those earlier days.

In the '30s and '40s it was a slower paced world. You could come roaring down to the ferry dock, and even if the ferry had dropped its gate, it would reverse itself and come back and pick you up. You knew the names of all the deckhands. When you went to the store you knew the names of the owners and they knew you. The people on the ferries were people you knew. It was absolutely charming.

But present-day Bainbridge is not without its charm as well. There are still friends one meets on the ferry and there is the chance to get away from the traffic and problems of big-city life in Seattle. There is the timeless fascination of the tides that wash against our bulkhead, and the enjoyment Ann and I get from entertaining our children and grandchildren on a summer day around the pool or on the beach.

The House We Live In—601

I was born in a great house, designed by a nationally famous architect. The very existence of that house gave me a lifetime interest in architecture, and may have had something to do with my marrying Anne Gould. Her father was the eminent architect Carl F. Gould, who designed the University of Washington campus and many of its buildings. He died before our marriage, and I regret that I did not have the opportunity to meet him. Annie knew all the famous architects, and when we had occasion to visit some of them we were always immediately ushered in by the receptionist who said that Mrs. Hauberg was the daughter of Carl F. Gould of Seattle.

Annie and I built the house on McGilvra and later the Bainbridge house, both of which were published in all the magazines. After my marriage to Ann Homer Brinkley, she and I moved to a house in the north end of Seattle, close to the city limits, and did a little remodeling. We put my pre-Columbian and Pacific Northwest Coast Indian collections in it, and that house also was written up nationally. About the third or fourth time that it took an hour to commute from downtown because of traffic jams, we decided we would move close to town. We specifically wanted to live in Washington Park. Ann was born just down the street from our present house, and lived there until she was eight years old.

We wanted to build a fine house, but I don't think we had in mind anything like we have now. Ann's cousin, Andrew Price, Jr. and his wife, Marianna, lived on this piece of property and put their house up for sale. When we bought it, I told Marianna we would be tearing down the house and she said that was OK. It was a nice old house, built in about 1908 and set well back from the corner. It probably had a superb view originally, but now all the trees had grown up so it had almost no view, even from the attic.

We started looking for architects. At a cocktail party at Gil Anderson's, we admired their house and they told us the architect was Jim Olson. When we visited the Hedreen house, just down the street, their architect also turned out to be Jim Olson. So we hired the firm of Olson Sundberg to do our house. We worked on the plans for a year and a half, trying to squeeze in everything we wanted. As a guide to what we wanted in the house on our lot at 601, I wrote a twenty-five-page booklet describing what we liked and did not like about our Northwood house. For example, we wanted higher ceilings, and this much room compared to that much room at Northwood. We didn't get into details of furniture or color or anything like that. We finally came down to pretty much writing the specifications for the architect's decisions about this house.

It was lots of fun to work with Olson Sundberg, a young firm and not as large as it is today. Their method of proceeding was interesting. Every Friday the entire staff of architects would go over all of the jobs the firm had, so the least established of their architects could see something they thought could be done, or critique something that might be done better or not at all. The whole firm pitched in on the planning of our house, and they did a magnificent job

We had a styrofoam model of the proposed house made, one-inch to one-foot. You could take the floors apart. It was my idea to make the model, which cost five or six thousand dollars. When we began to see what we had, all kinds of modest changes took place. One of the most interesting things about the model was that we had all the major paintings we were going to hang in the house photographed, and then the photographs were printed in a size to correspond with the exact scale of the model. We hung every picture in this little model before the house was even built, to make sure we could accommodate them all.

We had commissioned the Libenskys, world famous glass artists from Prague, to do a crystal column for our house at Northwood but they never got around to making it for that house. They work together as a team; he's the designer and she makes all the casts for the pieces they do. Finally it arrived in two huge boxes, which were stored at Artech. Jim Olson and Tom Kundig, the job captain, and Ann and I went down to Artech, took the lids off the boxes and measured the column.

Then the architects had to contend with where to place the column to best advantage. The decision was to position it in a pool at the end of the hall. The north side of the house is divided into a front hall, a gallery, and then the various rooms. The hall goes straight from the front door through to the pool. The Libensky column is just outside the window at the west end of the hall. We also opened up a part of the living room wall so we could see the crystal column from the living room.

I had also thought it would be great to have a skylight done by Ed Carpenter, a talented stained-glass artist who has done walls for important government and commercial builders, mostly in Oregon. Olson Sundberg called in Ed Carpenter and we came to the agreement that he would do a skylight. Ed worked very closely with the architects to perfect the skylight, which reflects sunshine through various shapes of glass with colors. The sun is refracted by a mirror through these pieces of glass and onto the walls.

Olson Sundberg was very flexible, and they were all excited about our project, which was a difficult challenge. We used every square foot permitted by the law, and every cubic foot allowed by the code. There is no way we could expand the house in any direction. In my twenty-five-page booklet I said we had traveled in southern France and Italy a lot, and wanted a house somewhat like a small Italian villa. We wanted it to be light in color. We didn't want overhangs that would make any of the rooms dark or gloomy. We wanted color inside the house as well as out. We wanted lots of light to be let in. The concrete pillars evolved, and the concrete floors with slate and terra cotta tile emerged through somebody's mind in the firm. The house was a year and a half in the planning and two and a half years in construction. When it was completed, it was a masterpiece.

In November 1992 we moved in. The *New York Times* published an article about the house on March 23, 1993 by Amalia Lui, their leading architectural critic. I remember vaguely taking her around and how enthusiastic she was, but I never realized what would it lead to. Her extensive article with pictures was reproduced in newspa-

601 in 2000

pers all over the world. We left Palm Springs a week after the article was published, and by the time we got home we had stacks of mail from all over the place—people wanting to see the house. Since then it has been visited by perhaps three or four thousand people. Groups from art museums all over the U.S.A. come through. We always have Jim Olson with us to show the house when groups have come through.

People still stop their cars and look up at the house.

One interesting group that came by included nine vice-presidents of Microsoft. The Microsoft billionaires (some of whom are buying two or more smaller homes and tearing them down to build a huge one) generally speaking are not very conscious of art and architecture, but efforts are being made to educate those who are receptive. A Microsoft executive who was then treasurer of the Seattle Art Museum arranged the tour. He was shocked that so many of his cohorts were spending all of their new money building rather hideous houses and not getting into very good art, so he organized a visit to four houses. In addition to our house, the tour included Jane Davis's, for her art collection as well as the location and general layout of her house, Dick Hedreen's, just down the street from us, then finally Jinny and Bagley Wright's house, an Arthur Ericson house.

The purpose of the tour was to acquaint the visitors not only with the fundamentals of good architecture, but also to note the way these houses complemented the type of art chosen by the home owner. Each of the four houses displayed a different kind of art collection. For example, Jinny Wright is on the cutting edge of modernism; Dick Hedreen is a little more conservative, but with prominent artists of the '70s and '80s and maybe the '90s; Jane has an eclectic mixture of everything. She has wonderful taste and her pictures are strong but not challenging. Everybody loves Jane's collection.

In Chapter 24, I discussed the art which my wife and I have collected over the years, the display of which was very important to us in designing the house in which we now live.

It has been rewarding to see the interest which our house has created, but the important part is that it exactly fits our needs. It was designed so that should either of us experience serious health problems as we grow older, the elevator and wide doorways will give ready access to a wheelchair. Building a house is a challenging experience. It should blend in with the community to a reasonable though not a slavish extent, offer the latest in technological advances which will provide ease of maintenance and access, but most importantly enhance your particular lifestyle and interests. Based on these criteria, Ann and I have been delighted with our house at 601.

Tatoosh

The annual, popular PONCHO auction in 1969 or 1970 featured a small prefabricated house. Annie Gould was fascinated by the concept of prefab, low cost housing, and bid it in. She then contacted the company that had built it and asked them to let her help design a second such house. Working with the company manager, she produced a design, which combined two "boxcars," fourteen feet by thirty-four feet, the maximum size for highway transport. These boxes were juxtaposed in such a manner as

The Instant House

to make for two bedrooms and a living room on one side of a hallway, with a bath-room and kitchen and dining room on the other side. The dining room opened onto the living room. Windows were large to enjoy views.

The plans for the house were transmitted to Glen Greener, my land manager of Pilchuck Tree Farms, and he poured the foundations, brought in water and electricity in advance of the arrival of the two "boxcars." He also developed a gravel road across the marsh on property I had bought for my "Tatoosh Development," which had failed—but at least I had a 135-acre tract of high ground in the midst of the Pilchuck Tree Farm property with great views of both the Cascades and Olympic Mountains.

The boxcars arrived and a crane placed each in place on Glenn's foundations. The bolting together and hooking up to water and electricity took only two hours! We named our new little house the Instant House. And so it was called for ten years.

Annie got carried away and ordered two more prefab houses of different sizes to join Instant in 1970. Both were transferred to other owners in a few years, one to Pilchuck Glass School, just one mile away up the hill and in need of an infirmary in case of accidents.

The 1970s became the years of Annie's and my marriage cooling and ultimate dissolution so the little house was little used. But after Ann Homer and I were mar-

The marsh and pond at Instant, with great views of the Cascades to the east

ried, we found it a great retreat where we could read, listen to records, and hike over the tree-farm roads. We spent dozens of weekends at our Tatoosh house over the next twenty years, only occasionally inviting friends or family to share it with us.

We added a beautiful bedroom and bath designed by Tom Bosworth starting in 1983. Our comfort was vastly increased with these two rooms. Large windows opened on every view, and bookshelves let us bring together a substantial library. The large walls went to large paintings by Northwest artists.

This idyll has been shattered by Ann's illness from strokes and seizures, but the place is ready for us upon any recovery on her part.

Meanwhile, the scores of trees of many species planted over the years have brought great color every fall. A two-acre hardwood forest resembling the forest my great-grandfather Hauberg left behind in Germany has made a start into this type of research in the Pacific Northwest.

Sue Hauberg, John Henry Hauberg, Jr., and
Fay Hauberg Page celebrate John's 85th birthday

CHAPTER 29

Family Events

Birthdays and Marriages

b Y THE YEAR 2001, ANN AND I HAVE A FULL COMPLEMENT OF CHILDREN AND grandchildren. Happy marriages have led to happy families whose progress through work and schools has been closely followed and chronicled.

Much of the annual events have been photographed by Fay Page and Elizabeth Brinkley Rosane, "Izzy," to most of us, and me. It would triple the size of this already lengthy opus if I used too many pictures. Following in Chapter 30 are a few from over the years.

Also, I would also like to record important dates, at the same time providing the family with a convenient chronicle.

Ann Homer Hauberg
born June 28, 1923
in Seattle, Washington
of Marion Wiley and Carl Homer

John Henry Hauberg, Jr.
born June 24, 1916
in Rock Island, Illinois
of Susanne Denkmann and John H. Hauberg

Married December 7, 1979

Children of Ann Homer and James F. Brinkley, Jr.:

James F. Brinkley III, born Dec. 1, 1948
Sheila Lukehart, born Sept. 27, 1951
  Married: Nov. 21, 1991
  Children: Jessie Lukehart Kindig,
    born Aug. 23, 1982
  David Michael Brinkley,
    born Jan. 30, 1997

Marion Brinkley, born Mar. 11, 1951
George Mohler, born Nov. 29, 1947
  Married: Nov. 16, 1985
  Children: Jenny Mohler,
    born Dec. 16, 1987
  Heather Mohler, born Apr. 27, 1990

Elizabeth Brinkley, born June 20, 1952
Andrew Rosane, born Feb. 16, 1955
  Married: Aug. 20, 1983
  Children: Olivia Rosane,
    born June 9, 1987

Alison Brinkley, born Mar. 29, 1955
Lawrence Kingsley, born June 16, 1960
  Married: Sept. 8, 1989
  Children: Marnie Kingsley,
    born May 8, 1991
  Ian Kingsley, born July 4, 1992

Children of Anne Gould Hauberg and John H. Hauberg, Jr.:

Fay Hauberg Page, born February 4, 1944 in Seattle, Washington
Nathaniel Blodgett Page, born April 19, 1944 in Boston, Massachusetts
   Married: June 17, 1967
      Children: Catherine (Carey) Blodgett Page, born April 3, 1974 in
         Cambridge, Massachusetts
      Ben Hauberg Page, born September 12, 1977 in Cambridge, Massachusetts
Sue Bradford Hauberg, born October 3, 1948 in Seattle, Washington

Relatives of Ann Homer Hauberg

Rosemary Homer (sister to Ann Homer) born February 28, 1926 in Seattle,
   Washington of Marion Wiley & Carl Norman Homer
George Arthur Blackstone, born September 30, 1922 in Hastings, Nebraska
   Married: June 11, 1955
   Children: Carl Homer Blackstone, born June 29, 1956 in Washington, D.C.
   Selden Prentice, born March 30, 1958
      Married: June 27, 1987
      Children: Katie Blackstone, born March 6, 1988
         Hilary Blackstone, born Oct.11, 1991
   Amy Grace Blackstone, born May 6, 1958

Charles Wiley Homer, born July 5, 1927 in Seattle, Washington
Elizabeth Lou Elwood, born June 23, 1928 in Omaha, Nebraska
   Married: June 17, 1950
   Children: Winifred Wiley Homer, born November 2, 1951
      Bruce Messer Smith, born October 28, 1951
         Married: August 25, 1973
         Children: Elizabeth Homer-Smith, born October 15,1976
            Rebecca Homer-Smith, born March 29, 1979
      Rosemary Elwood Homer, born August 13, 1953
      Michael Bruce Lanyon, born April 27, 1954
         Married: September 10, 1983
         Children: Charles Homer Lanyon, born April 19, 1985

Calendar Year Birthdays

January
2   Kinda Kayyali, 1975
9   Harriet Sweeney Fraunfelter, 1948
30 David Michael Brinkley, 1997

February
1   Sean Michael Sweeney, 1965
4   Fay Hauberg Page, 1944
7   Philip Miles Sweeney, 1945
16 Andrew Rosane, 1955
28 Rosemary Blackstone, 1926

March
6   Katie Blackstone, 1989
11 Marion Mohler, 1951
29 Alison Kingsley, 1955
29 Rebecca Homer Smith, 1979
29 Selden Prentice, 1959
31 Suzanne Sweeney Kayyali, 1941

April
3   Catherine Blodgett Page, 1974
11 Catherine Hauberg Sweeney, 1914
19 Nathaniel Blodgett Page, 1944
19 Charles Homer Lanyon, 1985
27 Bruce Lanyon, 1954
27 Heather Mohler, 1990

May
6   Amy Grace Blackstone, 1958
6   Mark Edward Sweeney, 1974
8   Marnie Kingsley, 1991
10 Eric Christopher Sweeney, 1967
20 Colin Gabriel Sweeney, 1985

June
9   Olivia Rosane, 1987
16 Lawrence Kingsley, 1960
20 Elizabeth Brinkley Rosane, 1952
23 Betty Lou Homer, 1928
24 John H. Hauberg, Jr., 1916
28 Ann Borodell Homer Hauberg, 1923
29 Carl Homer Blackstone, 1956

July
4   Ian Kingsley, 1992
5   Charles W. Homer, 1927
10 Eric Fraunfelter, 1947

August
15 Rosemary Homer Lanyon, 1953

September
1   John Sweeney, 1954
12 Benjamin Hauberg Page, 1977
27 Sheila Lukehart Brinkley, 1951
30 George Blackstone, 1922

October
3   Sue Bradford Hauberg, 1948
7   Randa Kayyali Zeneddine, 1970
9   Sandra Sweeney, 1942
11 Hilary Blackstone, 1991
14 Edward Sweeney, Jr., 1942
15 Elizabeth Homer Smith, 1976
28 Bruce Homer Smith, 1956

November
2   Winifred Homer Smith, 1951
29 George Mohler, 1947

December
1   Jim Brinkley III, 1947
2   Liana Catherine Sweeney, 1987
16 Jenny Mohler, 1987

Ann and John in Italy, 1984

CHAPTER 30
Family Photo Album

1980

Wow!

Above: Pages on Bainbridge; Above left: Pages in Rock Island at the Great House

Carey Page, first grade

Below: John Davis leads the Woodbrook Hunt at Pilchuck

Above: James F. Brinkley, III, Elizabeth Rosane and Marion Mohler

JHH's secretaries from 1950 to 2002: Corrine Reinbold, 1980 to present; Kathryn Hillman, 1965 to 1980; Grace Bartlett, 1950 to 1975

At Tatoosh

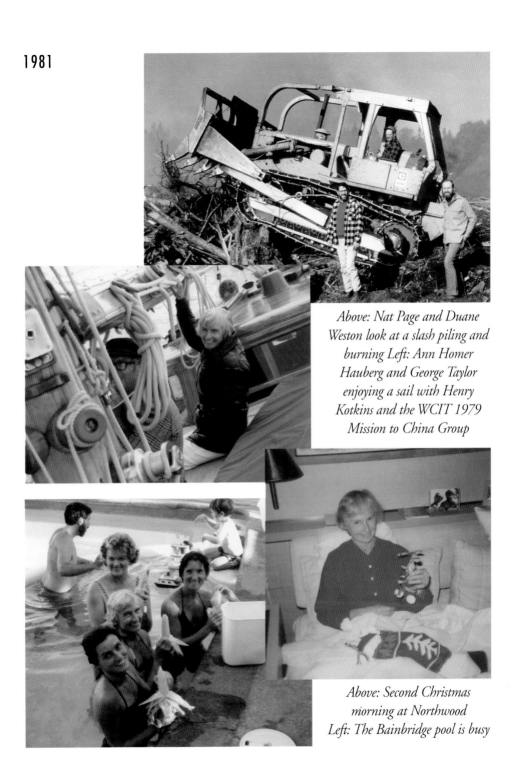

1981

Above: Nat Page and Duane Weston look at a slash piling and burning Left: Ann Homer Hauberg and George Taylor enjoying a sail with Henry Kotkins and the WCIT 1979 Mission to China Group

Above: Second Christmas morning at Northwood Left: The Bainbridge pool is busy

*Above: Fort Knox State Park,
near Bucksport, ME; Right: Fort
Louisbourg in Nova Scotia*

*With Kay Sweeney in Nova Scotia. At this point, Kay had houses in
Florida, Colorado, France, and Nova Scotia*

Left: Secretary's Day at the Pilchuck Tree Farm: left to right: Karen Gilbertson, Corrine Reinbold, Barbara Wood, Ann Homer Hauberg, Duane Weston, Fay Page, Nat Page; Center: JHH with Chihuly

Above: Mt. Rainier at Sunrise; Left: Sue, Ann, Fay with Ben and Carey at Pilchuck's Christmas Tree Sales

In Greece—Mykonos

Right: Ann and John–Delphi

Delphi

1983

Right: Our Northwood house and collections as photographed for Architectural Digest

Below: Izzy and Andrew's wedding day, August 20, 1983

The King of Spain, Juan Carlos, shakes Ann's hand at his country palace near Madrid

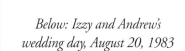

THE CLASS OF 1939 AWARD at the

Class Dinner, June 1, 1984

John Henry Hauberg, Jr.

I know that Paul Bunyan, legendary giant lumber-jack, and Babe, his Big Blue Ox, never realized that the annoying kid, John Hauberg, was following them around from the sawmill at Rock Island, Illinois, where the logs floated down the Mississippi from the white pineries of Minnesota and Wisconsin. After they were depleted, and before the income tax was invented, his grandfather Denkmann took yet another productive risk with partner and brother-in-law Weyerhaeuser and "went West" on a deal to acquire 1500 square miles of timber from the Northern Pacific Railroad and James J. Hill at Tacoma.

Back in Rock Island, John Henry Hauberg, Jr. soaked up sawdust, Black Hawk Indian history, YMCA hikes and plain good citizenship. He grew up into a module which Town and Country called "a tall lanky Gary Cooper-type", but which my mother earlier called "a bull-in-a-China shop" when he inadvertently kicked over a Chinese horse on his way into our library. Before the visit was over, in college days, he broke a lamp in the guest room, and left the boat untied after a party, so it floated down the St. Croix almost into the Mississippi. Mother said: "Bobs, wherever did you get this friend?". I replied, "Why, mother, he's my roommate at Princeton".

It was not long before John served others, including four years in the Army ending as a Captain in Occupied Germany. Returning to Seattle, he felt the tug of sylvi-culture and earned a degree in forestry, soon starting his private non-industrial forest, called Pilchuck Tree Farm. While waiting 35 years for the 20 square miles of trees to grow, he plunged into diverse educational, civic, cultural and church groups, and political organizations.

They could see a good man coming. He headed the Art Museum, managed the Symphony, trusteed Reed College, University of Puget Sound, Pacific Northwest Arts Center, Northwest Hardwoods Association, headed the Helen Bush School, and the State Republican finance committee. Big John expressed his vigorous personality: love of music, appreciation of art, and philosophy of trees as a renewable resource crop of the land. Quietly, not immune from life's personal tragedies and defeats, he accepted them and resolved to serve handicapped groups, and grow in stature.

Such a sustained, diverse leadership would exhaust a lesser man, but Johnny took it in easy Bunyanesque strides, though now, he concentrates on his educational goal of a small man-made forest with intensive management.

No challenge too big, no one's problem too small, this huge Medici of our class from the Pacific Northwest has brought a healthy influence to his region, and in so doing has reflected honor on Princeton University and our Class of 1939.

Hambone, in the name of everyone, we salute you!

JHH honored by classmates...

Carey at Four Winds

*Above: Maui; Right: Ann and Marion
on the beach in Maui*

*...I paid Bob Meech (above, seated to the right of Ann Homer Hauberg),
my senior year roommate, a huge amount to write this forty-five years later.*

With Kay at the Jewett wedding in Spokane

*Below: Vienna with Hugh Wynne,
president of our Princeton Class of 1939*

*Up the Rhine with '39,
Houghs and Haubergs*

1985

*Below: Marion with Ann
and sisters Izzy and
Alison, bridesmaids*

*Marion and George, married
on November 16, 1985*

Marion and George's wedding party, Mercer Island, Washington

Bainbridge golfers: JHH, Jr., Ann Homer Hauberg, Nat Page and grandson Ben Page

With Rosanes at the National Gallery in Washington D.C

George Mohler and John at Tatoosh

The balloon and basket are stretched out ready to be filled with hot air (easy part)

Above and left: Up in a balloon over France

Right: The landing was rough

Below: Paris. The Picasso Museum

Rosemary Blackstone and Ann Homer Hauberg on a "barge" on the Nivernais Canal in France; barging, bicycling, and ballooning on the Nivernais Canal in Burgundy

Below: With the Blackstones, Lew and Sonja Johnson, Alison and Tecla Wurlitzer

*A picnic with Alison in
Cezanne country, Southern
France in April*

*Alison and John prepare a picnic
in Southern France*

*Alison and John at sister Kay
Sweeney's house in France;
note "long legs"*

Right: At the top of Mt. Haleakala, the weather station in January; Below: Pilchuck Glass School, Fay and Laura Partridge with "Chihulys" on the lawn

Above: At the Sunset Club family Christmas party; Left: Marion and George Mohler

1987

Thanksgiving tennis in Carmel

*Maui golf with Sheff
and Patty Phelps*

*Left: How we looked
in 1987*

Below: Olivia arrived June 9,
mother and Grandmother doing well

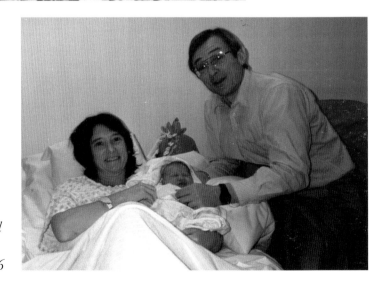

Andrew and Izzy

Right: Marion and
George welcome
Jenny, December 16

Below: The Pages and the Burkes

The Pages take a cross-country vacation in a motor home

The Pages: Stan, Nat, Carey, Ben, and Sally

Right: Ben with Luke. All photos on the page by my daughter, Fay.

1988

Poppa's annual Christmas visit to the Page's

A hale and hearty family in 1988…

Baseball buddies:
Ben and Nat Page

…and in 1926, too

The YWCA portrait, Rock Island, Illinois

Ann and John relaxing on Bainbridge

Izzy and Olivia, Marion and Jenny

Below: Wrights, Rawns, Padelfords, Knudsens, and Haubergs at the 4 K compound at Kihei

Marion and George at Tatoosh

Ann and John visited Raphael's Sistine Madonna in Dresden, which had made a lasting impression on JHH in 1926

Above and right: We spent two days and nights with Christian, Furst von Steinfurt zu Bentheim, and his forester von Brockhausen, who said the Prince would not let him cut down this tree. "Not old enough." And to the right is the Prince's moated castle at Steinfurt. The language barrier was formidable, but with Brockhausen's help, we all got along fine

*Left: The infamous
Berlin Wall was not
to come down until
1989 when the
Communists gave up
East Germany and
Communist rule…*

*Right:…which is
a contrast to
American freedom
and democracy. We
joined our neighbors
in the traditional
July Fourth flag
raising at the
country club on
Bainbridge Island*

Left: Moscow!

1989

Alison Brinkley & Lawrence Kingsley
wed—September

Ann & John in the garden of Baron Thyssen
— Bornemisza, Lugano, Switzerland

A toast to the bride

Princeton Class of 1939 at our 50th reunion, with wives, children, and grandchildren

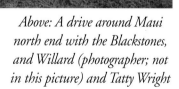

Above: A drive around Maui north end with the Blackstones, and Willard (photographer; not in this picture) and Tatty Wright

Left: And a drive into a tropical climate in mid-France with sister Kay and Hans and Marietta Schneider to see bamboo growing

Right: Meanwhile – Ann's yoga and bridge group, Knudsens, Rawns, Hills, and Lenore McIntyre relax in our Bainbridge pool

Left: Amid a swarm of Sweeneys, Eric Fraunfelter and Harriet are married on September 8

Right: The Seattle Art Museum broke ground for its new building with trustees Jacob Lawrence and George and Ayami Tsutakawa

1990

The family golfers

A visit from the Homer-Smiths

Carey's 16th Birthday, April 3

Below: Rosanes at Tatoosh

In the pool at Northwood in December; Below: The Reimers and Schneiders salute. A Denkmann family gathering in San Antonio.

Selden and Katie; Below: Alison and Lawrence Kingsley

Right: Summer Sunday night on the beach

1991

Left: James Brinkley III, Sheila Lukehart and Jessie Kindig, November 21, 1991

Below: Jim Brinkley, Jr., Mary Jane Burns Brinkley, Dwight and Adda Lukehart, Jim, Sheila, Jessie, Ann, JHH, and Olivia

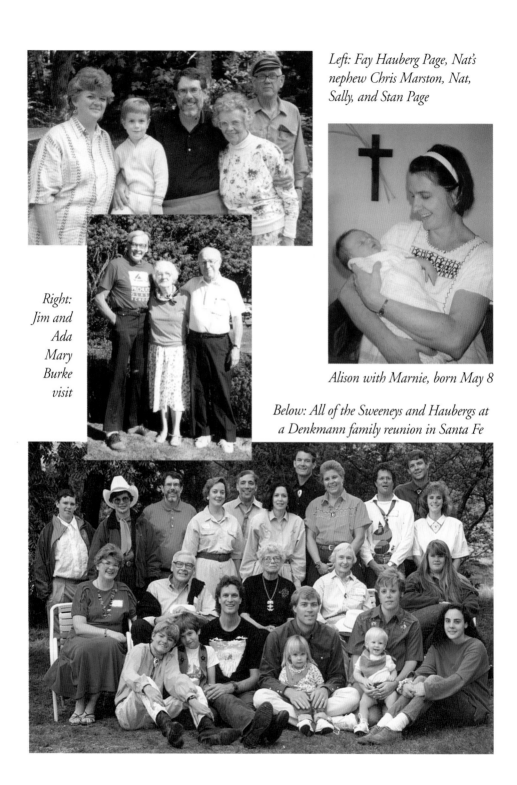

Left: Fay Hauberg Page, Nat's nephew Chris Marston, Nat, Sally, and Stan Page

Right: Jim and Ada Mary Burke visit

Alison with Marnie, born May 8

Below: All of the Sweeneys and Haubergs at a Denkmann family reunion in Santa Fe

With Izzy and Andrew in Ottawa

Andy and Marianna Price, previous owners of the property, inspect the new house at 601. Below: Sue has a lovely house too

Three Princeton roommates and their wives in Florida in February. Lucia Uihlein, Rita Murrie, Eddie Uihlein, Dick "Pinkie" Murrie, and JHH

1992

JHH baked an apple pie

Sheila and Jim Brinkley

Grandmother and Marnie

Ann and Sheff

Sue with more ribbons

The Homers at Salishan

Our beautiful new house – 601

Left: Jessie and Jim

Below: Carey's graduation from Bush

Olivia
Left: Ben in the play,
"Once in a Lifetime"

1993

Ann Homer Hauberg on Bainbridge Island

Our Ted Carpenter-designed skylight does its stuff on a sunny summer day at 601

Kitchell, Wesselhoefft, Robinson, Hauberg at Fourth of July picnic on Bainbridge

Cousins Marietta and Hans Schneider at Pilchuck Tree Farm

Tennis finalists at the Country Club: Ben Page at left and Bob Kitchell at right

Future finalists: Heather, Ian, Jenny, and Marnie

Left: Marnie, Heather, Jenny, and Olivia

JHH designed this playhouse for the kids

Lawrence Kingsley with Marnie and Ian

Jim III, Jessie Kindig, and Sheila Lukehart enjoy the beach

The Carl Blackstones at the annual Christmas party of Ann and JHH

Ann and JHH visit Canyonlands. This is Bryce Canyon

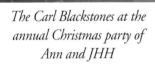

Left: Our summer pcinic, a favorite event

1994

A bigger machine to harvest smaller timber

Jessica Pilar and Sally Page, Fay's niece & mother-in-law

Somebody's turkey; Thanksgiving at the Pages on Mercer Island

Left: Ike Kampmann & Beechie with class of 39 on the Rhone from Marseille to Lyon

Bainbridge!

Kay at Castillon du Gard;
Below: JHH's pies are about a
year apart

Ann brought dresses from Sweden

A little row…

A bit of snow…

An ancient giant makes way for newer life

A rebellious upstart? From left: Nat, Ben and JHH

1995

A Bainbridge summer

Our fourth every-five-year visit to the Mt. St. Helens eruption of 1980 showed a little greening in the blast zone

Left: The Seattle Art Museum organized a fine trip to several areas of China. A high point was a boat ride on the Li River through its famous hills painted in so many Chinese scrolls.

Following China, Ann and I went
on to Cambodia and to ancient
culture at Angkor Wat

Left: The lovely Hotchkiss Chapel where I sang in the choir sixty years ago. About thirty of us came back to our sixtieth class reunion in June out of a graduating class of ninety

Old friends, Nute and Kitchell

Below: Older cousins, Ada Mary Lyford and Jim Burke

Below: Our Tatoosh house, now twenty-five, gets ever lovelier

1996

Our Joint 153rd Birthday Party on Bainbridge

JHH and Ann at the Joint 153rd Birthday Party

Below: Baking cookies at 601 house, Olivia and Grandmother Ann

Ben's graduation from Bush, June 1996

Below: Family picnic at Colby by the Lake

Carey's graduation from Colby College, May 1996

*First seven presidents of Pilchuck Glass
School. From left to right: McCarthy,
Kitchell, Hauberg, Seidl, Anderson,
Hughbanks, and Haley*

*At a Denkmann family reunion
at Salishan in Central Oregon*

*Another reunion of Pilchuck Glass School Artists and
Founders, with Ann are Dale Chihuly, Fritz Dreisbach,
and Italo Scanga, at the Seattle Museum of History and
Industry*

1997

Lake Alamoosook, Maine
with Stan and Sally Page

Nana Sally and her three grandsons, Ben
Page, Genaro Lopez, and Chris Marston

Ann and her three daughters, Alison, Marion, and Izzy

At Tatoosh, Jessie's tree is up, but its planters are out

Ann's tribe on Bainbridge

David Michael Brinkley gets his first bath on Bainbridge

Christmas at Jim III's

Sheff Phelps received, belatedly, the Distinguished Flying Cross. He led his observation crew in locating the Japanese fleet at Truk during WW II

Izzy's graduation from Seattle University's Teacher Training School

1998

Right: Sue has a huge sale of her things as she prepares to sell her ranch. Fay Page, her loyal sister, and Gloria and Ted Snook, her houseparents, assist.

Grandchildren on Bainbridge

A Christmas with Carl and Selden Blackstone, Ann's nephew, and Selden's mother, Mrs. Prentice

This (top left) is the high prairie of western Illinois where Haubergs claimed and settled in 1850...and this (middle left) is the western foot-hill area of the Cascade Range in Puget Sound country where a recently planted forest is being cleared of brush piles on Pilchuck Tree Farm

The Hauberg family reunion brings us back to Rock Island and the Great House

1999

*Rosemary and George Blackstone
visit us on Bainbridge*

*John's niece Harriet and Eric
Fraunfelter from Washington,
D.C., call*

Right: All of Ann's children

Our past catches up

The Kingdome— a
pile of rubble

Right: Ann, Olivia,
and Marion

Right: Ann and JHH visit the Mt. St. Helens 1980 eruption for the fifth time every-five-years

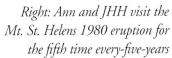

Left: The overlook at Pike and Boren and the old Plymouth Congregational Church columns donated to JHH by the church elders and given to the City of Seattle by JHH

A 1920s forest in the background awaits a new one at Pilchuck Tree Farm

*The kids __do__ look at
my albums!*

A lot of happy people

Cousins!

Daughter Sue and Dad

Grandchildren Olivia and Carey

Daughter Fay and
Dad

Sisters Ada Mary
Burke and Helen
Simpson, my cousins

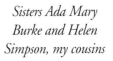

Classmates

Democracy, Why Not Now?

In 1960 the Republican National Finance committee members and their spouses were invited to dinner at the White House with President and Mrs. Dwight D. Eisenhower. What a thrill!

Annie and I flew east from Seattle with evening gown and dinner jacket and stayed with sister Kay Sweeney. We discovered that our tablemates were to be Melville (Mel) Grosvenor for Anne and Mrs. Summerfield, the Postmaster General's wife for me. Both were close friends of Kay.

Kay invited Mrs. Summerfield to lunch and a swim in the pool to discuss the coming evening with us. Annie had brought only a short evening gown and was suddenly concerned that it might not be appropriate. There was still the afternoon to buy a longer gown. Mrs. Summerfield said she would call Pat Nixon, the Vice-President's wife for advice. Mrs. Nixon said she was going to wear a short evening gown, so that was that!

We thought we would take a taxi to the White House, but Kay said that would be difficult because the taxi driver's credentials would have to be checked. Anyway, Jesse, Kay's butler and chauffeur, had driven her and Edward to the White House on several occasions and would be honored to take us.

Jesse donned his driver's cap, was saluted at the White House gate, and swept us right up to the White House door, the one that faces Lafayette Square. We were escorted by a White House naval aide, a young ensign, to a desk to check in, receive a card telling us where we were to sit, and then taken by the ensign to the East Room where the dinner party was assembling. The ensign also showed us where we were to stand as a couple, for the introduction to the President and his wife and their guests of honor. Meanwhile, we could move about the East Room to mingle with our friends until a signal would tell us to return to our "spot" on the East Room floor.

Although I had been a National Committeeman since 1956, we had never been invited to a White House dinner or even met the President. The aides soon told us to return to our place in line. A band struck up "Ruffles and Flourishes" and the President's party entered and took places. Their guests of honor were the Philippines President Ferdinand Marcos and his wife Imelda. We guests executed a right face and went in a circle until we came up to the president.

The Eisenhowers obviously had prepared for the party. As I was introduced by an aide to Ike, as everyone called him, he said, "How nice of you to come all the way from Seattle to join us tonight," and then turned to Mamie and said, "Here are the Haubergs from Seattle." Mrs. Eisenhower then introduced us to the Marcoses. We returned to our "spot." Another musical flourish and the President's party left for the dining room. We did not move until they had arrived at their seats.

Our card, given to us at the door, had instructions on how, exactly, to get to our seats. My task was easy because Mrs. Summerfield had been to many of these dinners before. Our seats were between Secretary of State John Foster Dulles and his partner, and California Senator William Knowles and his partner. Mrs. Eisenhower had arranged the tables to join the head table—so we could all say we sat at the same table with the President! The President, before we all sat down, told us that Mamie had made all the flower arrangements for this "table" for about 150 of us, who gave her a big hand.

During the dinner I had an opportunity to ask John Foster Dulles what he thought was the basic necessity for any nation's democracy. He instantly replied, "Christianity." And I have thought that over many times since.

Each pair of chairs was monitored and served by a waiter. The Eisenhower dinnerware was beautiful. The dinner itself was delicious. Marcos' after dinner speech was short. The Navy Glee Club was to the President's taste back in the East Room after dinner. I felt enormous pride in our country and its leadership.

In the year 2000, the world is still suffering from violence, chaos, poverty, disease and corruption. Some of these apply even to wealthy, well-educated democracies such as the U.S.A. and to established dictatorships, such as Cuba, China, and Russia.

What sorts of thing have to be resolved before an orderly democracy (or is that an oxymoron?) can take over and survive?

Here is a list that comes to my mind:
1. Reduction of the hate level between peoples of racial, tribal, and religious differences
2. Reduction of differences between the haves and the have-nots.
3. Universal education. Literacy.
4. Elimination of corruption, the will to enforce laws affecting all peoples
5. A military subservient to elected leaders.

How would a program leading to all the above, or even one of them, begin? Where would you start? Would John Foster Dulles' "Christianity" be a true starting place? How would you move a country when almost all its soil is worn out, with no sanitation, little education, widespread disease, and centuries-old tribal or racial or religious hatreds dividing its people into two or more camps? Will the highly educated, reasonably wealthy Israelis become comfortable co-existing with Palestinians, who have lived in that area for hundreds of years?

In two Weyerhaeuser mills on the Thompson River of British Columbia one hires only Hindus, the other only Pakistanis, both people thousands of miles from their native countries yet bringing their hatreds with them.

One has to believe that democracy is a very precious jewel. We Americans for the most part have agreed to disagree peacefully. But among us, others are eager to resort to violence to get their way, because they feel it is the only way to get our attention. But our attention for the most part lasts only a short time. Unless the violence turns to taking lives or destroying property, we forget quickly. How fortunate are those protesters to live in the United States!

So I do not agree with John Foster Dulles that Christianity is the necessary first stepping-stone to democracy. Christ preached love, perhaps the only prophet who did. Ironically and unfortunately, millions of people over the centuries have gone to war bearing the banner of Jesus Christ. However, most democratic nations are Christian. But Christ also preached hope, and those people without hope may never try to reach democracy.

Perhaps respect for each other comes about when we all need each other. In the mid-1800s, immigrants came to the American prairie and needed each other to help harvest crops, to midwife for each other, or just to have friends and some sort of society. Certainly the Pilgrims and Puritans needed each other and created many of our institutions of democracy. Yet Roger Williams and his Congregationalists in Rhode Island put to death others who came there with different beliefs.

Disease control and population control go hand in hand in many countries and are problems to be resolved before a successful economy can be established. Ignorance and poverty delay the development of an economy. A military-supported dictatorship encourages corruption instead of an evenhanded enforcement of laws.

Currently, in the year 2000, many countries that do not have democracy are on the threshold of achieving it because they possess many of the basic requirements of good land, education, good health, a fairly good economy with jobs for most, and a political structure that can be changed. Let's hope they reach a true democracy soon, Israelis, Christians, Muslims, Buddhists, Hutus, Tutsis, Pakistanis, Hindus, haves, have-nots, or whatever.

In May 2000, the news is that the Catholic IRA and the Irish Republican Army have agreed to lay down their weapons, and are ready to reconcile differences with the Protestant, basically British, North Irelanders. Who will be next? Or is the current situation comfortable to both of them like an American football rivalry?

Will the wealthy democracies help improve education and health, help suppress violence and corruption, and bring opposing parties to a peace table? Do we who live in flourishing democracies have the will to bring about the right conditions for democracy wherever there is none at the moment? It is a most difficult task.

History is a pattern of timeless moments.—T.S. Eliot

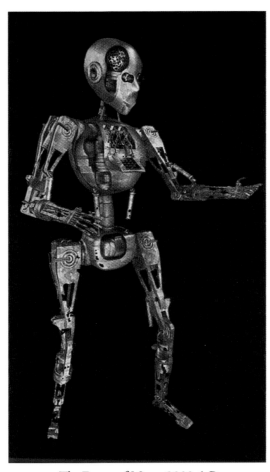

The Future of Man – 3000 A.D.
and only 250 years old

EPILOGUE

d

AD DIED AT 11:30 AM ON APRIL 5, 2002, AFTER A TWO AND ONE HALF WEEK BATTLE for his life in Swedish Hospital in Seattle. He died of heart failure due to the bacteria, streptococcus piogenes, which had invaded his body through the removal of a corn on his foot. He had not told the doctor he had artificial knee joints and an artificial shoulder joint. I don't think he understood that he needed to be taking antibiotics whenever he had surgery. Evidently, bacteria are attracted to artificial joints and are impossible to clean out. His legs swelled and the bacteria got into the blood stream to attack his heart and lungs. His strong Hauberg constitution helped him almost make a recovery, but the initial damage was too great to overcome. Fortunately, many friends and family members had time to visit and pay their respects. He died without pain. At one point a nurse asked him what he'd like for a drink and he said, "How about a martini?" He had his sense of humor to the end.

He was a terrific father, friend, colleague, and philanthropist. He loved life as can be seen in his memoirs. He came from a strong extended family that loved to do things together and believed in serving their community. Dad brought his confidence and financial means both to enjoy life and solve problems. In the 1970s, he may have taken on more than even he could handle successfully and I know he was disappointed that some of his dreams and plans didn't come true. Yet he had much to be proud of. At his 85th birthday party at the Sunset Club, he thoroughly enjoyed the accolades from over one hundred of his best friends and closest family.

I want to set the record straight on one point. Even though I had won the Washington State Equitation Championship and qualified to ride in Madison Square Garden, Dad didn't let me go. I was only in the 7th or 8th grade but he didn't want me to miss a week of school in November! Note that in the 1950s, this was well before Billy Jean King's win over Bobby Riggs and Title IX legislation. Women athletes weren't important at all. Before Dad died, I told him that this was one of the great disappointments of my life and he apologized. He hadn't understood. He was proud of the time and effort Nat and I spent with our own children, and he enjoyed all his grandchildren and step-grandchildren tremendously, including all the girls! He encouraged many people to follow their passion to make a contribution to society and make the most of their talents.

His funeral was held at St. Mark's Cathedral on May 3, 2002. Over 900 people attended. Mimi Gates, director of the Seattle Art Museum, Ralph Munro, former Washington Secretary of State, Duane Weston, head forester for Dad's Pilchuck Tree Farm, Sheffield Phelps, his best friend, neighbor, and fellow businessman, and his grandson, Benjamin Hauberg Page, eulogized Dad and his many accomplishments. Some of his ashes have been scattered on the tree farm. A basalt bench, by Julie Speidel, at "Inspiration Point" looks west at the beautiful San Juan Islands, the sunset, Skagit Valley, and his beloved trees. The rest of his ashes are interred at Lakeview Cemetery, next door to the Seattle Asian Art Museum, where he is joined by his beloved Ann (d. April 4, 2003) and many other prominent Seattle citizens. We will never forget you, Dad!

> *And down the distance*
>
> *With dying note and swelling*
>
> *Walk the resounding way*
>
> *To the still dwelling*
>
> —A.E. Housman
>
> *—Fay Hauberg Page, Spring, 2003*

REFERENCES

A Midwestern Family: 1848–1948, John Henry Hauberg, Sr., 1950

Weyerhaeuser and Denkmann: Ninety-five years of Manufacturing and Distribution of Lumber, John Henry Hauberg, Sr., 1957

Hauberg Family History, Delbert L. Brewer, 1985

Memoirs, Marx D. Hauberg, 1923

The John H. Hauberg (Sr.) Historical Essays, O. Fritiof Ander, editor, 1954

Hauberg Homestead: Since the Indians Left 1851–1941, John Henry Hauberg, Sr., 1941

Rock Island Argus, Tuesday, April 29, 1941, section 3 page 9

Hauberg Family Tree

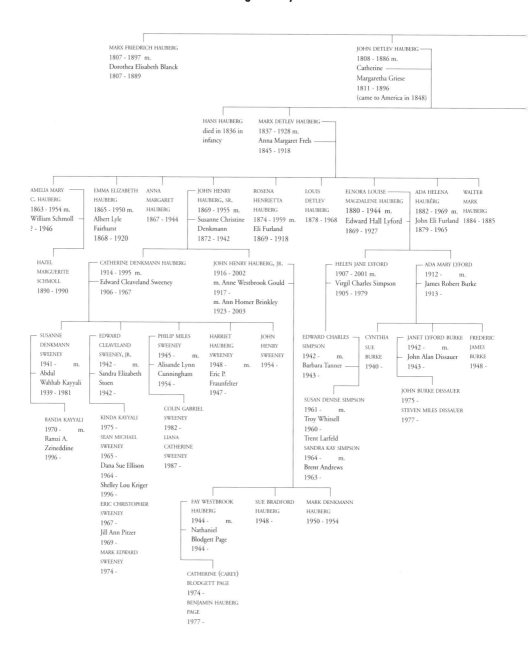

MARX FRIEDRICH HAUBERG
1807 - 1897 m.
Dorothea Elisabeth Blanck
1807 - 1889

JOHN DETLEV HAUBERG
1808 - 1886 m.
Catherine
Margaretha Griese
1811 - 1896
(came to America in 1848)

HANS HAUBERG
died in 1836 in
infancy

MARX DETLEV HAUBERG
1837 - 1928 m.
Anna Margaret Frels
1845 - 1918

AMELIA MARY
C. HAUBERG
1863 - 1954 m.
William Schmoll
? - 1946

EMMA ELIZABETH
HAUBERG
1865 - 1950 m.
Albert Lyle
Fairhurst
1868 - 1920

ANNA
MARGARET
HAUBERG
1867 - 1944

JOHN HENRY
HAUBERG, SR.
1869 - 1955 m.
Susanne Christine
Denkmann
1872 - 1942

ROSENA
HENRIETTA
HAUBERG
1874 - 1959 m.
Eli Furland
1869 - 1918

LOUIS
DETLEV
HAUBERG
1878 - 1968

ELNORA LOUISE
MAGDALENE HAUBERG
1880 - 1944 m.
Edward Hall Lyford
1869 - 1927

ADA HELENA
HAUBERG
1882 - 1969 m.
John Eli Furland
1879 - 1965

WALTER
MARK
HAUBERG
1884 - 1885

HAZEL
MARGUERITE
SCHMOLL
1890 - 1990

CATHERINE DENKMANN HAUBERG
1914 - 1995 m.
Edward Cleaveland Sweeney
1906 - 1967

JOHN HENRY HAUBERG, JR.
1916 - 2002
m. Anne Westbrook Gould
1917 -
m. Ann Homer Brinkley
1923 - 2003

HELEN JANE LYFORD
1907 - 2001 m.
Virgil Charles Simpson
1905 - 1979

ADA MARY LYFORD
1912 -   m.
James Robert Burke
1913 -

SUSANNE
DENKMANN
SWEENEY
1941 -   m.
Abdul
Wahhab Kayyali
1939 - 1981

EDWARD
CLEAVELAND
SWEENEY, JR.
1942 -   m.
Sandra Elizabeth
Stoen
1942 -

PHILIP MILES
SWEENEY
1945 -   m.
Alisande Lynn
Cunningham
1954 -

HARRIET
HAUBERG
SWEENEY
1948 -   m.
Eric P.
Fraunfelter
1947 -

JOHN
HENRY
SWEENEY
1954 -

EDWARD CHARLES
SIMPSON
1942 -   m.
Barbara Tanner
1943 -

CYNTHIA
SUE
BURKE
1940 -

JANET LYFORD BURKE
1942 -   m.
John Alan Dissauer
1943 -

FREDERIC
JAMES
BURKE
1948 -

RANDA KAYYALI
1970 -   m.
Ramzi A.
Zeineddine
1996 -

KINDA KAYYALI
1975 -
SEAN MICHAEL
SWEENEY
1965 -
Dana Sue Ellison
1964 -
Shelley Lou Kriger
1996 -
ERIC CHRISTOPHER
SWEENEY
1967 -
Jill Ann Pitzer
1969 -
MARK EDWARD
SWEENEY
1974 -

COLIN GABRIEL
SWEENEY
1982 -
LIANA
CATHERINE
SWEENEY
1987 -

SUSAN DENISE SIMPSON
1961 -   m.
Troy Whitsell
1960 -
Trent Larfeld
SANDRA KAY SIMPSON
1964 -   m.
Brent Andrews
1963 -

JOHN BURKE DISSAUER
1975 -
STEVEN MILES DISSAUER
1977 -

FAY WESTBROOK
HAUBERG
1944 -   m.
Nathaniel
Blodgett Page
1944 -

SUE BRADFORD
HAUBERG
1948 -

MARK DENKMANN
HAUBERG
1950 - 1954

CATHERINE (CAREY)
BLODGETT PAGE
1974 -
BENJAMIN HAUBERG
PAGE
1977 -

Note: To the children of the eighth generation of Haubergs and the seventh generation of

418

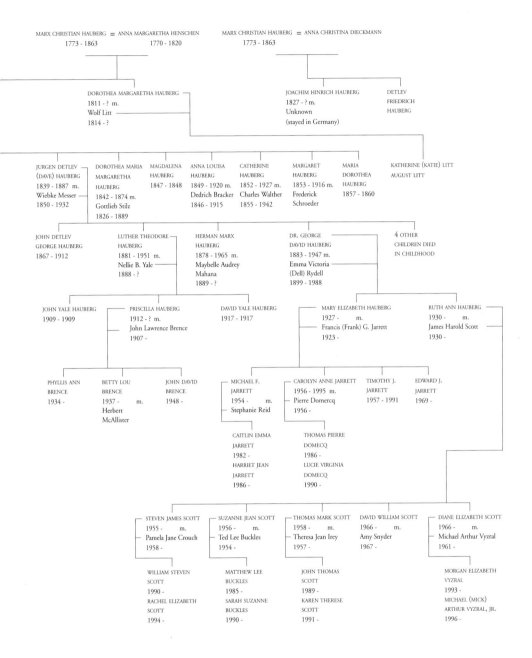

MARX CHRISTIAN HAUBERG = ANNA MARGARETHA HENSCHEN
1773 - 1863   1770 - 1820

MARX CHRISTIAN HAUBERG = ANNA CHRISTINA DIECKMANN
1773 - 1863

DOROTHEA MARGARETHA HAUBERG
1811 - ? m.
Wolf Litt
1814 - ?

JOACHIM HINRICH HAUBERG
1827 - ? m.
Unknown
(stayed in Germany)

DETLEV
FRIEDRICH
HAUBERG

JURGEN DETLEV
(DAVE) HAUBERG
1839 - 1887 m.
Wiebke Messer
1850 - 1932

DOROTHEA MARIA
MARGARETHA
HAUBERG
1842 - 1874 m.
Gottlieb Stilz
1826 - 1889

MAGDALENA
HAUBERG
1847 - 1848

ANNA LOUISA
HAUBERG
1849 - 1920 m.
Dedrich Bracker
1846 - 1915

CATHERINE
HAUBERG
1852 - 1927 m.
Charles Walther
1855 - 1942

MARGARET
HAUBERG
1853 - 1916 m.
Frederick
Schroeder

MARIA
DOROTHEA
HAUBERG
1857 - 1860

KATHERINE (KATIE) LITT

AUGUST LITT

JOHN DETLEV
GEORGE HAUBERG
1867 - 1912

LUTHER THEODORE
HAUBERG
1881 - 1951 m.
Nellie B. Yale
1888 - ?

HERMAN MARX
HAUBERG
1878 - 1965 m.
Maybelle Audrey
Mahana
1889 - ?

DR. GEORGE
DAVID HAUBERG
1883 - 1947 m.
Emma Victoria
(Dell) Rydell
1899 - 1988

4 OTHER
CHILDREN DIED
IN CHILDHOOD

JOHN YALE HAUBERG
1909 - 1909

PRISCILLA HAUBERG
1912 - ? m.
John Lawrence Brence
1907 -

DAVID YALE HAUBERG
1917 - 1917

MARY ELIZABETH HAUBERG
1927 -   m.
Francis (Frank) G. Jarrett
1923 -

RUTH ANN HAUBERG
1930 -   m.
James Harold Scott
1930 -

PHYLLIS ANN
BRENCE
1934 -

BETTY LOU
BRENCE
1937 -   m.
Herbert
McAllister

JOHN DAVID
BRENCE
1948 -

MICHAEL F.
JARRETT
1954 -   m.
Stephanie Reid

CAROLYN ANNE JARRETT
1956 - 1995 m.
Pierre Domercq
1956 -

TIMOTHY J.
JARRETT
1957 - 1991

EDWARD J.
JARRETT
1969 -

CAITLIN EMMA
JARRETT
1982 -
HARRIET JEAN
JARRETT
1986 -

THOMAS PIERRE
DOMECQ
1986 -
LUCIE VIRGINIA
DOMECQ
1990 -

STEVEN JAMES SCOTT
1955 -   m.
Pamela Jane Crouch
1958 -

SUZANNE JEAN SCOTT
1956 -   m.
Ted Lee Buckles
1954 -

THOMAS MARK SCOTT
1958 -   m.
Theresa Jean Irey
1957 -

DAVID WILLIAM SCOTT
1966 -   m.
Amy Snyder
1967 -

DIANE ELIZABETH SCOTT
1966 -   m.
Michael Arthur Vyzral
1961 -

WILLIAM STEVEN
SCOTT
1990 -
RACHEL ELIZABETH
SCOTT
1994 -

MATTHEW LEE
BUCKLES
1985 -
SARAH SUZANNE
BUCKLES
1990 -

JOHN THOMAS
SCOTT
1989 -
KAREN THERESE
SCOTT
1991 -

MORGAN ELIZABETH
VYZRAL
1993 -
MICHAEL (MICK)
ARTHUR VYZRAL, JR.
1996 -

Denkmanns, we apologize for not being able to include your names due to space limitations.

Denkmann Family Tree

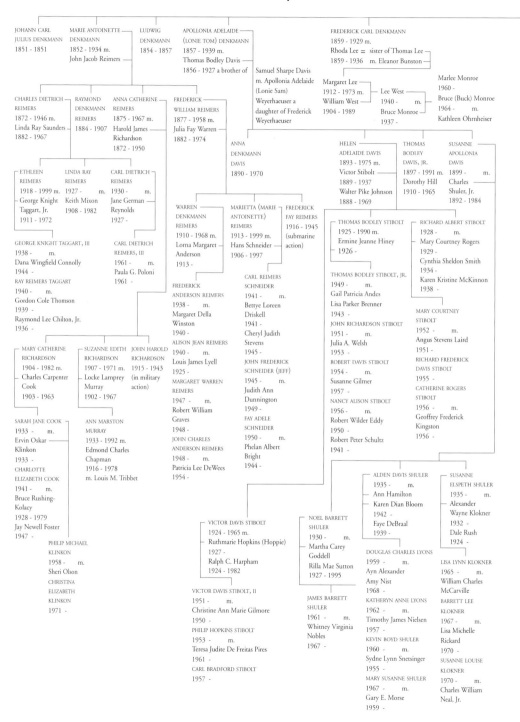

JOHANN CARL
JULIUS DENKMANN
1851 - 1851

MARIE ANTOINETTE
DENKMANN
1852 - 1934 m.
John Jacob Reimers

LUDWIG
DENKMANN
1854 - 1857

APOLLONIA ADELAIDE
(LONIE TOM) DENKMANN
1857 - 1939 m.
Thomas Bodley Davis
1856 - 1927 a brother of

Samuel Sharpe Davis
m. Apollonia Adelaide
(Lonie Sam)
Weyerhaeuser a
daughter of Frederick
Weyerhaeuser

FREDERICK CARL DENKMANN
1859 - 1929 m.
Rhoda Lee = sister of Thomas Lee
1859 - 1936 m. Eleanor Bunston

Margaret Lee
1912 - 1973 m.
William West
1904 - 1989

Lee West
1940   m.
Bruce Monroe
1937 -

Marlee Monroe
1960 -
Bruce (Buck) Monroe
1964 -
Kathleen Ohrnheiser

CHARLES DIETRICH
REIMERS
1872 - 1946 m.
Linda Ray Saunders
1882 - 1967

RAYMOND
DENKMANN
REIMERS
1884 - 1907

ANNA CATHERINE
REIMERS
1875 - 1967 m.
Harold James
Richardson
1872 - 1950

FREDERICK
WILLIAM REIMERS
1877 - 1958 m.
Julia Fay Warren
1882 - 1974

ANNA
DENKMANN
DAVIS
1890 - 1970

HELEN
ADELAIDE DAVIS
1893 - 1975 m.
Victor Stibolt
1889 - 1937
Walter Pike Johnson
1888 - 1969

THOMAS
BODLEY
DAVIS, JR.
1897 - 1991 m.
Dorothy Hill
1910 - 1965

SUSANNE
APOLLONIA
DAVIS
1899 -   m.
Charles
Shuler, Jr.
1892 - 1984

ETHLEEN
REIMERS
1918 - 1999 m.
George Knight
Taggart, Jr.
1911 - 1972

LINDA RAY
REIMERS
1927 -   m.
Keith Mixon
1908 - 1982

CARL DIETRICH
REIMERS
1930 -   m.
Jane German
Reynolds
1927 -

WARREN
DENKMANN
REIMERS
1910 - 1968 m.
Lorna Margaret
Anderson
1913 -

MARIETTA (MARIE
ANTOINETTE)
REIMERS
1913 - 1999 m.
Hans Schneider
1906 - 1997

FREDERICK
FAY REIMERS
1916 - 1945
(submarine
action)

THOMAS BODLEY STIBOLT
1925 - 1990 m.
Ermine Jeanne Hiney
1926 -

RICHARD ALBERT STIBOLT
1928 -   m.
Mary Courtney Rogers
1929 -
Cynthia Sheldon Smith
1934 -
Karen Kristine McKinnon
1938 -

GEORGE KNIGHT TAGGART, III
1938 -   m.
Dana Wingfield Connolly
1944 -
RAY REIMERS TAGGART
1940 -   m.
Gordon Cole Thomson
1939 -
Raymond Lee Chilton, Jr.
1936 -

CARL DIETRICH
REIMERS, III
1961 -   m.
Paula G. Poloni
1961 -

FREDERICK
ANDERSON REIMERS
1938 -   m.
Margaret Della
Winston
1940 -
ALISON JEAN REIMERS
1940 -   m.
Louis James Lyell
1925 -
MARGARET WARREN
REIMERS
1947 -   m.
Robert William
Graves
1948 -
JOHN CHARLES
ANDERSON REIMERS
1948 -   m.
Patricia Lee DeWees
1954 -

CARL REIMERS
SCHNEIDER
1941 -   m.
Bettye Loreen
Driskell
1941 -
Cheryl Judith
Stevens
1945 -
JOHN FREDERICK
SCHNEIDER (JEFF)
1945 -   m.
Judith Ann
Dunnington
1949 -
FAY ADELE
SCHNEIDER
1950 -   m.
Phelan Albert
Bright
1944 -

THOMAS BODLEY STIBOLT, JR.
1949 -   m.
Gail Patricia Andes
Lisa Parker Brenner
1943 -
JOHN RICHARDSON STIBOLT
1951 -   m.
Julia A. Welsh
1953 -
ROBERT DAVIS STIBOLT
1954 -   m.
Susanne Gilmer
1957 -
NANCY ALISON STIBOLT
1956 -   m.
Robert Wilder Eddy
1950 -
Robert Peter Schultz
1941 -

MARY COURTNEY
STIBOLT
1952 -   m.
Angus Stevens Laird
1951 -
RICHARD FREDERICK
DAVIS STIBOLT
1955 -
CATHERINE ROGERS
STIBOLT
1956 -   m.
Geoffrey Frederick
Kingston
1956 -

MARY CATHERINE
RICHARDSON
1904 - 1982 m.
Charles Carpenter
Cook
1903 - 1963

SUZANNE EDITH
RICHARDSON
1907 - 1971 m.
Locke Lamprey
Murray
1902 - 1967

JOHN HAROLD
RICHARDSON
1915 - 1943
(in military
action)

SARAH JANE COOK
1933 -   m.
Ervin Oskar
Klinkon
1933 -
CHARLOTTE
ELIZABETH COOK
1941 -   m.
Bruce Rushing-
Kolacy
1928 - 1979
Jay Newell Foster
1947 -

ANN MARSTON
MURRAY
1933 - 1992 m.
Edmond Charles
Chapman
1916 - 1978
m. Louis M. Tribbet

PHILIP MICHAEL
KLINKON
1958 -   m.
Sheri Olson
CHRISTINA
ELIZABETH
KLINKON
1971 -

VICTOR DAVIS STIBOLT
1924 - 1965 m.
Ruthmarie Hopkins (Hoppie)
1927 -
Ralph C. Harpham
1924 - 1982

NOEL BARRETT
SHULER
1930 -   m.
Martha Carey
Goddell
Rilla Mae Sutton
1927 - 1995

ALDEN DAVIS SHULER
1935 -   m.
Ann Hamilton
Karen Dian Bloom
1942 -
Faye DeBraal
1939 -

SUSANNE
ELSPETH SHULER
1935 -   m.
Alexander
Wayne Klokner
1932 -
Dale Rush
1924 -

DOUGLAS CHARLES LYONS
1959 -   m.
Ayn Alexander
Amy Nist
1968 -
KATHERYN ANNE LYONS
1962 -   m.
Timothy James Nielsen
1957 -
KEVIN BOYD SHULER
1960 -   m.
Sydne Lynn Snetsinger
1955 -
MARY SUSANNE SHULER
1967 -   m.
Gary E. Morse
1959 -

LISA LYNN KLOKNER
1965 -   m.
William Charles
McCarville
BARRETT LEE
KLOKNER
1967 -   m.
Lisa Michelle
Rickard
1970 -
SUSANNE LOUISE
KLOKNER
1970 -   m.
Charles William
Neal, Jr.

VICTOR DAVIS STIBOLT, II
1951 -   m.
Christine Ann Marie Gilmore
1950 -
PHILIP HOPKINS STIBOLT
1953 -   m.
Teresa Judite De Freitas Pires
1961 -
CARL BRADFORD STIBOLT
1957 -

JAMES BARRETT
SHULER
1961 -   m.
Whitney Virginia
Nobles
1967 -

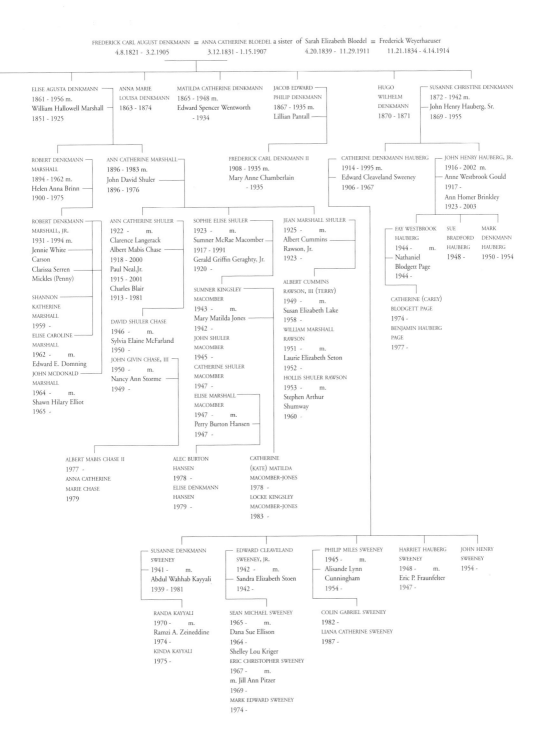

FREDERICK CARL AUGUST DENKMANN = ANNA CATHERINE BLOEDEL a sister of Sarah Elizabeth Bloedel = Frederick Weyerhaeuser
4.8.1821 - 3.2.1905   3.12.1831 - 1.15.1907   4.20.1839 - 11.29.1911   11.21.1834 - 4.14.1914

ELISE AGUSTA DENKMANN
1861 - 1956 m.
William Hallowell Marshall
1851 - 1925

ANNA MARIE
LOUISA DENKMANN
1863 - 1874

MATILDA CATHERINE DENKMANN
1865 - 1948 m.
Edward Spencer Wentworth
- 1934

JACOB EDWARD
PHILIP DENKMANN
1867 - 1935 m.
Lillian Pantall

HUGO
WILHELM
DENKMANN
1870 - 1871

SUSANNE CHRISTINE DENKMANN
1872 - 1942 m.
John Henry Hauberg, Sr.
1869 - 1955

ROBERT DENKMANN
MARSHALL
1894 - 1962 m.
Helen Anna Brinn
1900 - 1975

ANN CATHERINE MARSHALL
1896 - 1983 m.
John David Shuler
1896 - 1976

FREDERICK CARL DENKMANN II
1908 - 1935 m.
Mary Anne Chamberlain
- 1935

CATHERINE DENKMANN HAUBERG
1914 - 1995 m.
Edward Cleaveland Sweeney
1906 - 1967

JOHN HENRY HAUBERG, JR.
1916 - 2002 m.
Anne Westbrook Gould
1917 -
Ann Homer Brinkley
1923 - 2003

ROBERT DENKMANN
MARSHALL, JR.
1931 - 1994 m.
Jennie White
Carson
Clarissa Serren
Mickles (Penny)

SHANNON
KATHERINE
MARSHALL
1959 -
ELISE CAROLINE
MARSHALL
1962 -   m.
Edward E. Domning
JOHN MCDONALD
MARSHALL
1964 -   m.
Shawn Hilary Elliot
1965 -

ANN CATHERINE SHULER
1922 -   m.
Clarence Langerack
Albert Mabis Chase
1918 - 2000
Paul Neal,Jr.
1915 - 2001
Charles Blair
1913 - 1981

DAVID SHULER CHASE
1946 -   m.
Sylvia Elaine McFarland
1950 -
JOHN GIVIN CHASE, III
1950 -   m.
Nancy Ann Storme
1949 -

SOPHIE ELISE SHULER
1923 -   m.
Sumner McRae Macomber
1917 - 1991
Gerald Griffin Geraghty. Jr.
1920 -

SUMNER KINGSLEY
MACOMBER
1943 -   m.
Mary Matilda Jones
1942 -
JOHN SHULER
MACOMBER
1945 -
CATHERINE SHULER
MACOMBER
1947 -
ELISE MARSHALL
MACOMBER
1947 -   m.
Perry Burton Hansen
1947 -

JEAN MARSHALL SHULER
1925 -   m.
Albert Cummins
Rawson, Jr.
1923 -

ALBERT CUMMINS
RAWSON, III (TERRY)
1949 -   m.
Susan Elizabeth Lake
1958 -
WILLIAM MARSHALL
RAWSON
1951 -   m.
Laurie Elizabeth Seton
1952 -
HOLLIS SHULER RAWSON
1953 -   m.
Stephen Arthur
Shumway
1960 -

FAY WESTBROOK
HAUBERG
1944 -
Nathaniel
Blodgett Page
1944 -

CATHERINE (CAREY)
BLODGETT PAGE
1974 -
BENJAMIN HAUBERG
PAGE
1977 -

SUE
BRADFORD
HAUBERG
1948 -

MARK
DENKMANN
HAUBERG
1950 - 1954

ALBERT MABIS CHASE II
1977 -
ANNA CATHERINE
MARIE CHASE
1979

ALEC BURTON
HANSEN
1978 -
ELISE DENKMANN
HANSEN
1979 -

CATHERINE
(KATE) MATILDA
MACOMBER-JONES
1978 -
LOCKE KINGSLEY
MACOMBER-JONES
1983 -

SUSANNE DENKMANN
SWEENEY
1941 -   m.
Abdul Wahhab Kayyali
1939 - 1981

RANDA KAYYALI
1970 -   m.
Ramzi A. Zeineddine
1974 -
KINDA KAYYALI
1975 -

EDWARD CLEAVELAND
SWEENEY, JR.
1942 -   m.
Sandra Elizabeth Stoen
1942 -

SEAN MICHAEL SWEENEY
1965 -   m.
Dana Sue Ellison
1964 -
Shelley Lou Kriger
ERIC CHRISTOPHER SWEENEY
1967 -   m.
m. Jill Ann Pitzer
1969 -
MARK EDWARD SWEENEY
1974 -

PHILIP MILES SWEENEY
1945 -   m.
Alisande Lynn
Cunningham
1954 -

COLIN GABRIEL SWEENEY
1982 -
LIANA CATHERINE SWEENEY
1987 -

HARRIET HAUBERG
SWEENEY
1948 -   m.
Eric P. Fraunfelter
1947 -

JOHN HENRY
SWEENEY
1954 -

Index